Witnessing Slavery

Wisconsin Studies in American Autobiography

William L. Andrews, General Editor

Witnessing Slavery

The Development of Ante-bellum Slave Narratives

Second Edition

FRANCES SMITH FOSTER

The University of Wisconsin Press

The University of Wisconsin Press
1930 Monroe Street, 3rd floor
Madison, Wisconsin 53711-2059

3 Henrietta Street
London WC2E 8LU, England

www.wisc.edu\wisconsinpress

Printed in the United States of America

Library of Congress Cataloging-in-Publication Data
Foster, Frances Smith.
    Witnessing slavery : the development of ante-bellum slave
narratives / Frances Smith Foster.
    238 p.   cm. — (Wisconsin studies in American autobiography)
Originally published: Westport, Conn.: Greenwood Press, 1979.
With new introd., chapter, and supplementary bibliography.
Includes bibliographical references (pp. 167, 177) and index.
ISBN 0-299-14214-0 (paper)
    1. American prose literature—Afro-American authors—History and
criticism. 2. American prose literature—19th century—History and
criticism. 3. Slaves—United States—Biography—History and
criticism. 4. Afro-Americans—Biography—History and criticism.
5. Autobiography—Afro-American authors. 6. Slavery and slaves in
literature. 7. Narration (Rhetoric) I. Title. II. Series.
PS366.A35F6   1994
818'.3080989073—dc20   93-34490

ISBN-13: 978-0-299-14214-8 (pbk.: alk. paper)

*For Mabel Josephine Gullette Smith
and Quinton Theodore Smith*

Contents

Preface

OF THE MORE than six thousand extant works generally labeled as slave narratives, the writings vary in content and structure and range from one-page interviews to four-hundred-page books. They share, however, the common theme of the black's struggle for freedom from bondage in the United States of America. Variously hailed as "among the most remarkable productions of the age" and as "a new department to the literature of civilization" and condemned as "those literary nigritudes—those little tadpoles of the press," personal narratives by slaves were published separately and in newspapers, magazines, anthologies, court records, church documents, and state and federal reports. Best-sellers in the ante-bellum period, by the end of Reconstruction they were virtually impossible to obtain. Ignored or maligned by early twentieth-century historians and literary critics, in the past decade they have become primary sources for the current reassessments of American slavery and of American literature.

It has been 133 years since Wendell Phillips rejoiced that "the time has come when the 'lions write history.'" Often during that period black narrators exclaimed as did the Invisible Man, "I have also been called one thing and then another while no one really wished to hear what I called myself." Yet, from the colonial era to the present time, there has been no generation which did not make its contribution to the black person's stories of bondage and freedom in the United States. Personal experience has been replaced by scholarly research or folklore as the last survivors of slavery have died. But the tradition continues. Twentieth-century works such as *The Autobiography of Miss Jane Pittman* by Ernest Gaines (1966), *Jubilee* by Margaret Walker (1966), *Flight to Canada* by Ishmael Reed (1976), and *Roots* by Alex Haley (1976) are consciously modeled after the ante-bellum slave narratives. Others such as Richard Wright's *Black Boy* (1945), James Baldwin's *Go Tell It on the Mountain* (1952), Claude Brown's *Manchild in the Promised Land* (1965), and Cecil Brown's *The Life and Loves of Mr. Jiveass Nigger* (1969) incorporate many of the dominant slave narrative characteristics.

There are significant differences between early slave narratives and contemporary versions, however. Ante-bellum slave narratives were presented as nonfiction. Prefaces, letters of reference, affidavits, news clippings, copies of legal documents, or other materials were published with each narrative to assure the reader of its validity. Most contemporary bondage and freedom accounts are presented as autobiographical fiction. Authors admit the assumption of poetic license in order to achieve aesthetically respectable works. The protagonist is still a representative black trying to achieve recognition of his manhood within an alien society, but the focus has shifted. There are few obvious appeals to the sympathy and charity of white readers. The protagonists exhibit more strength and more inclination to fight and to think their ways to freedom—independent of white support. The majority of their achievements are now credited to their abilities to manipulate their environments intellectually. The pathetic descriptions of meager diets, inadequate housing, and unending labor have given way to more angry and cynical observations about the reasons for these deprivations. The enemy is more generally white racism rather than the inhuman actions of some whites. The bondage and freedom of the twentieth-century works are a metaphor of psychological and social situations which differ significantly from the antebellum era. Slave narratives were didactic writings, created as a response to specific needs of a specific society; through the influence of their social ambience, these narratives were adapted to changing expectations, assumptions, and needs within that environment. This study examines not only the forms of separately published slave narratives but also the social context and literary traditions within which they changed in order to determine relationships among them. The most important elements of the narratives were race and slavery, and as race became synonymous with slavery and as racial discrimination became institutionalized in the United States, the slave narrative became increasingly distinct from other forms of American literature.

Slave narratives began as variations of personal narratives more like than unlike their analogues in the American Colonial Period. They evolved into a distinct and separate kind of writing definable in form and content and in relation to cultural matrix. There were two periods during which strong public interest in Afro-Americana encouraged a particularly significant amount of writing and publishing activity among blacks who had been enslaved. Both of these periods produced writings which were a continuation of the slave narrative tradition. Each period also incorporated ideas and techniques heretofore uncommon in the narrative. The existence of two chronological phases in the history of slave narratives does not prove an evolution from simple to complex or from primitive to sophisticated. Rather, these phases demonstrate clusters of structural and thematic characteristics which are limited fairly accurately by the following dates: 1760-1807 and 1831-65. The greatest number of separately published works and the most highly developed literary presentations emerged in the 1831-65 period. Therefore, after exploring the problems of cultural matrix and precursors to slave narratives, the study focuses upon these antebellum narratives.

Acknowledgments

I RECOGNIZE THE importance of the Ford Foundation's Graduate Fellowships for Black Americans and the University of Iowa's 1974 Institute on Afro-American Culture in enabling me to research slave narratives. I appreciate the strong support and encouragement offered in various ways and at various times by my friends and colleagues Elsie Adams, George Gross, Darwin Turner, John Waterhouse, and Sherely Anne Williams. My special thanks to him who has been there from the beginning, patiently prodding and always believing, Roy Harvey Pearce. And to my husband and children, my profound thanks.

Introduction to the
Second Edition

I WROTE *Witnessing Slavery* because I wanted to make a case for the importance of slave narratives as literary texts, but it was not a totally academic exercise. Reading slave narratives had changed my life. Prior to my discovery of these first person accounts of life in slavery and the attempt to become free, I had known virtually nothing about African American culture before the twentieth century and I had cared even less. "Slavery" was a worrisome word that connoted a time in the distant pass when my kinspeople had been oppressed so hard they could not stand. "Slaves" were but the ragged remnants of a once proud African lineage who plowed and picked, nursed and cleaned, waited and prayed for their deliverance from bondage. "Freedmen" were an embarrassment. They had been so devastated by their years of enslavement that they could not exercise the rights to participate in the political and intellectual arenas that the Union army had won for them. They would not even demand their forty acres and a mule. A child of the Martin and Malcolm era, I could see no value in trying to connect my Black and Proud self with folks who had worked from sunup until sundown and had produced only a few haunting spirituals and some Brer Rabbit stories from the experience.

I had taken a couple of courses in African American literature and I had earned two degrees in English, but I had never heard of the hundreds of published first person narratives by former slaves who had emancipated themselves using whatever means necessary. Back in the sixties, when I took my first courses in what was then called "black literature," I had read a little of Wheatley, Dunbar, Chesnutt, and Cullen, but I had been taught that the early African American writers were of the "mocking bird school"—imitating the songs of others, unable to or disinterested in singing their own. I preferred the monstrous Bigger to his, and my, Uncle Tom. Like Ralph Ellison's Invisible Man, I pondered the possible answers to "What did *I* do to be so black and blue?" With James Baldwin, I argued for the fire next time even as I secretly sought an African American equivalent to Michelangelo. And since the dominant approach to teaching literature was an uneasy mixture of formalism and sociology, I embraced the Black Arts movement and found no fault with the pronouncement of Leroi Jones (soon-to-be Imamu Amiri Baraka) that the majority of the literature written for publication prior to the current moment was not much to boast of. Claiming Jean Toomer, Lorraine Hansberry, and Langston Hughes as exceptions that proved the rule, I, too, asserted that "in most cases the Negroes who found themselves in a position to pursue some art, especially the art of literature, have been members of the Negro middle class, a group that has always gone out of its way to cultivate *any* mediocrity, as long as that mediocrity was guaranteed to prove to American . . . that they were not really who they were, i.e. Negroes."[1] Having come of age with MoTown, I knew very little about blues, jazz or the spirituals, but in concert with my black college sisters and brothers, I kept up with Jones who declared that "Only in music, and most notably in blues, jazz, and spirituals . . . has there been a significantly profound contribution by American Negroes" (106). The past was a burden to bear, an obstacle we would overcome. My money was on the cultural revolution being waged by the new black generation.

Still, I was curious about slavery. I felt a contradiction between the Sambo, Mammy, and Topsy images and the few spirituals and trickster tales I had heard. I wanted to reconcile the strength, imagination, resiliency, and love depicted in the stories told me by family and friends with those that I saw in print. In 1974, when Darwin Turner[2] offered a summer seminar on slave narratives, I applied. There I read the testimonies of those who had been slaves. The previously worrisome word became

1. Leroi Jones, "Myth of a Negro Literature," in Jones, *Home: Social Essays* (New York: William Morrow, 1966), pp. 105–6.
2. Scholar, critic, and poet, Darwin T. Turner helped build the Afro-American Studies Program at the University of Iowa. Mentor and friend to countless young professors, he offered a series of summer seminars at which, over the years, virtually every important scholar, writer and student in the discipline convened.

the flesh of brave and intelligent and ambitious people named Frederick and Harriet and Ellen and William and Solomon who bore witness to their experiences and to my heritage. Returning to the University of California at San Diego, I convinced two professors, Roy Harvey Pearce and John Waterhouse, that there was a literature of slavery from the slaves' point of view and that there were enough of these stories to justify at least one quarter of independent study. I set about identifying and reading everything I could that might fit under the rubric.

It took more than one quarter. A legacy from the sixties had been a plethora of publications. Arno Press, Negro Universities Press, Johnson Publishing Company, Rhistoric Publications, and others had issued entire libraries of reprinted texts that included many slave narratives. After Watts, San Francisco State, and the Black Student Unions, university librarians in California had purchased microfiche copies of "Negro" literature by the drawer full. Once I knew what to look for, I did not have to leave San Diego to find what I then thought were more than enough narratives for my study.

The question of what to do with them, how to read them right, became my next concern. Most of the critical discussions that I found were by historians who debated their value for revealing "the truth" about slavery. Ulrich B. Phillips dismissed slave narratives on the grounds that most "were issued with so much abolitionist editing that as a class their authenticity is doubtful."[3] Stanley Elkins was agreeable to making a few allowances. He judged some of Frederick Douglass's insights to be "valuable," but then *My Bondage and My Freedom*, he declared, was "obviously not the work of an ordinary slave."[4] Kenneth Stampp conceded an "urgent need for data" from the slaves' points of view but he concluded that "direct evidence from the slaves themselves is hopelessly inadequate."[5]

On the other side were Eugene Genovese, John Blassingame, and others who asserted that since any personal narrative was limited and subjective, those of slaves had at least the same standing as those of

3. Ulrich B. Phillips, *Life and Labor in the Old South* (Boston, 1929), p. 219.

4. Stanley Elkins, *Slavery: A Problem in American Institutional and Intellectual Life* (Chicago: University of Chicago Press, 1959), pp. 3–4.

5. Quoted in John W. Blassingame, *Slave Testimony: Two Centuries of Letters, Speeches, Interviews, and Autobiographies* (Baton Rouge: Louisiana State University Press, 1977), p. xi.

their owners. Genovese argued that the published accounts of "runaway slaves" could be "illuminating," and would suffice as historical evidence provided that one exercised "enormous care." He cautioned that they could be as "misleading in their honesty and accuracy of detail as in their fabrications."[6] John Blassingame used a different tactic. Like Elkins, he suggested that personal accounts by ordinary slaves might be problematic, but that was a minor problem, since most of the published narratives were by exceptional slaves. Blassingame countered the arguments of those like Phillips by focusing upon the good character of the abolitionist editors. "Any study," he declared, "must begin with an assessment of the editors . . . [who were] an impressive group of people noted for their integrity." Blassingame shores this argument by asserting, "One indication of the general reliability of the edited accounts is that antebellum southern whites challenged so few of them."[7]

In general, the historians, and the few literary scholars who had written about slave narratives, were primarily concerned with verisimilitude. Their studies discussed the biographical and social contexts of the texts, catalogued the details of slave life and the attitudes portrayed, queried the relationship of amanuenses and editors, and analyzed the points where "the slave's experience began and that of the antislavery recorder left off."[8]

It seemed to me that they were protesting too much. Obviously a fugitive slave who published his odyssey was not "ordinary," but this very subjectivity belied the monolithic Sambo stereotype of passive acquiescence. I could understand Ulrich B. Phillips's reluctance to credit the narrators' dialogic litanies of abuse for he had decided that "the plantation was a parish, or perhaps a chapel of ease." But since there was abundant evidence that slaves were brutally exploited, I couldn't fathom why historians who had long since abandoned the paternal planter concept would not accept the slaves' stories at face value. I was especially intrigued by the uniformity of the narrators' epiphanies of

6. Eugene Genovese, *Roll, Jordan, Roll: The World the Slaveholders Made* (New York: Random House, 1974), pp. 675-76.

7. John Blassingame, *Slave Testimony: Two Centuries of Letters, Speeches, Interviews, and Autobiographies* (Baton Rouge: Louisiana State University Press, 1977), pp. xvii-xxiii.

8. Gilbert Osofsky, *Puttin' On Ole Massa* (New York: Harper, 1969), p. 12.

literacy and the many examples of resourcefulness, self-esteem, and an indomitable determination to be as free as they could. I was not bothered by the silences about racism in the North, the underground railroad, or the black support networks because I had been caught up in the flights to Canada, following the shining North Star that led to the promised land. So what if names had been changed to protect the innocent or if the dialogue echoed that of sentimental novels? These texts constructed vivid images through powerfully evocative language. The sameness of their stories across time, place, and circumstance suggested another kind of truth. They made me a witness to my past and suggested new perspectives on the literature of the present.

I realize more fully now than I did then that we must continuously reexamine the assumptions and priorities of academic theory and practice, but I was not totally naive when I began this study. My struggle to obtain a bibliography of slave narratives and the prevalence of questions about authenticity and authority were disquieting. Why, I wondered, should I refrain from serious consideration of these works until I could verify who wrote what word at what time and under what circumstances? Certainly literacy was uncommon among slaves but it was also uncommon among women and indeed among most antebellum Americans. If we were not to be bothered by the relationships between editors and white women, for example, why this skepticism for blacks? Why the overwhelming need to verify that the author of record did in fact insert each comma and comment? I was satisfied that the plays attributed to William Shakespeare were worthy of close reading even though definitive texts—and concrete evidence that he wrote all the plays attributed to him—did not exist. I decided that I did not have to delay a consideration of the text and social context of slave narratives until I had first answered the riddle of who really wrote them. As far as I was concerned, such questions needed to be pursued by those who considered them important. For me, they had the same relevance as trying to establish the exact date of John Keats's death when it was the "Ode to a Grecian Urn" that engaged my imagination and stimulated my curiosity.

Witnessing Slavery was my attempt to join the conversation about slave narratives and to enlarge it. When I began, I was less interested in inventing a new methodology than in trying to describe the texts as I saw them. New Criticism was still the prevailing approach to literature and I felt it appropriate to focus upon the structure and content of slave narratives. But, I was also greatly influenced by the historicism then reviving once more, an approach to literary history that had greater affinities to formalism and placed more emphasis upon "the work" than does today's version. The New Historicism of the seventies provided models for examining these narratives within the contexts of both the antebellum period and our own rediscovery. Readers may also recognize a bit of archetypal methodology, a dash of feminism, more than a suggestion of black aestheticism, and hints of other approaches. In general I took the best of whatever critical approaches seemed helpful and began to construct a systematic way of studying what I believed was a literary genre that had profoundly shaped the development of African American literature. Implicit in my discussion was the idea that this tradition was also integral to American literature's engagement with the myths of selfhood and social renewal that were at the foundation of America's civil and cultural ideology in the late eighteenth and early nineteenth centuries.

Today, slave narratives are accepted as a legitimate literary genre. Some scholars of Native American autobiography, Mexican American *testimonios,* and other kinds of nineteenth century writings have found the ideas about slave narratives useful in their own studies. The rediscovery of literary production by African Americans, women, and other previously ignored groups, as well as the emergence of the autobiographical form and popular culture as respectable academic pursuits, have taken the conversation in complicated, exhilarating, occasionally perplexing, and increasingly playful directions.

The title for my book, *Witnessing Slavery,* came to me as I was completing the project. My original goal had been to examine this body of autobiographical writings by former slaves not from the perspective of historical accuracy or data, but as writings that somehow had the power to reveal, to transform, and to transcend. It was not that mimesis was unimportant. Certainly the narratives offered unique and valuable information about slavery as it was experienced by slaves themselves. Slave narratives are eyewitness accounts narrated by the participants, not by chance observers passing through the South nor strangers made sympathetic by philosophical or religious convictions. They are precious records of what certain individuals who had actually been enslaved had actually seen, heard, and felt about "the peculiar institution." These witnesses had been imprisoned in the house of bondage and escaped to tell the tale. Others could reject or refute their perspectives but the authority of "Nobody Knows the Trouble I Seen" and the accounts of "How I Got Over" could be claimed only if they had been earned. While many could describe the arrival of fugitives to the sanctuaries that they provided, no freeperson could duplicate the urgency of those who had actually run a thousand miles to freedom. When one could write, as Frederick Douglass did, "My feet have been so cracked with the frost, that the pen with which I am writing might be laid in the gashes,"[9] there is a power that surpasses that of mere journalism.

The ability of slave narratives to make me a witness to slavery undermined the arguments of those who asserted that their value lay in the accuracy of representation of the actual. So what if some details were omitted or conversations of some twenty years earlier were rendered verbatim? There are qualities of equal or greater value than historical accuracy and generic purity. I was particularly struck by the written narratives' similarity to stories I had learned in Sunday School. Their representation of the present in terms of the past, their ability to recast the Judeo-Christian myth and combine Egypt and Moses and the River Jordan, and their characterization of the narrator as one reborn or sometimes even as another Christ figure all testified to the efficacy of reading slave narratives as a particular kind of autobiographical literature. The persistence of images of crucifixion, death, and resurrection had to mean something more than incomplete or inadequate assimilation of white missionaries' Christianity. Even then I recognized that, like the testimonies of the Saved in Afro-Protestant prayer meetings and praise services, slave narrators were claiming to have been born into a new life and they were asserting the authority of direct revelation to provide answers to questions unasked and problems not yet solved.

On some points, I was very deliberate about going against the grain. On others, I made casual decisions that I now realize fundamentally affected the outcome of my study. My decision to eliminate the anthologies of slave autobiographies, the third person accounts, and those

9. *Narrative of the Life of Frederick Douglass, an American Slave* (New York: Doubleday, 1963), p. 29.

that were obviously "fictionalized" was pragmatic. The sheer volume of material had to be cut to a size I could deal with. What I didn't fully appreciate was that my choice to focus upon separately published and relatively straightforward texts effectively excluded virtually all the narratives written by women. Bibliographical sources had estimated that only 12 percent of the known published narratives were by women; but losing that 12 percent relegated at least half the population to the sidelines. It left my study with only *Incidents in the Life of a Slave Girl* to represent the experiences of slave women, and I had been sufficiently impressed by the controversy surrounding the identity of the author and the narrative's stylistic differences to avoid giving that text the weight it deserved. Consequently, a major weakness in *Witnessing Slavery* is that it seriously slights slave women's narratives. The resultant discussion is of a genre which I would now more accurately describe as antebellum slave narratives by men.

I tried to correct this in subsequent studies. Even before *Witnessing Slavery* appeared, I had already published "Ultimate Victims: Black Women in Slave Narratives," an article that explored the causes and effects of the depiction of African American women in representative texts.[10] As I continued to explore the role of gender in African American literary development, I became part of a community of scholars, mostly African American women, whose questions and concerns helped revolutionize African American critical study. Included in this second edition of *Witnessing Slavery,* directly following this introduction, is the essay " 'In Respect to Females . . .': Differences in the Portrayals of Women by Male and Female Narrators," which was among the earliest to call attention to the literary function of gender in the slave narratives. This essay was the starting place for my full length study of early African American women writers[11] and it has served as a catalyst for other studies of gender in African American and other literatures.

In choosing to reprint my original study without revision, I have forgone the opportunity to employ the theoretical tools that the emergence of African American studies, women's studies, and other

10. *Journal of American Culture* 1 (1978): 845–54.
11. Frances Smith Foster, *Written by Herself: Literary Production of African American Women, 1746–1892* (Bloomington: Indiana University Press, 1993).

areas of critical investigation have given us to further dismantle the master's house.[12] Overall, this is not a major problem; *Witnessing Slavery* is still the only study of its kind and it provides a discussion that is uniquely suited to those just being introduced to slave narratives. Still, there are places where I would prefer that the emphasis were altered or the examples extended. For example, my discussion of "Social and Literary Influences upon Ante-bellum Slave Narratives" is basically correct about the restraints and limits encountered by black writers seeking to influence white readers in the mid-nineteenth century. It argues convincingly about the narrators' understanding of the assumptions and conventions of their white readers. But while it mentions some of their defensive strategies, the chapter aborts its discussion of the narrators' offensive rhetorical maneuvers and it glosses over the relationship between the narrators and their black readers. Though it suggests that African American culture provided African American writers with "an additional set of references," and that racial identity did in fact create a "kind of tension peculiar to Afro-American literature,"[13] the chapter does not sufficiently pursue the implications of those ideas. Working from a present perspective, I would give more attention to the influences of African and African American literary traditions upon the slave narrators' propensity to favor particular characterizations and to emphasize particular aspects of their experiences.

I continue to believe that slave narrators emphasized certain elements of their experience and employed certain kinds of plots and characters in order to convince white readers to support anti-slavery activity. But, equally important is the fact that the narrators wanted (and their African American readers expected them) to correct, complete, or challenge those stereotypes and the half-truths. I see more clearly now how it was that slave narrators deliberately manipulated Anglo American discursive conventions and expectations as a means of developing authority but I am adamant that such manipulation did not require them to dismiss the interests and needs of the African Americans to whom

12. Here I am alluding to the now classic presentation that Audre Lorde gave for "The Personal and the Political Panel" at the Second Sex Conference, New York, September 29, 1979.

13. *Witnessing Slavery* (Westport, Ct: Greenwood Press, 1979), p. 64. Subsequent references are from this edition and found in the text.

they also wrote and for whom they hoped to speak. In part, this insight is a direct result of developments in, and my introduction to, two disciplines that literary scholars have not yet fully acknowledged or begun to appreciate—Afrocentric and theological studies.

When reading the works of liberation ethicists such as Katie G. Cannon and Vincent L. Wimbush, I found models by which I could better explain how slave narrators navigated between opposing forces. For example, in discussions of the contradictions within Christian theory and practice, Katie G. Cannon is one of several who argues that African Americans practiced a "hermeneutics of suspicion"[14] that filtered what was heard and what was read through culturally constructed sieves. Liberation ethicists argue that African Americans have always understood the need to "consider the source" and that they were constantly attentive to ideas that might be wrong or hurtful to the well-being of their community. Using an argument firmly grounded in the hermeneutics of suspicion concept that " 'there is no value-free space,' "[15] Vincent L. Wimbush asserts that "the question of *origins* is of minor importance—in isolation from concern about *function*. The question about the relevance or potential power of critical methods . . . must be addressed ultimately in terms of a people's history, and how such methods could service that people in its present situation."[16] Wimbush further argues that a more persistent question was: "What . . . for African Americans should/do the texts *mean?*" (50). Such statements testified to efficacy of those writers upon which I based *Witnessing Slavery* and revived my interest in continued exploration of the narratives.

The work of liberation theologists and church historians in reconstructing the development of Afro-Protestantism reminds us to resist the temptations to collapse cultures, and to ignore important differences both within and between communities. Studies of the complexities of theological arguments and of congregant responses in slave religion

---

14. Cannon, Katie G., "The Bible from the Perspective of the Racially and Economically Oppressed," in *Scripture: The WORD beyond the Word*, Edited by Nancy A. Carter (New York: Women's Division, The General Board of Global Missions of the United Methodist Church, 1985), pp. 35–40.

15. Cannon, *Bible*, p. 36.

16. Wimbush, Vincent L., "Historical/Cultural Criticism as Liberation: A Proposal for an African American Biblical Hermeneutic," *Semeia* 47 (1989): 44.

also challenge our persistent inclinations to favor secular studies over religious ones and to view the nineteenth century from a twentieth century perspective. This is a much needed corrective, for all too often scholarship has been contaminated by an ideology of progressive intelligence that assumes we are more intelligent and sophisticated than our ancestors were. Otherwise, why have we so readily repeated dictums of sociologists, anthropologists, and folklorists that African Americans had a complex and nuanced oral and material culture—that they could speak volumes through drums and banjos, stories and jokes, dances and songs and even clothing styles—but that their transition from oral to written arts necessitated the loss of subtlety or linguistic agility? Why else have we agreed that slaves could "read" people's actions but not their words, that they could wear the mask without losing face, that the performance was not the thing itself? The work of our sisters and brothers in the divinity schools in reconstructing the function and future of religion in African American society reminds us that in the nineteenth century, as now, the everyday experiences of most African Americans encouraged them to recognize and deal with the ways of white folks. That earlier work provides an opening for additional study of African American reader response theory.

Another important influence upon my current thinking is the pioneering work of African American Studies scholars, especially those in folk culture and linguistics. Since the seventies, many African American speech act theorists have also identified rhetorical strategies that are deliberate, though subtle, challenges to the discourse of the dominant. One of the most intriguing of these acts by its very nature defies precise definition. Known variously as "signifying," "masking," "shucking," "marking," or "diss-ing" (few scholars, or practitioners, agree on exactly what distinguishes one term from another or upon the contextual clues that verify which activity is indeed occurring), the term eludes precise definitions, but Claudia Mitchell-Kernan's definition of signifying as "ways of encoding messages and meanings which involve, in most cases, an element of indirection."[17] conveys the basic idea. Mitchell-Kernan further describes "signifying" as a black folk

17. Claudia Mitchell-Kernan, "Signifying," in *Mother Wit From the Laughing Barrel: Readings in the Interpretation of Afro-American Folklore*, edited by Alan Dundes (Englewood Cliffs: Prentice-Hall, 1973), p. 311. All subsequent references are from this source and are given in the text.

concept that assumes the complexity of communication by requiring the receiver to "attend to all potential meaning carrying symbolic systems in speech events—the total universe of discourse [this requires readers to assume] . . . the *given context* and, most importantly, . . . [the] *additional context* from [their] background knowledge of the world" (314). For example, both personal background knowledge about the speaker and "expectations based on role or status criteria enter into the sorting process" (314).

As one very brief example of how recognition of "signifying" can influence our reading of slave narratives, consider the many implications of the following passage from *Incidents in the Life of a Slave Girl.*

> *Benjamin reached* New York *safely, and concluded to stop there until he had gained strength enough to proceed further. It happened that* my grandmother's *only remaining son* had sailed for the same city on business for his mistress. *Through God's providence,* the brothers met. You may be sure it was a happy meeting. "O Phil," exclaimed Benjamin, "I am here at last." Then he told him how near he came to dying, almost in sight of free land, and how he prayed that he might live to get one breath of free air. He said life was worth something now, and it would be hard to die. *In the old jail he had not valued it; once, he was tempted to destroy it; but something, he did not know what, had prevented him; perhaps* it was fear. He had heard those who profess to be religious declare there was no heaven for self-murderers; and as his life had been pretty hot here, he did not desire a continuation of the same in another world. "If I die now," he exclaimed, *"thank God, I shall die a freeman."*[18] (italics added)

The cadence of, and many phrases in, this paragraph are those used in some of the most popular Bible stories of slavery, bondage, and deliverance in both the Old and the New Testaments. The first sentence echoes any number of biblical flights. Not only has Jacobs rechristened her uncle Joseph Benjamin but the pun on her own name and phrases such as "it happened that, "only remaining son," and "through God's providence" suggest, in particular, the stories of Rachel and Jacob and

18. Harriet A. Jacobs, *Incidents in the Life of a Slave Girl, Written by Herself* (Cambridge: Harvard University Press, 1987), p. 25. Subsequent references are from this edition and are given in the text.

their children, each of whom is readily identified with slavery. While a fugitive in Mesopotamia, Jacob indentured himself for seven years in order to be free to marry Rachel. But as had happened in Harriet Jacobs's own family, the servant was betrayed by his master. Rachel, whose name is also associated with the woman who wept for her children lost in captivity, died giving birth to Benjamin. When their other son, Joseph, was sold into slavery, Benjamin was their only remaining son. During a famine, Jacob allowed his sons by other women to travel to Egypt in search of food, but he refused to let Benjamin go until Joseph, in order to test his brothers' mettle and to bring about the reunion and deliverance for his entire family, demanded he be sent. There is not a one-to-one correspondence between the two stories, but both are clearly linked by more than issues of slavery, survival, freedom, and risk taking. In a blessing attributed to Moses, Benjamin is characterized as "The beloved of the Lord, he dwells in safety by him" (Deut. 33:13). In the paragraph quoted above, Jacobs attributes her Benjamin's escape to God's providence. The biblical Benjamin was characterized as aggressive but generous ("Benjamin is a ravenous wolf, in the morning devouring the prey, and at evening dividing the spoil." Gen. 49:27). Such a description applies to Benjamin's attempt to have his brother join him in freedom. And finally, this same paragraph also evokes the traditional conversion experience of the Afro-Protestant church. In many autobiographical accounts, African American writers testify to a sequence of emotional crises that include the conviction of being trapped, the impulse to commit suicide, the unexplained restraint from that act, and their ultimate salvation.[19]

I am inclined to believe that the "hermeneutics of suspicion," which black liberation theologists maintain characterizes Afro-American religion, is rooted in, and a manifestation of, "signifying;" but my point here is that African Americans had long ago created a method of challenging, chastising, correcting, or complementing indirectly—of persuading when they appear to be informing, of saying one thing and meaning another, of assuming that "every good bye ain't

19. See, for example: *God Struck Me Dead: Religious Conversion Experiences and Autobiographies of Ex-Slaves,* edited by Clifton H. Johnson, (Philadelphia: Pilgrim Press, 1969); *Spiritual Narratives* edited by Sue E. Houchins (New York: Oxford University Press, 1988); and *Sisters of the Spirit,* edited by William L. Andrews (Bloomington: Indiana University Press, 1986).

gone.'' And, as we understand from the scholarship on spirituals, work songs, folk tales, and other cultural behaviors, often these modes of communication were so indirect, so disguised, that some of us could be present, listening, and even participating and not have a clue that there was more than one agenda being pursued. Though William Wells Brown, Harriet E. Wilson, Frederick Douglass, and others made a profession of explaining black life to white people, as African Americans and/or former slaves, they were heirs to the same cultural contexts, aesthetic concerns, and communicative modes as those of whom they wrote or spoke. Their acquisition of literacy and the rhetorical strategies common to the Anglo American tradition did not require that they discard their own. It is a bit naive to assume that they would abandon the discourse of indirection in general or of signifying in particular, communicative modes that informed and characterized their folk tales, their spirituals, and, especially, their daily interactions with whites in favor of apologetic appeals to sensitivity and Christian principals simply because they were writing instead of speaking. It seems more likely that they would adopt and adapt various strategies to achieve their ends.

The exploration of these and other ideas would require more time and space than is fitting for an introduction. Suffice it to say that *Witnessing Slavery* would be another book were I to write it now; still, its basic idea that slave narratives are first-person accounts of life in slavery and the pursuit of freedom similar to but distinct from other autobiographical writings would remain. The concept of slave narratives as literary texts that intended to explain, persuade, assert, and prevail via the power and the magic of ''the word'' would continue to be fundamental. And, the assumption that text and social context are inextricably so interwoven that any serious attempt to understand the writing ought not stray too far from its sources would continue to underlie it all.

"In Respect to Females...": Differences in the Portrayals of Women by Male and Female Narrators

EVEN BEFORE THE *Roots* phenomenon, maybe even before the forceful presentations of writers and scholars such as Arna Bontemps, Charles Nichols, Eugene Genovese, and John Blassingame, the watermelon-loving, dancing and singing, docile and dull Sambo image had been pretty well abandoned. Not only do many Americans now know of Frederick Douglass, Richard Allen, and George Washington Carver, but they embrace these outstanding achievers, along with Kunte Kinte and Chicken George, as examples of the heroic spirits once enslaved. Mention the slave woman, however, and noble images fade. They see her as victim—to be pitied, perhaps—but neither respected nor emulated. In the popular imagination, she stands on the auction block, nameless, stripped to the waist, her infant just sold from her arms, waiting to be claimed by yet another licentious master. Phillis Wheatley, Vyry, and Miss Jane Pittman notwithstanding, the common association of slave women is with fornication. From Clotel to Kizzy, our most frequent images of slave women are as victims of illicit sexual intercourse and as childless mothers.

There are many reasons for this. First of all, the forced selling of children from slave mothers and the rape of slave women were frequent events. No matter what percentage of the slave population cliomatricians and other contemporary historians may decide was actually involved in such matters, the fact will remain that slave women were subject to sexual abuse far beyond that of other groups of nineteenth-century women. The increasing presence of mulatto slaves would be adequate documentation even if reports by abolitionists, journalists, and tourists had not so frequently emphasized such cases. American slavery was an abomination, and sexual exploitation contributed to its hideousness.

A second reason for the tenacity of the image of the slave woman as sexual victim is the slave narratives. Widely accepted as being, if not the slave's own true story of slavery, at least the versions of slave life most sympathetic to the slaves, most slave narratives stereotyped slave women as sexually exploited beings. Most slave narratives, however, were related by men. Narratives by slave women present a significantly different perception of slave women. It is this discrepancy which has not been duly noted, and it is this neglect of slave women's versions of their lives that is a basic reason for the perpetuation of the current and inadequate image of women slaves.

There is no reason to believe that male narrators deliberately set out to demean or to misrepresent slave women. Both social attitudes toward women and literary conventions made the distortion of slave women probable in narratives that featured male protagonists.

The slave narrative was a special kind of autobiographical writing. Written after the individual writer's freedom had been achieved, these accounts were designed to enlighten audiences about the facts of slavery and to excite them to work for the abolishment of the institution and of racial discrimination. Closely akin to Indian captivity narratives, the prisoner-of-war accounts, the religious autobiographies, and the temperance testimonies of their time, the slave narratives were rigidly patterned, didactic works. Their generic conventions made it necessary that all characters—including to some extent the protagonist—be types. The narrator was symbol, the one who by God and good luck got away, the spokesperson for the thousands remaining in the wilderness. It was the narrator's life with which the narrative was specifically concerned. The lives of other slaves were noted as supplementary evidence. The protagonist would have to be female if an extended depiction of a slave woman was to be expected.

Moreover, black men shared the nineteenth century's predilection for defining women in terms of manners, morals, and motherhood and for limiting the female protagonist to the genteel writing designed for the woman reader. Few male slave narrators appear to notice that their pictures of slavery were largely masculine. One who did is revealing. Says Moses Roper, "It will be observed, that most of the cases here cited are those in respect to males. Many instances, however, in respect to females might be mentioned, but are too disgusting to appear in this narrative."[1] Roper, like most male narrators, refers to slave women en masse as "the females" or "the women" and presents slave women primarily as examples of the extremes of the depravity to which slave-holders descended and of the degradation to which black men, through their inability to protect and to provide, were forced.

An example of the treatment given slave women by male narrators is the description by William Craft who implies that for the woman, rape or seduction is virtually inevitable:

> It is a common practice in the slave States for ladies, when angry with their maids, to send them to the calaboose, . . . and have them severely flogged; and I am sorry it is a fact, that the villains to whom those defenseless creatures are sent, not only flog them as they are ordered, but frequently compel them to submit to the greatest indignity. Oh! if there is any one thing under the wide canopy of heaven horrible enough to stir a man's soul, and to make his very blood boil, it is the thought of his dear wife, his unprotected sister, or his young and virtuous daughters, struggling to save themselves from falling a prey to such demons!
>
> It is a common practice for gentlemen (if I may call them such), moving in the highest circles of society, to be the fathers of children by their slaves, whom they can and do sell with the greatest impunity; and the more pious, beautiful, and virtuous the girls are, the greater the price they bring, and that too for the most infamous purposes.
>
> Any man with money (let him be ever such a rough brute) can buy a beautiful and virtuous girl, and force her to live with him in a criminal connection; and as the law says a slave shall have no higher appeal than the mere will of the master, she cannot escape, unless it be by flight or death.[2]

1. Moses Roper, *The Narrative of the Adventures of Moses Roper* (1838; rpt. Philadelphia: Rhistoric, 1967), p. 26.
2. William Craft, *Running a Thousand Miles to Freedom, or the Escape of William and Ellen Craft from Slavery* (1860) in *Great Slave Narratives*, ed. Arna Bontemps (Boston: Beacon Press, 1969), pp. 274–75.

Craft's comment that the indignities to which these defenseless creatures are subjected are enough to make a man's blood boil is certainly not intended to belittle the brutal effect upon the women, but it does remind us that maltreatment of women is often considered an affront to the men with whom the women are associated. If the slave woman could escape only "by flight or death," then the aberration of a system that prevents the stronger members of a group from fulfilling their responsibilities to their dependents is clearly shown. The psychological dejection of those men who could not protect their women is then included as another burden of slavery. Josiah Henson, for example, makes clear the double bind of the slave men when he says the only incident he can remember from his childhood was the "appearance one day of my father with his head bloody and his back lacerated. It seemed," explains Henson, "the overseer had sent my mother away from the other field hands to a retired place, and after trying persuasion in vain, had resorted to plain force to accomplish a brutal purpose. Her screams aroused my father from his distant work. . . ."[3]

The slave narrators are careful to blame the lust and greed of white men for these situations. Henry Bibb, among others, claims it is this licentiousness that sustains the institution of slavery:

> the strongest reason why southerners stick with such tenacity to their "peculiar institution," is because licentious white men could not carry out their wicked purposes among the defenseless colored population as they do without being exposed and punished by law, if slavery was abolished. Female virtue could not be trampled under foot with impunity, and marriage among the people of color kept in utter obscurity.[4]

In narrative after narrative by male slaves, graphic portrayals of sexual abuse of slave women by white men abound. (Rare indeed is any reference to sexual abuse of slave men by white women, and homo-

---

3. Josiah Henson, *Truth Stranger than Fiction: Father Henson's Story of His Own Life* (1858; rpt. New York: Corinth Books, 1962), pp. 2–3.

4. Henry Bibb, *Narrative of the Life and Adventures of Henry Bibb, and American Slave* (1849) in *Puttin' On Ole Massa*, ed. Gilbert Osofsky (New York: Harper and Row, 1969), p. 169.

sexuality is never mentioned.) The effect is a monolithic characterization of slave women as utter victims. When slave women tell their
stories, however, they barely mention sexual experiences and never
present rape or seduction as the most profound aspect of their existence. Though they document the trauma and grief of sexual exploitation and physical abuse beyond the comprehension of most nineteenth-century (and twentieth-century) white women, the slave
women's works do not center around these tragedies. From their narratives it is repeatedly clear that slave women saw themselves as far
more than victims of rape and seduction. Though they wrote to witness
slavery's atrocities, they also wrote to celebrate their hard won escape
from that system and their fitness for freedom's potential blessings. In
their autobiographical accounts are the likes of Sojourner Truth and
Harriet Tubman, the stories of strong, courageous, and spirited
women.

There is more than a hint of dignity and self-satisfaction when
Elizabeth Keckley begins her narrative by saying, "My life has been
an eventful one."[5] Though she calls herself a "feeble instrument" of
God, she clearly sees herself as a significant figure in human history
when she asserts that "a wrong was inflicted upon me; a cruel custom
deprived me of my liberty, . . . I would not have been human had I
not rebelled. . . . through me and the enslaved millions of my race, one
of the problems was solved that belongs to the great problems of human
destiny" (xii).

The switch in characterization of slave women from passive victims
to heroic actors is partly due to the fact that slave women are protagonists and thus expected to exhibit more complex and positive traits
and to engage in a greater variety of experiences than when all women
are secondary characters. However, slave women's narratives also
present more positive images of secondary female characters, devote
more discussion to familial relationships, and rely less upon litanies of
beatings and mutilations of other slaves. This seems to indicate a subtle
difference in the values of male and female slave narrators. Male narrators interpret as supplements to their own experiences that which they

---

5. Elizabeth Keckley, *Behind the Scenes: Thirty Years a Slave and Four Years in the
White House* (1868; rpt. New York: Arno Press, 1968), pp. 38–39. Subsequent references
are from this edition and are noted parenthetically in the text.

saw and deemed significant of other slaves' experiences as a means of enhancing their descriptions of the crippling power of slavery. Female narrators present those incidents that most affected their development, those experiences that in Keckley's words "influenced the moulding of my character" (18), and by implication or direct statement, they extend their positive characteristics to other slaves. Rather than elaborating upon the weight of their oppression, the women emphasize the sources of the strength with which they met that force.

As an example, consider the way female narrators treat sexual harassment, instances that Moses Roper considered so "disgusting." When slave women relate episodes of sexual harassment in their lives, they do so to render more clearly the tenor of their courage and faith. Harriet Jacobs devotes considerably more space to her sexual persecution than most slave women do, yet her description seems merely an elaboration of what the other women might have said. Compare the earlier cited statement by William Craft concerning the perils of slave women and Harriet Jacobs' analysis of her own situation.

In a chapter titled, "The Trials of Girlhood," she notes that "the degradation, the wrongs, the vices, that grow out of slavery, are more than I can describe. They are greater than you would willingly believe."[6] She says that slave children become "prematurely knowing in evil things" (27), but she indicts not only the slaveholding men but the slave mistresses and American society in general when she states, "There is no shadow of law to protect her [the slave women] from insult, from violence, or even from death. . . . The mistress, who ought to protect the helpless victim, has no other feelings towards her but those of jealousy and rage." (26–27). Jacobs, however, makes it clear that not every slave woman suffers seduction or rape. She says, "Even the little child . . . will learn before she is twelve years old, why it is that her mistress hates *such and such a one* among the slaves" (27, emphasis mine).

When Jacobs enters a liaison with a white man, it is not the effect upon her male relatives that she chronicles, but it is her grandmother's response that she notes. Her grandmother's extreme reaction shows

---

6. Harriet Jacobs, *incidents in the Life of a Slave Girl* (1861; rpt. New York: Harcourt Brace, Jovanovich, 1973), p. 27. Subsequent references are from this edition and are noted parenthetically in the text.

that such conduct was not so common as to be easily excused by other slave women. When her grandmother discovered the affair, she exclaimed, "I had rather see you dead than to see you as you now are. You are a disgrace to your dead mother." Tearing her mother's wedding ring from Jacobs' hand, her grandmother proclaimed, "Go away! and never come to my house again" (57). Though later grandmother and granddaughter were reconciled, Jacobs reports that her grandmother "did not say, 'I forgive you,' " but that "she looked at me lovingly with her eyes full of tears. She laid her old hand on my head and murmered, 'Poor child! Poor child!' "(58).

Though Harriet Jacobs was driven to desperation by her licentious master, by her own account she was not completely defenseless. She was not seized, beaten, and raped. She was propositioned for several months by her master who occasionally threatened but more often begged, pleaded, and cajoled. He sent notes and gifts and eventually began to build her a small house in the woods as a bribe for her consent. Rather than the object of physical violence, Jacobs describes herself as a person confronted with a serious dilemma. She knew that alone she could not avoid her master indefinitely. Because her master had denied her request to marry a black suitor, she decided to revenge herself and at the same time to make her own position more secure. "I knew what I did, and I did it with deliberate calculation" (54), she says. "I knew nothing would enrage Dr. Flint [her master] so much as to know that I favored another; and it was something to triumph over my tyrant even in that small way" (55). She chose an unmarried professional man, who had befriended her earlier and whose interest had begun to have a less platonic tone. She candidly stated that

> to be an object of interest to a man who is not married, and who is not her master, is agreeable to the pride and feelings of a slave, if her miserable situation has left her any pride or sentiment. It seems less degrading to give one's self, than to submit to compulsion. There is something akin to freedom in having a lover who has no control over you, except that which he gains by kindness and attachment. (55)

Sexual exploitation of slave women is verified by Harriet Jacobs in her narrative. Indeed, in her life, it was a signifcant factor for a few years. In spite of this, she was able to exercise some control over her situation.

In exchange for sexual favors, she gained two well-loved children, an adoring—if in our eyes irresponsible—lover, and protection from the advances of her master. More importantly, in her narrative, sex is but one aspect of her life. These incidents are covered in a relatively brief portion, near the beginning of her work. The emphasis of Jacobs' narrative is upon her attempts to win freedom for herself and her children, her seven years of hiding in an attic, her dangerous escape to freedom, her success in finding jobs, and the reunion of her family in the North. Neither her sexual misuse nor her slave existence were enough to destroy her self-confidence. Her self-esteem was so strong that as a fugitive slave she rejected all efforts to legalize her freedom by paying her master's price. When she received word that her manumission had been purchased, she wrote one of her benefactors, "I thank you for your kind expressions in regard to my freedom; but the freedom I had before the money was paid was dearer to me. God gave me *that* freedom; but man put God's image in the scales with the paltry sum of three hundred dollars . . ." (210).

In the narrative by Elizabeth Keckley, sexual victimization is covered in one paragraph:

> I was regarded as fair-looking for one of my race, and for four years a white man—I spare the world his name—had base designs upon me. I do not care to dwell upon this subject, for it is one that is fraught with pain. Suffice it to say, that he persecuted me for four years, and I—I—became a mother. The child of which he was the father was the only child that I ever brought into the world. If my poor boy ever suffered any humiliating pangs on account of birth, he could not blame his mother, for God knows that she did not wish to give him life; he must blame the edicts of that society which deemed it no crime to undermine the virtue of girls in my then position. (38-39)

Keckley's brief acknowledgment of her sexual persecution is more typical of that by most female narrators than is Harriet Jacobs', but like Jacobs', it is less an admission of fraility than it is an attack upon a society that condones such an atmosphere within which some women must live.

Elizabeth Keckley, like other women narrators, provides another dimension to the slave narratives' theme of physical violence. In addi-

tion to villainous overseers and brutal masters, they describe the malev-
olent influences and direct violence of slave mistresses, thus elaborating upon a dimension of the Southern belle that most narrators
omit. Not only does this modify the stereotype of the Southern white
woman, but the slave woman's necessity to defend herself against
women as well as men converts the sexual victim image into a more
general target of affliction, one with which both men and women can
more readily identify. Keckley recalls the vindictiveness of a mistress
who, feeling that the slave woman was too proud, persuaded a man to
whip her. Shortly after her day's work had ended, the man called
Keckley into his study and told her, "I am going to whip you, so take
down your dress this instant." Says Keckley:

> Recollect, I was eighteen years of age, was a woman fully developed and
> yet this man coolly bade me take down my dress. I drew myself up
> proudly, firmly, and said: "No, Mr. Bingham, I shall not take down my
> dress before you. Moreover, you shall not whip me unless you prove the
> stronger." (33)

Mr. Bingham overpowers Keckley. She describes the beating as one of
"excruciating agony," but in contrast to male narrators' descriptions
of women's sufferings, she neither moaned nor wailed. "I was too
proud to let my tormentor know what I was suffering," she recalls. "I
closed my lips firmly, that not even a groan might escape from them,
and I stood like a statue while the keen lash cut deep into my flesh"
(34). When the beating was over, she went to her master to protest but
was beaten by him as well. Says Keckley, "My spirit rebelled against
the unjustness that had been inflicted upon me, and though I tried to
smother my anger and to forgive those who had been so cruel to me,
it was impossible" (35). The persecution continued for several weeks
and Keckley tells how she fought back, biting and kicking and chastising the man for his cruelty until finally he "burst into tears, and declared that it would be a sin to beat me any more" (37).

    She writes "in the shady side of forty" with pride in her achieve-
ments. With her fortitude and skills, she had purchased herself and her
son and established herself as the most sought-after dressmaker in
Washington society. Elizabeth Keckley is more concerned with describing her success as a modiste and her reputation as a professional

for whose services the ladies in society competed and of whose friendship Mrs. Jefferson Davis and Mrs. Abraham Lincoln boasted than
with chronicling her victimization.

Susie King Taylor's work centers around her experiences as a laun-
dress, a nurse, and a teacher during the Civil War. In her first chapter,
"A Brief Sketch of My Ancestors," she places herself in a context of
strong and courageous slave women. She begins her narration by saying, "My great-great-grandmother was 120 years old when she died."[7]
Taylor continues what is essentially a matrilineal account by sum-
marizing the achievements of her great-grandmother Susanna, "one
of the noted midwives of her day," and her grandmother Dolly whose
skill in marketing, laundry work, and domestic service "made a good
living for her." In a digression which apparently typifies her ancestry,
Taylor describes her grandmother's reaction to the loss of her life
savings when the Savannah Freedmen's Savings Bank collapsed: "She
felt it more keenly, coming as it did in her old age, when her life was
too far spent to begin anew; but she took a practical view of the matter, for she said, '. . . If the Yankees did take all our money, they freed
my race; God will take care of us' " (3). In a later chapter, Taylor informs us that her widowed mother, after the war, opened a grocery
store and parlayed the profits into the largest real estate holdings in
town.

There is no hint of sexual abuse endured by Taylor or other slave
women and she refuses to present herself or her family as significantly
different from many others. In the paragraph before she notes her
mother's economic success after freedom, Taylor begins, "One thing
I have noticed among my people in the South: they have accumulated
a large amount of real estate, . . . and all that is needed is the protection
of the law as citizens" (64). As a fugitive during the war her reply to
a Northern officer who was impressed by her education and manners
also stresses her identification with most slaves. When he tells her,
"You seem to be so different from the other colored people who came
from the same place as you did," she replies, "No! the only difference
is, they were reared in the country and I in the city" (9).

---

7. Susie King Taylor, *Reminiscences of My Life in Camp* (1902; rpt. New York: Arno
Press, 1968), p. 9. Subsequent references are from this edition and are noted parenthetically in the text.

Taylor's inclusion of the stories of women who survived slavery and prospered in freedom is not unique among slave women writers. And, more often than not, these women are their mothers or grandmothers. While their family members are presented as examples of many other slave women, their inclusion counters the image of the childless mother as the prototype.

Amanda Berry Smith attributes much of her success to the example of her mother. Smith was an itinerant preacher who after obtaining her freedom, traveled extensively through the eastern United States and to India, England, and Africa as well. Her narrative describes the difficulties she encountered as a black woman with little formal education or money who aspired to the ministry, but having had a mother who was "equal to any emergency,"[8] she had ample incentive to persevere. "My mother was a great economist," she recalls. "She could make a little go a great ways. She was a beautiful washer and ironer, and a better cook never lifted a pot. I get my ability in that (if I have any) from my dear mother. Then withal she was an earnest Christian, and had strong faith in God, as did also my grandmother" (148). This Christian and domestic mother was also quite spirited and that too seems to have influenced Smith's life. One instance that she relates concerns her mother's involvement with the undergroundrailroad. Once, the family was awakened by slavecatchers, and though there were no fugitives in their home that night, Smith relates that her mother "sprang up, and as she ran downstairs she snatched down father's cane, which had a small dirk in it; she went up and threw open the door, pushed father aside, but he got hold of her, but O, when she got through with those men! They fell back and tried to apologize, but she would hear nothing" (153). The effect of this episode was such that as long as two years later, Smith tells us that slavecatchers would come to their house with search warrants but refuse to enter saying to her father," We have heard your wife is the devil. . . . You know, Sam, we don't want any trouble with her, you can tell us just as well" (155).

---

8. Amanda Berry Smith, *An Autobiography: The Story of the Lord's Dealing with Mrs. Amanda Smith, the Colored Evangelist* (1893) in *Black Women in Nineteenth-Century American Life,* ed. Bert James Loewenberg and Ruth Bogin (University Park: Pennsylvania State University Press, 1976), p. 147. Subsequent references are from this edition and are noted parenthetically in the text.

Annie Louise Burton portrays a similar maternal heritage. An argument with her mistress resulted in Burton's mother's first whipping. The event so enraged her mother that she ran away and was not heard from for three years. When she returned, the Civil War had just ended. Her mistress refused to release her children so the mother kidnapped Annie and her siblings. When two men appeared at Burton's mother's door, demanding the return of the children, the woman not only refused but threatened to enlist the aid of the Union soldiers. Says Burton, "The young men left and troubled us no more."[9]

Obviously, not all slave women distinguished themselves as did these here cited, and it was not the intention of the slave women narrators to imply that such was the case. Nor is there any reason to believe that slave women tried to suggest that they were any more heroic than slave men or that they tried to diminish the intensity of suffering and pain that can result from sexual exploitation. It is less a matter of contradictions between the male and female versions of female slavery than it is an awareness on the part of the writers as to what examples are most appropriate to their individual ends and what images are most accurate according to their own perceptions.

Slave women saw themselves as supplementing the work towards the progress of their race. Harriet Jacobs in her preface declares that she is contributing her efforts to those of other anti-slavery writers while concentrating upon the members of the sex she knows best. "I want to add my testimony to that of abler pens," she says, "to convince the people of the Free States what Slavery really is," but she intends specifically to "arouse the women of the North to a realizing sense of the condition of two millions of women at the South, still in bondage, suffering what I suffered, and most of them far worse" (xiv). Susie King Taylor, after the war, is compelled to write not only to "show how much service and good we can do to each other and what sacrifices we can make for our liberty and rights," but also to show that "there were 'loyal women,' as well as men, in those days, who did not fear shell or shot . . ." (vi).

The number of slave narratives published by men far exceeds those

---

9. Annie Louise Burton, *Memories of Childhood's Slavery Days* (1909), in *Black Women in Nineteenth-Century American Life*, ed. Bert James Loewenberg and Ruth Bogin (University Park: Pennsylvania State University Press, 1976), p. 100.

published by women, and thus the slave's self-portrayal is dominated by male features. Male narrators' use of slave women's experiences was limited by the generic conventions of slave narratives as well as by their conventional nineteenth-century male notions of woman's place. As a result, slave women were stereotyped as sexual victims. Women narrators, because of those same generic conventions and their differing view of woman's place, present stronger, more complex portraitures of their sex. Through their likenesses we gain a different perception of the courage and perserverance not only of the narrators but also of the women who did not write their stories. To recognize their presence gives us a more complete picture of our past, and this we should strive for not only in respect to females, but in respect to ourselves.

Witnessing Slavery

1

Slave Narratives
and Their Cultural Matrix

SLAVE NARRATIVES ARE the personal accounts by black slaves and exslaves of their experiences in slavery and of their efforts to obtain freedom. Written after the physical escape had been accomplished and the narrators were manumitted or fugitive slaves, these narratives were retrospective endeavors which helped the narrators define, even create, their identities as they attempted to relate the patterns and implications of their slavery experiences. More important, the narratives soon became the attempts of black slaves and exslaves to alter and, eventually, to abolish an institution which was increasingly vital to the continued prosperity of their white audience.

Though some are aesthetically superb and rank with the best literature, the slave narratives were not created for a limited audience of refined and cultivated sensibilities. On the other hand, they bear only limited resemblance to authentic black folk literature. Although some commercialization is apparent in the latter part of their development, slave narratives maintain integrity and do not come under the category of "mass culture." The authors of slave narratives usually wrote in a simple, direct style with a realistic eye upon the needs and expectations of a variety of readers. They attempted to urge the various elements of society to realize their collective need to eliminate injustices and to work for a unity of peace and understanding.

The narrators sought to inform their readers of the inhuman and immoral characteristics of slavery. They tried to communicate with an audience with which they did not share cultural or moral concerns—an audience, in fact, which was increasingly certain that

3

real and significant differences between whites and blacks necessitated vigilance lest there develop undue social and intellectual intercourse between them. At the same time, this audience was increasingly aware that blacks were the foundation of what could well be the most profoundly important institution in America. Thus the narrators could expect a certain amount of interest in their experiences and attitudes, but they could not assume sympathy for their beliefs. The narrators hoped to persuade their readers to accept not only the autobiographical truth of their message, but also the necessity for every individual's working against the institution of slavery. They had to do this without raising suspicions that they were advocating social equality or seriously challenging theories of racial superiority. Thus slave narratives were didactic writings, created as a response to the specific needs of a specific society. As a genre, the slave narratives were influenced by their social ambience, and they were adapted to the changes of expectations, assumptions, and needs within that environment.

The earliest slave narratives vary only slightly from other personal narratives of their time. Like the others, they tell of geographical explorations, oceanic adventures, and encounters with Indians. They, too, place a great emphasis upon the religious implications of the narrator's experiences. Like other personal narratives, the slave narratives chronicle incidents in an individual's experience, and they provide the reader with insights into an individual's mind as well as into the structure and working of that individual's society. In the slave narratives, as in other autobiographical literature, the authors are keenly interested in the clues provided by the narrated experiences about their identities and about the ultimate significance of their lives. They investigate the process of their spiritual and emotional development and try to assess the effects of social and familial relationships upon the ways in which they see themselves. Statements and arguments about philosophical, political, and religious beliefs are interspersed throughout their stories of physical bondage and escape.

Their combination of autobiographical and social concerns is perhaps one of the secrets of the early popularity of slave narratives. The colonists favored art that was relevant to their particular circumstances to such an extent that, according to James D. Hart, "Books were often judged by the amount of help they furnished the reader in his quest for worldly advancement.''[1] Slave narratives, like other personal narratives, were especially popular because they illustrated religious and political truths while relating interesting and exciting true-to-life adventures.

Although they were, in the beginning, simply a variation of the personal narrative tradition in American literature, slave narratives soon emerged as a distinct genre recognizable by its form, content, and relation to the cultural matrix. As the sociohistorical experiences of the narrators became more obviously different from those of their audience, their writings reflected this change.

Race was the most crucial factor in the development of the slave narratives because in the United States the slaves' experiences of bondage and freedom were a product of race. It is doubtful that American slavery began as a result of racial prejudice. Winthrop Jordan, in fact, declares it was merely a coincidence: ''At the start of English settlement in America, no one had in mind to establish the institution of Negro slavery. Yet in less than a century the foundations of a peculiar institution had been laid.''[2] Regardless of intentions, however, by the end of the seventeenth century a system of racial slavery heretofore unknown to the English world had evolved. This peculiar institution framed the relationship between the black narrator and a virtually all-white readership. As the differences in experiences between the races became more institutionalized, the differences between the perceptions and values of the races increased. The communication process had to respond to these differences, and the response accordingly helped to shape and to inform slave narratives.

The search for spiritual identity in the slave narratives was complicated by the desire to use incidents in the narrator's life as examples of the experiences of many others like him. As a result, the slave narrator increasingly focused upon the effects of a dehumanizing environment upon his race rather than upon his own individuality. In most cases the desire to recognize oneself and to be recognized as a unique individual had to counter the desire to be a symbol, and it created the tension that is a basic quality of slave narratives.

The problem of distinguishing between the individual self and the community self and the desire to present the symbolic nature of one's personal experiences while maintaining one's own inimitability is traditional for autobiographical writers. For the slave narrator the question is complicated by his status as a black man in the United States. When white writers realize a dichotomy between their individual perceptions and the expectations of society, they must weigh one legitimate role against another. Egoism confronts socialization. The tension is internalized because the white writer is a member of the society that he is addressing. Slave narrators were not recognized as members of the same society as their audience. The slave narrator was an alien whose assertions of common humanity and civil rights conflicted with some basic beliefs of that society that he was addressing. The differences between personal and group preferences must be dealt with in that context.

Black men usually desired the same freedoms and responsibilities that white society reserved for itself. As a black, the narrator shared these desires. As a nonwhite, he knew these desires were socially unacceptable to white society. The social expectations which he had to consider were divided into the expectations of the dominant white society and the expectations of the subordinate black society. His personal goals had to be considered against two different and sometimes opposite sets of social expectations.

The evidence of increasing alienation between whites and blacks is myriad. A comparison of the British explorers' first reactions to black men and the attitudes exhibited by their descendants in the United States provides an adequate summary. In 1564 John Hawkins described the natives of Africa by saying, "These people are all blacke, and are called Negros, without any apparell, saving before their privites."[3] Robert Baker, in his poetic descriptions of his expeditions to Africa about the same time, writes:

> And entering in, we see
> a number of blacke soules,
> Whose likelinesse seem'd men to be,
> but all as blacke as coles.
> Their Captaine comes to me
> as naked as my naile,
> Not having witte or honestie
> to cover once his taile.[4]

In these examples of sixteenth-century commentary on Africans it is obvious that the color of the Africans and their different social mores set them apart. The early explorers are condescending, but they have little doubt that these are men who come from some sort of definable society. Although Baker's statement that "likelinesse seem'd men to be" could indicate some doubt about their humanity, he had before that declared them "soules" and his next line indicates his reservation stemmed from their unusual color. However, his comment about "their Captaine" not only implies recognition of the existence of a social structure but bears censure because the naked African is not accepting Baker's assumption that men should be clothed. Had Baker considered him inhuman, his nudity would not have been remarkable.

Concern over the humanity of the African seemed to be more pronounced among Europeans (including those in the American colonies) who had not ventured into Africa and whose contact was limited primarily to observation of slaves. According to Philip D. Curtin in *The Image of Africa:*

> Most men connected with the slave trade, and even the West Indian planters (to say nothing of the enlightened travellers with their ethnographic and humane interests), were less inclined to emphasize racial factors than those who stayed in England. . . . The travellers often condemned individual Africans as bad men—or all Africans as savage men—but they left the clear impression that Africans *were* men.[5]

As time passed, many whites found it convenient to consider blacks as a category outside that of *Homo sapiens*. Evidence of this attitude is found in a 1680 rebuttal by the Reverend Morgan Godwin to the belief that a "disingenuous and unmanly *Position* had been formed; and privately *(and as it were in the dark)* handed to and again, which is this, That the Negro's, though in their figure they carry some resemblances of Manhood, yet are indeed *no Men.*" Godwin tried to refute this idea by saying that

> the consideration of the shape and figure of our *Negro's* Bodies, their Limbs and Members; their Voice and Countenance, in all things according with other Mens; together with their *Risibility* and *Discourse* (Man's peculiar Faculties) should be sufficient Conviction. How

should they otherwise be capable of *Trades*, and other no less Manly imployments; as also of *Reading and Writing*; or show so much Discretion in Management of Business; eminent in divers of them; but wherein (we know) that many of our own People are *deficient*, were they not truly Men?[6]

By the eighteenth century many whites, especially in the North, accepted blacks as members of the human species; then the debate shifted to racial hierarchy. The kinds of issues addressed are evident in Thomas Jefferson's public declarations. In 1784 he wrote, "The opinion that they [the blacks] are inferior in the faculties of reason and imagination, must be hazarded with great diffidence." He continues, however, "I advance it therefore as a suspicion only, that the blacks, whether originally a distinct race, or made distinct by time and circumstances, are inferior to whites both in body and mind."[7] By 1792 Jefferson was still skeptical, as the exchange between Benjamin Banneker and him indicates. Banneker states: "I suppose it is a truth too well attested to you, to need a proof here, that we are a race of beings who have long labored under the abuse and censure of the world; that we have long been looked upon with an eye of contempt; and that we have long been considered rather as brutish than human, and scarcely capable of mental endowments." He urges Jefferson to "embrace every opportunity to eradicate that train of absurd and false ideas and opinions which so generally prevails with respect to us."[8] Jefferson's reply indicates that he was not fully convinced of the natural equality of races but that "No body wishes more than I do, to see such proofs as you exhibit, that nature has given to our black brethren talents equal to those of the other colors of men."[9]

The Constitutional Convention of 1800 presented a compromise on the issue by declaring that for purposes of taxation and representation, the black slave was to be counted as three-fifths of a man, but for all other purposes he remained property. In *The Black Image in the White Mind*, George M. Fredrickson reports:

In 1859, two years after the Supreme Court's decision in the Dred Scott case denying American citizenship to all Negroes, Abraham Lincoln noted that some Northern Democrats were now asserting openly that when the Declaration of Independence spoke of "all men" this did not include Negroes. Although a believer in black inferiority, Lincoln was not willing to go so far as to countenance a doctrine that demoted the Negro "from the rank of a man to that of a brute."[10]

As the research, such as that by William F. Shockley and Arthur Jensen, and the response to that research in the past decade indicate, the significance of race in determining the degree of humanity has never been resolved in American society.

The black, who in the ante-bellum society attempted to define himself and to assess the factors which had made him as he was, found that the process of communicating this knowledge to a group which had doubts about his human status and which was guilty of his enslavement was fraught with special problems. He had to overcome the incredulity of persons whose surprise that a black could write overshadowed any attempt to understand or to consider what he was writing about. He had to convince his readers to accept the validity of his knowledge and conclusions, which in many instances profoundly contradicted their own. Furthermore, if he was to obtain their sympathy and aid, he had to do this in a manner which did not threaten or embarrass his readers.

For some narrators the difficulty of these tasks was compounded because they not only had to affirm for their readers the validity of their perceptions, but they also had to reaffirm that validity for themselves. This need was a direct result of the cultural matrix within which the black narrators existed. In a white society that questions and ultimately denies the humanity of blacks, it is difficult for blacks to take their humanness for granted. In such an environment most narrators needed continually to defend their own humanity to their readers and to themselves. As racist attitudes created an increasingly dehumanizing atmosphere for black narrators, their narratives reflected their intensified struggles to affirm their humanness.

Comparisons between the slave narratives by Africans and those by Afro-Americans reveal the effects of racism upon the attitudes of the narrators and the issues addressed in their writings. The narrators who began their lives in Africa maintained a strong sense of who they were and what they should be about throughout their enslavement. In their writings "our manners," "our buildings," and "our lives" are the bases for information, comparisons, and judgments.

In describing his introduction to white civilization, Olaudah Equiano often makes comparisons such as the following:

> I was astonished at the wisdom of the white people in all that I saw; but was amazed at their not sacrificing, or making any offerings, and eating with unwashed hands, and touching the dead. I likewise could not help remarking the particular slenderness of their women, which I did not at first like; and I thought they were not so modest and shame-faced as the African women.

Equiano's appreciation for some features of European civilization and astonishment at the barbarity of other aspects indicate the existence of some external set of values by which he can judge such factors. For many years he entertained the idea of returning home "and thought if I could get home what wonders I should have to tell."[11]

Such tendencies to compare cultures did not seemingly diminish with time. After sixty years in American slavery, Venture Smith still considered himself an African in exile and evaluated incidents in terms of his own country. After relating an incident when he was cheated out of some money, he says:

> Such a processing as this committed on a defenseless stranger, almost worn out in the hard service of the world, without any foundation in reason or justice, whatever it may be called in a Christian land, would in my native country have been branded as a crime equal to highway robbery. But Captain Hart was a *white gentleman*, and I a *poor African*, therefore it was *all right, and good enough for the black dog.*[12]

In contrast, a major concern of the Afro-American slave was to discover and preserve proof of his right to disagree with whites, for the Afro-American was born into a denial of human respect. Henry Bibb explains:

I was born May 1815, of a slave mother . . . and was claimed as the property of David White Esq. . . . I was *flogged up*; for where I should have received moral, mental, and religious instruction, I received stripes without number, the object of which was to degrade and keep me in subordination. I can truly say, that I drank deeply of the bitter cup of suffering and woe. I have been dragged down to the lowest depths of human degradation and wretchedness, by Slaveholders.[13]

The Afro-American narrator had no direct experience in any other society and often knew no more of his own personal history than the season of his birth or the appearance of his mother. His predicament was more completely one of exclusion from the only society he knew than of introduction to a new and hostile one. He often emphasized that he was a native of this country and, in fact, related to some of its oldest or most prominent citizens. His confrontation was not with contrasting values of an alien society but with alien ideas concerning his place in society. His comparisons were between his freedom as a child and his bondage as an adult, between his role as slave and the roles of whites as masters. Insofar as might makes right, his recognition of personal impotence threatened his acceptance of the validity of his perceptions. His comparisons were supported by references to differences between the ideals which Christianity and the American society extol and the failures of slaveholders to live up to these values. Hence the Afro-American narrator is likely to evoke the Bible as his authority and to compare his bondage with that of the children of Israel.

The narratives of Afro-American slaves also indicate there were differences between African and Afro-American slaves. Charles Ball implies racial differences when he tells of his grandfather's "great contempt for his fellow slaves, they being, as he said, a mean and vulgar race, quite beneath his rank, and the dignity of his former station." To Ball, a black born in U.S. slavery, his grandfather held "strange and peculiar notions of religion." Among other things, the old African maintained that

the religion of the country was altogether false, and indeed, no religion at all; being the mere invention of priests and crafty men, who hoped thereby to profit through the ignorance and credulity of the multitude. In support of this opinion, he maintained that there could only be one true standard of faith, which was the case of his country.[14]

Apparently, Africans were more successful in rejecting psychological and physical enslavement than Afro-Americans. John Hope Franklin reports that

> overseers found it necessary to develop a practice of "breaking in" the newcomers. In some areas they were distributed among the seasoned, or veteran, slaves, whose duty it was to teach the newly arrived slaves the ways of life in the New World. In other places the newcomers were kept apart and supervised by a special staff of guardians and inspectors who were experienced in breaking in those Negroes who might offer resistance to adjusting in their new environment.[15]

Afro-American narrators report no such formal breaking in procedures for them. Many discuss the phenomenon of "niggerbreakers" in the United States, but, as a rule, "nigger-breakers" were required for unruly individuals and not for whole groups. Furthermore, in many accounts of confrontations between a "nigger-breaker" and a slave, the narrators note that the slave was African.

Austin Steward recounts the occasion when slaves defied the patrollers' attempts to break up a slave party. Steward makes much of the leader's heritage, describing him as "an athletic, powerful slave, who had been but a short time from his 'fatherland,' whose spirit the cowardly overseer had labored in vain to quell." He was "a gigantic African, with a massive, compact frame, and an arm of great strength" who "clenched his powerful fist, and declared that he would resist unto death, before he would be arrested by those savage men." This African led some twenty-five slaves in a rebellion that alarmed the total community.[16]

J. W. C. Pennington maintains the Afro-American slave was in a defenseless state because slavery eliminated a viable Afro-American culture. "To estimate the sad state of a slave child," he says, "you must look at it as a helpless human being thrown upon the world without the benefit of its natural guardians. It is thrown into the world without a social circle to flee to for hope, shelter, comfort, or instruction." Pennington makes it clear that it is not simply a deprived childhood that he laments when he says,

> Whatever may be the ill or favoured condition of the slave in the matter of mere personal treatment, it is the chattel relation that robs him of his manhood, and transfers his ownership in himself to another. It is this that transfers the proprietorship of his wife and children to another. It is this that throws his family history into utter confusion, and leaves him without a single record to which he may appeal in vindication of his character, or honour.
>
> . . .
>
> Suppose insult, reproach, or slander should render it necessary for him to appeal to the history of his family in vindication of his character, where will he find that history? He goes to his native state, to his native country, to his native town; but nowhere does he find any record of himself *as a man*.[17]

For the Afro-American narrator, life is a series of attempts to discover and proclaim his validity in spite of his perceived defects. The Afro-American's narratives most often end with a commitment to continue the struggle for recognition, "to contend," as Henry Bibb declares, "for the natural equality of the human family, without regard to color, which is but fading *matter*, while *mind* makes the man."[18]

The evolution of slave narratives began more from social reality or historical imperative than from literary consciousness. The peculiar nature of their situation and their intent made compromise mandatory for slave narrators. The nature of these compromises determined the form and content of the narratives.

It was vital to the slave narrators that they maintain in their works a close relationship with the reality of the Afro-American experience. It was also necessary that they avoid unnecessarily antagonizing their audience. Yet, as the experiences of black slaves in the United States became more distinct from those of any other group, their writings had to reflect these changes; and, as slavery became more brutal, its depictions had to become more brutal also. The narrator's fidelity to the reality of the American slave experience was at the risk of offending many Americans who, regardless of their humanitarian beliefs, were, after all, members of the society being criticized. Moreover, the narratives ran the risk of alienating segments of people because the accounts of slavery presented an unsavory view of the South in particular and the United States in general. This made the narratives potentially offensive to American nationalists, though popular with those in the North who encouraged regionalism and with those in England who still smarted over the result of the War of Independence.

This dilemma is illustrated in Ephraim Peabody's mixed review, "Narratives of Fugitive Slaves." His enthusiasm is obvious when he says:

> We place these volumes without hesitation among the most remarkable productions of the age—remarkable as being pictures of slavery by the slave, remarkable as disclosing under a new light the mixed elements of American civilization, and not less remarkable as a vivid exhibition of the force and working of the native love of freedom in the individual mind.

The praise is tempered with caution, however, when, in the midst of what is intended as a highly sympathetic review, he complains that "these books give the impression that the Slave States constitute one vast prison house, of which all the whites without exception are the mere keepers, with no interest in the slaves further than they can be made subservient to the pleasure or profit of their owners. But this is far from the case." He advises slave narrators to give what he considers *"more balanced views of slavery."* He further warns that he will not condone any "censorious, loose, and violent treatment" of slavery because it would antagonize antislavery southerners and northerners having personal ties to the South who would otherwise help the movement.[19]

Slave narrators, especially those of the nineteenth century, were in a difficult situation. They wished to contradict the masters' version of slavery by presenting the black slave's views, and they wanted to do this with an audience and with supporters who were more closely related by culture and vested interests to the masters than to the slaves. Their narratives show great efforts to appease without neutralizing their position. It became almost axiomatic that for every two or three bad experiences related, one good experience must be recounted.

The manner in which comparisons between the United States and Britain were handled shows how this was done. Slave narrators considered Britain a more enlightened and hospitable country than the United States. Such bias could easily be interpreted as anti-Americanism and as such would seriously impede any attempts by blacks to change any American institution. The narrators had to develop a compromise that would allow them to gain American sympathizers without sacrificing their strong appreciation for the antislavery positions of other countries. Their decision to ignore as foci of attacks sources of slavery such as racism, discrimination, and economics and to concentrate upon the weakness of the institution was one compromise because this reduced the number of persons in the United States who were obviously being criticized and focused discussions of Britain's merits upon one area: slavery.

The narrators' appreciation of Britain was based upon that country's antislavery reputation. Although Britain was heavily involved in the slave trade, it never developed a strong system of slavery at home. During the War of Independence and the War of 1812, the British gained favor with blacks by promising freedom to all fugitive slaves who joined them. The reports of early narrators who had experienced both forms of slavery encouraged favorable attitudes toward Great Britain. Writers such as Olaudah Equiano and James Gronniosaw ignored the responsibility of England for the situation in its colonies and severely criticized U.S. treatment of black slaves in the New World. While many favorable references to "dear old England" are made, horrendous incidents are reported as commonplace in the West Indies and southern United States. Equiano contrasts his degradation in the United States with the comfort he experienced in England by declaring that soon after his arrival in England, he was "almost an Englishman" and felt not only "quite easy with these new countrymen, but relished their society and manners." This ease and sense of belonging was possible in England, he maintains, in spite of his condition of enslavement. On the other hand, even after winning his freedom, his treatment in Georgia was such that he could hardly wait "to take a final farewell of the American quarters of the globe."[20]

There was, however, sufficient nationalism in the United States to require diplomacy. Equiano does not condemn the entire New

World. He describes Robert King, his master in the West Indies, as a Quaker from Philadelphia who "possessed a most amiable disposition and temper, and was very charitable and humane."[21] The problem, as Equiano presents it, is that there were very few masters like King, and those persons were not capable of protecting their slaves from exploitation by the majority of inhabitants in that area.

When Parliament abolished slavery in Britain and all British colonies in 1833, the pro-British flavor of the narratives became even more pronounced. When the Compromise of 1850 allowed the expansion of slavery into the territories and made fugitive slaves unsafe in any area of the United States, slave narratives began to display anti-American tendencies. It is not uncommon to find narratives in which the writers' displeasure is directed not only against slaveholders but against the U.S. government as well. Their bitterness is obvious when Ellen and William Craft report they "thought it best, at any sacrifice, to leave the mock-free Republic, and come to a country where we and our dear little ones can be truly free."[22]

In order to minimize the antagonism which could result from such declarations, the narrators usually tried to explain their repatriation as unavoidable. The Crafts concede:

> We shall always cherish the deepest feelings of gratitude to the Vigilance Committee of Boston (upon which were many of the leading abolitionists), and also to our numerous friends, for the very kind and noble manner in which they assisted us to preserve our liberties and to escape from Boston, as it were, like Lot from Sodom. . . . Oh! may God bless the thousands of unflinching disinterested abolitionists of America, who are labouring through evil as well as through good report, to cleanse their country's escutcheon from the foul and destructive blot of slavery, and to restore to every bondman his God-given rights.[23]

Others, such as Lewis Clarke, indicate the lengths to which they went to avoid repatriation and the depths of their desires to remain in the areas of their births. Clarke went first to Cincinnati, then to Cleveland, but in both places he was not safe. Finally, he moved to Canada. His relief at being free is mixed with sorrow for, as he explains:

A strange sky was over me, a new earth under me, strange voices all around; even the animals were such as I had never seen. A flock of prairie-hens and some black geese were altogether new to me. I was entirely alone; no human being, that I had ever seen before, where I could speak to him or he to me.
And could I make that country ever seem like *home*?[24]

Clarke, when he admits that he would have preferred remaining in Kentucky, tries to assuage not only any ideas of un-Americanism but also the fears of northerners that hoards of exslaves would migrate north if slavery were abolished:

Some people are very much afraid all the slaves will run up north, if they are ever free. But I can assure them that they will run *back* again, if they do. If I could have been assured of my freedom in Kentucky, then, I would have given anything in the world for the prospect of spending my life among my old acquaintances where I first saw the sky, and the sun rise and go down.[25]

The slave narrators' ability to praise Britain for its antislavery attitudes without appearing to be anti-American may even have been a factor in their popularity in the United States, for, in spite of their strong nationalism, many Americans still deferred to Great Britain as a model for cultural and social living. At any rate, the exslaves' willingness to include positive images of Americans prevented pro-British biases from being a significant obstacle to the narratives' success when published in the United States.

The initial stages in the evolution of the slave narratives are directly related to the changes in the institution of slavery. The first writings were autobiographical narratives of the authors' lives and experiences as slaves. The narratives included descriptions of the structure and practices of slavery. As slavery became more inhumane, the narratives began to expose its abuses and to agitate for the abolition of the slave trade. Finally, they began to defend blacks as legitimate and respectable members of the human race and to focus upon the perniciousness of a system which pretended otherwise. They began to demand the immediate elimination of all forms of slavery. During this process, the basic concerns of the narratives became increasingly compatible with those of antislavery societies.

This is one reason for the fact that the majority of the nineteenth-century narratives were published in cities which were centers of antislavery action: Boston, Philadelphia, New York, and London. Some narratives, such as Frederick Douglass's and William Wells Brown's, were actually printed in the offices of abolitionist societies. It became increasingly common for narrators to acknowledge their friends' suggestions that they relate their slave experiences to support antislavery movements. Two prefatory statements, one written in 1789 and the second in 1848, illustrate not only the changing emphasis of slave narrators but also their stylistic evolution from philosophic arguments to outright propaganda.

In *The Interesting Narrative of the Life of Olaudah Equiano, or Gustavus Vassa, the African*, Equiano says he is writing to satisfy his friends' requests and to promote more humanitarian treatment of blacks. In the first paragraph of Chapter 1 he states:

> I believe there are a few events in my life, which have not happened to many: it is true the incidents of it are numerous, and, did I consider myself an European, I might say my sufferings were great: but when I compare my lot with that of most of my countrymen, I regard myself as a *particular favourite of Heaven*, and acknowledge the mercies of Providence in every occurence of my life. If then, the following narrative does not appear sufficiently interesting to engage general attention, let my motive be some excuse for its publication. I am not so foolishly vain as to expect from it either immortality or literary reputation. If it affords any satisfaction to my numerous friends, at whose request it has been written, or in the smallest degree promotes the interests of humanity, the ends for which it was undertaken will be fully attained, and every wish of my heart gratified.[26]

In the entire narrative, Equiano rarely alters the dispassionate and modest tone of his prefatory remarks. He philosophically presents a problem and then suggests the logical solution. His denial of personal involvement, beyond the desire to please his friends and to make a small contribution to "the interests of humanity," is in accordance with accepted standards of gentlemanly humanitarianism. He relies upon irony and understatement even when it could be misinterpreted. An example is the statement, "... did I consider myself an European, I might say my sufferings were great; but when I compare my lot with that of most of my countrymen. . . ." It is possible to read this as a remark about common deprivations in African society when compared with European society. Only when reading the narrative itself does it become apparent that his "countrymen" are those Africans who are also enslaved and "the interests of humanity" with which he is so concerned are those of antislave trade partisans.

Fifty-one years later, the focus and style of slave narratives had radically altered. *The Fugitive Blacksmith; or, Events in the History of James W. C. Pennington* is more directly antislavery. Pennington begins:

> The question may be asked, Why I have published anything so long after my escape from slavery? I answer I have been induced to do so on account of the increasing disposition to overlook the fact, that THE SIN of slavery lies in the chattel principle, or relation. Especially have I felt anxious to save professing Christians, and my brethren in the ministry, from falling into a great mistake. My feelings are always outraged when I hear them speak of "kind masters,"— "Christian masters,"—"the mildest form of slavery,"—"well fed and clothed slaves," as extenuations of slavery; I am satisfied they either mean to pervert the truth, or they do not know what they say. The being of slavery, its soul and body, lives and moves in the chattel principle, the property principle, the bill of sale principle; the cart-whip, starvation, and nakedness, are its inevitable consequences to a greater or less extent, warring with the dispositions of men.[27]

Pennington also denies any egotism in his motives, but he exhibits personal conviction that his experiences and his opinions concerning the lessons of his life are worthy of public notice. His desire to use his narrative as an all-out attack on slavery is blatant, and he has little use for polite discussion. His is the rhetoric of the evangelist, of the crusader whose cause demands rapid and extreme measures. There is no subtlety in comments such as, "I am satisfied they either mean to pervert the truth or they do not know what they say."

Despite their increased radicalism, the slave narratives were widely read and proved to be immensely helpful to the antislavery efforts. A quotation from *Chronotype*, a popular antislavery paper, illustrates the fervor with which some abolitionists espoused the publication of slave narratives:

This fugitive slave literature is destined to be a powerful lever. We have the most profound conviction of its potency. We see in it the easy and infallible means of abolitionizing the free states. Argument provokes argument, reason is met by sophistry; but narratives of slaves go right to the heart of men. We defy any man to think with patience or tolerance of slavery after reading Bibb's narrative, unless he is one of those infidels to nature who float on the race as monsters, from it, but not of it. Put a dozen copies of this book into every school, district, or neighbourhood in the free states, and you might sweep the whole north on a thorough-going liberty platform for abolishing slavery, everywhere and everyhow. Stir up honest men's souls with such a book and they won't set much by *disclaimers*; they won't be squeamish how radically they vote against a system which surpasses any hell which theology has ever been able to conjure up.²⁸

Slave narratives, however, were not supported by abolitionists only. There are four major reasons for their widespread popularity. Some writers, such as James Gronniosaw and Olaudah Equiano, emphasized their conversions and other religious experiences. Consequently, their works were also useful for the religious and moral education and persuasion of their readers. Others, like Frederick Douglass and William Wells Brown, included discussions of the social and political relevance of their experiences. They enjoyed an especially good market during the pre-Civil War period, for they provided details about the life-styles and attitudes of southern whites and blacks for many who simply wanted to know more about the South.

A third reason for the popularity of many slave narratives was that under the label of education, scenes of violence and cruelty were presented which not only could awaken moral outrage against slavery but at the same time did satisfy the public's appetite for sensationalism. In the introductory essay to *Four Fugitive Slave Narratives*, Robin Winks states the argument thus: "The fugitive slave narratives were the pious pornography of their day, replete with horrific tales of whippings, sexual assaults, and explicit brutality, presumably dehumanized and fit for Nice Nellies to read precisely because they dealt with black, not white, men."²⁹

The fourth reason for the popularity of slave narratives is a result of the first three. As it became financially advantageous to print slave narratives, publishers encouraged sales through various promotional techniques. An interesting example is the case of *Slavery in the United States: A Narrative of the Life and Adventures of Charles Ball, a Black Man, Who Lived Forty Years in Maryland, South Carolina, and Georgia as a Slave.* First published in Lewiston, Pennsylvania, in 1836, it was moderately successful and, in fact, was reissued in New York, Pittsburgh, and London. Twenty-two years later, when the popularity of slave narratives was at its all-time high, Ball's narrative was, as John Nelson describes it, "seized upon, condensed slightly, bound in a fiery red cover, with great wavering gilt letters staring out at the reader, and handed out to an eager public under the astonishing title *Fifty Years in Chains.*"[30] With the eager assistance of the commercial publishers, the slave narratives in the nineteenth century became the equivalent of the twentieth-century Westerns. Arna Bontemps elaborates upon this when he says,

> Like the Westerns, they also created a parable of the human condition, but with them the meaning was different. Their theme was the fetters of mankind and the yearning of all living things for freedom. In this context the perils of escape and the long journeys toward the North Star did not grow tiresome with repetition until a new myth, the Western, replaced the earlier one.[31]

It is impossible to ascertain the number of slave narratives which were published. In *Many Thousands Gone: The Ex-slaves' Account of Their Bondage and Freedom,* Charles Nichols estimates "thousands" of extant narratives.[32] Marion Starling claims that there are more than 6,000 slave narratives still in existence.[33] The statements of Nichols and Starling, however, refer to the entire spectrum of writings commonly included under the rubric "Slave Narrative." These writings range from court records and broadsides to the more than 2,000 interviews recorded as part of the Federal Writers' Project in the 1930s and those in anthologies like Benjamin Drew's *The Refugee,* which is composed of 400 thumbnail sketches from interviews of fugitives living in Canada. If we consider only those narratives which were written by persons who had been legally enslaved in the United States, the number is considerably smaller. Nichols's bibliography of separately published slave narratives

lists 85 titles. Starling's bibliography presents data on 142. In spite
of the absence of exact figures for separately published slave narratives extant, it is certain that with the slave narrative, as is usual
with most kinds of popular literature, those still in existence represent
a small portion of those which were written.

Quantity is not the only indication of a genre's popularity. Nonetheless, an idea of the public's predilection for the slave narratives
can be seen by the number of editions printed and copies sold during the time in which they were being written. *A Narrative of the
Most Remarkable Particulars in the Life of James Albert Ukowsaw
Gronniosaw, an African Prince, as Related by Himself*, first published in 1770, had 12 editions by 1814 and had been published in
both Britain and the United States and translated into Celtic. *The
Interesting Narrative of the Life of Olaudah Equiano*, published
in 1789, had gone through 36 editions by 1837. Equiano's narrative, which had 8 editions in its first five years, was published in
England, Ireland, and the United States and translated into Dutch
and German. Statistics of other slave narratives demonstrate the
same kind of public appeal. Moses Roper's narrative, published
in 1839, was still selling after 11 editions. Frederick Douglass's
1845 narrative had 7 editions in four years, and William Wells
Brown's 1847 work sold 4 editions in its first year. Father Josiah
Henson's story was first published in 1849 and sold 6,000 copies in
three years. Eventually, when it was revealed that he served as the
model for Mrs. Stowe's Uncle Tom, his narrative totaled 100,000
sales. As the Civil War approached, sales figures of slave narratives
grew even greater.[34]

To put this in some perspective, consider that in 1849, the same
year that Father Henson's story was published, Thoreau's *Week
on the Concord and Merrimack River* appeared. In four years, it
sold 219 copies. In 1853, Hawthorne's royalties on *Mosses from an
Old Manse* equaled $144.09. In 1853, Harper's warehouse fire
destroyed all but 60 copies of *Moby Dick*. But, as James D. Hart
points out, "these presumably satisfied the demand for ten years,
since the book was not reissued until 1863. The reprint, even though
it moved faster than an average of six copies a year, did not sell
enough to warrant a third printing before 1892."[35] On the other
hand, sentimental novels were far more popular than the slave

narratives. Fanny Fern's *Fern Leaves from Fanny's Portfolio* sold 70,000 copies in one year. Susan Warner's *The Wide, Wide World* had 14 editions in two years and in the third year, the semiannual royalties totaled $4,500.00.

Most of the slave narratives were not intended for exactly the same audiences as Thoreau's, Melville's, or even Hawthorne's works. Yet a comparison between sales figures for their works and those of slave narratives which were published during the same period shows that the contemporary audiences of Douglass, Brown, and Henson were far larger than those of three of the literary figures most revered today. On the other hand, it is apparent that the real experiences of the slave narratives did not appeal to as many persons as the imaginary plights of many sentimental heroines. The slave narratives were not mass culture writings or fictitious accounts concocted to appeal only to the heightened sensibilities of romantic females or any other mass audience. The narrators' desire to inform and to convert their audiences could accommodate some preconceived expectations, but, after this, the stories of bondage and freedom had to be told as their particular world view necessitated. Their popularity is astounding when one considers how precarious their situation was.

2

Blacks in Colonial Literature

THE HISTORY OF the slave narratives begins before the appearance of blacks as central figures in American prose writings. Their origins are in the stories of bondage and freedom which are contained in the first records of the black experience in America, in the records of the establishment of the colonies themselves. Unfortunately, any documents which may have been written by blacks at this time are not extant. In fact, the earliest information is culled from material which was not written specifically to discuss blacks in the colonies. It is found in census reports, court cases and laws, journals, letters and travel descriptions, proclamations and sermons, and poems and essays. In short, it is in the matters of public experience which comprise the majority of what is now accepted as colonial American literature.

Since the written expression from the colonies during the early seventeenth century was pretty much confined to inventories, reports, and other public record keeping, it is not surprising that the first notations about blacks are primarily statistical. Nonetheless, these records provide information about the arrival of blacks in the British colonies, the number of black inhabitants, and their places of residence. The manner in which the data are recorded gives some information about the status of blacks in the colonies and the attitudes with which they were perceived. The infrequency and shallowness of the earliest references to blacks testify to the level of significance which the whites accorded their presence. Later writings help document the increased concern and the proportionately increased distinctions made between whites and blacks, servants and slaves.

In the mid-seventeenth century, the documents begin to reveal the reactions of the blacks to these distinctions. The appearance of laws which prescribe their rights and responsibilities indicates that black perceptions of their status differed from the ideas of the white colonists. The records of court cases and the settlements of these cases also give ideas about white society's increasing resistance to black claims of personal sovereignty. Such information contributes substantially to our understanding of the evolution of the unique form of slavery which developed in the United States and the correspondingly unique expressions of those enslaved within that institution.

The earliest documents that mention blacks in the colonies were written by John Rolfe. In a 1620 letter to Sir Edwin Sandys, treasurer of the Virginia Company, Rolfe wrote that the year before a Dutch man-of-war "brought not anything but 20. and odd Negroes, which the Governor and Cape Marchant bought for victualles . . . at the best and easyest rate they could."[1] John Smith's *Generall Historie of Virginia* includes another letter by Rolfe, who is apparently referring to that same cargo when he states that "about the last of August came in a dutch man of warre that sold us twenty Negars."[2] Whether these "twenty Negars" were the first blacks to be imported into the colonies is not known; nor is it clear that their status differed appreciably from that of any other indentured servants. What is certain is that blacks were in servitude at that time and that their first mention in American literature is as merchandise.

The next references to blacks appear in 1624. Documents in this year give clues that differences in the status of white and black servants already existed. The "List of the Livinge and Dead in Virginia," which was prepared by the representatives of the Virginia Company of London, showed twenty-two blacks living in the colony. As Alden T. Vaughan has pointed out, "What is most striking about the appearance of these blacks in the census is that although most of them have been in America for five years, none is accorded a last name and almost half are recorded with no name at all. . . . By contrast, very few entries for non-Negroes have incomplete names."[3]

The 1625 census was a more ambitious effort than that of 1624. It listed not only the names of all the white inhabitants, including indentured servants, but also their ages, the dates they arrived in Virginia, and the ships upon which they rode. The census further provided a list of the possessions of each free family. Again, however, the information about blacks is cursory. In most cases, they are listed at the end of the "servants" section and referred to as "Negro Men 3 Negro Women 5" or "Negro woman and a young child of hers." Obviously, the difference in the recording techniques was not a matter of servitude or freedom, but a matter of race.

Documents from other colonies indicate the presence of black enslavement in the early seventeenth century. John Winthrop's notation that in 1638 "The Salem ship, the *Desire*, returned from the West Indies . . . and brought some cotton, and tobacco, and negroes, etc."[4] is clear evidence of the slave trade in colonial Massachusetts. Although the trading of slaves was their primary involvement, slavery did exist as a legitimate institution in the New England colonies. In New Netherland and the Middle Colonies, in Maryland and the Carolinas, the records show blacks were legally enslaved by the second half of the seventeenth century. Such early evidence leads to the conclusion that in the colonies of North America the status of blacks was never the same as that of whites, whether free or not.

By 1640, there is clear evidence that an institution of slavery based on racial differences was emerging. For example, court records show that in the 1640s some blacks were in slavery for life and their children were inheriting their status. Probably the most famous example of the emerging trend toward legal discrimination based on race is the case in which the Virginia General Court tried and sentenced three servants who had fled to Maryland. Two, a Dutchman and a Scotsman, were sentenced to an additional year of labor for their masters and three years of labor for the colony, but the court decreed that "the third being a negro named John Punch shall serve his said master or his assigns for the time of his natural life here or else where."[5]

The status of blacks continued to decline as the century continued. In 1643, the Virginia legislature declared that white women who engaged in field work were no longer subject to taxation but that all adult men and all Negro women were to be taxed. Racial discrimination was obvious when the lawmakers declared:

Whereas some doubts, have arisen whether negro women set free were still to be accompted tithable according to a former act, *It is declared by this grand assembly* that negro women, though permitted to enjoy their freedome yet ought not in all respects to be admitted to full fruition of the exemptions and impunities of the English, and are still lyable to payment of taxes.[6]

Most colonies forbade blacks the right to bear arms, and in 1660 Connecticut forbade them to enter military service. In 1663, Maryland presented a law that made slaves of all blacks, including those who were already free, and including any blacks born in the colony regardless of the status of the mother. There were, to be sure, some blacks who were not only free but prosperous. At least one, Anthony Johnson of Virginia, owned black slaves himself. But such situations were becoming more the exception than the rule.

The mid-seventeenth-century cases of Elizabeth Key and of Fernando give further idea of the deteriorating status of blacks.[7] About 1655, Key's attorney, William Greensted, sued for her freedom on three grounds: Her father was a free man, and British common law awarded children the status of their fathers; she had been baptized; and she had been sold for a term of nine years and that period had expired. The jury granted her freedom.

Fernando, ten years later, was not so favorably treated. In August 1667 at the Lower Norfolk County Court he sued for his freedom. He claimed that, as a Christian and former resident of England, he should serve no longer than English bondsmen served. The justices declared that there was no cause for action and dismissed the suit.

Several historians have noted evidence that the conversion to Christianity gave a colonial black a higher status, that in fact conversion or baptism could entitle a slave to freedom. Since both Key and Fernando cited their religious affiliations as grounds for their manumission, their cases seem to support this theory. The success of Key and the failure of Fernando give further clues to the increasing disparity between the attitudes of whites and those of blacks concerning the role of blacks in the new world. Key won her freedom in 1655 or 1656. In December 1662, the General Assembly decided that the status of the mother determined the status of the children, a decision which prevented any child born of a slave from using his paternity to achieve freedom. In September 1667, the General Assembly adopted a law that stated "conferring of baptisme doth not alter the condition of the person as to his bondage of freedome."[8] The case of Fernando, then gives direct evidence of the institutionalization of racism, which so greatly influenced the development of the slave narrative.

A brief study of the writings in which blacks are first mentioned provides a variety of valuable insights into the changing environment that caused a changing literature. For example, the clues that the cases of Key and of Fernando give about the role of religion in the social mobility of slaves are also valuable in assessing a characteristic of the nineteenth-century slave narratives. The slave narrators, a large percentage of whom were ministers, emphasized their Christianity. Almost without exception, the narrators give detailed descriptions of their conversion experiences and their habitual piety. They testify to the sustaining power of their Christian faith during the trials of slavery and during their efforts to escape that non-Christian institution. Although there are other reasons why they would desire to promulgate their faith, certainly a compelling motivation for such emphasis upon the author's religious beliefs would be the idea that the conversion to Christianity, though no longer deemed sufficient by the entire society to merit automatic liberty, would have enough residual impact to dispose their readers to more sympathetic attitudes.

Of more immediate importance is the fact that these early writings support the assertion that the difference between the narratives of blacks and the narratives of whites grew in proportion to the difference in the social expectations developed by and for these two groups. Consequently, as society made increasingly sharp distinctions between blacks and whites, the goals of their written expressions became increasingly distinct.

This contention is more obviously supported in surveys of the narratives which were written by blacks in the eighteenth century. In these narratives one directly encounters the black's perspective for the first time. It is easy to observe the differences in the attitudes and experiences of narrators such as Briton Hammon (1760), James Gronniosaw (1770), and Olaudah Equiano (1789). However, the information which exists in the seventeenth-century writings provides documentation of the peculiar situation which surrounded the existence of blacks and their failure to accept this situation. Already there is evidence of attempts by blacks to escape servitude, by both flight and litigation, and evidence of the failure of whites to afford the same treatment to blacks as to nonblacks. Already we have stories of bondage and freedom.

The stories of bondage and freedom became more coherent as the increasing number of black slaves in the colonies caused the disparities to become more obvious. By 1700 the slave population had grown to such an extent that in the New England colonies, where the black population was smallest, the ratio of blacks to whites was 1 to 10. Despite this small percentage, the growing presence of black residents helped nurture in the Puritans an uneasiness of conscience which had existed since the first cargo of black slaves arrived in New England. On June 24, 1700, Samuel Sewall published the first significant antislavery document, *The Selling of Joseph.* The acknowledged motivations for Sewall's essay demonstrate that slavery had become not only a philosophical but a practical problem. In the essay, the philosophical concern is revealed by Sewall's choice as epigraph the quotation from the English Puritan divine William Ames, which stated that "Forasmuch as *Liberty* is in real value next unto *Life:* None ought to part with it themselves, or deprive others of it, but upon most mature Consideration." Sewall's first sentence addresses the practical problem: "The Numerousness of them under their Slavery, hath put many upon thinking whether the Foundation of it be firmly and well laid; so as to sustain the Vast Weight that is built upon it."[9] Notations in Sewall's diary show how the philosophical and practical combined to produce *The Selling of Joseph:*

> Having been long and much dissatisfied with the Trade of fetching Negros from Guinea; at last I had a strong Inclination to Write something about it; but it wore off. At last reading Bayne, Ephes. about servants, who mentions Blackamoors; I began to be uneasy that I had so long neglected doing anything. When I was thus thinking, in came Bro Belknap to shew me a Petition he intended to present to the Gen Court for the freeing a Negro and his wife, who were un-

justly held in Bondage. And there is a Motion by a Boston Comittee to get a Law that all Importers of Negros shall pay 40^S p̄ [sic] head, to discourage the bringing of them. And Mr. C. Mather resolves to publish a sheet to exhort Masters to labour their Conversion. Which makes me hope that I was call'd of God to Write this Apology for them; Let his Blessing accompany the same.[10]

The Selling of Joseph confronts two major concerns: the religious validity of slavery as well as the potential physical threats to the emerging Puritan society.

It is a matter of record that about this same time a slave named Adam had solicited Judge Sewall's help in obtaining the freedom promised him by his owner, John Saffin, and that Sewall, Saffin, and Adam became embroiled in a legal battle that lasted several years. In 1701 Saffin published *A Brief and Candid Answer to a Late Printed Sheet, Entituled, The Selling of Joseph.* In this pamphlet, Saffin details his problems with Adam and presents what has been described as "The first in a long American line, prototype of the Bible defense of slavery in the era of Calhoun, in which scriptural snippets are manipulated to fortify a theology of white superiority and black bondage."[11]

The Selling of Joseph is responsible for beginning the first serious discussion of slavery in New England society and American literature. When it is considered with several entries in Sewall's diary and with certain events which occurred after its publication, *The Selling of Joseph* gains importance as the publication most directly responsible for the first written account of sequential incidents in the life of a black slave on the North American continent. From it and Saffin's rebuttal, from personal diaries, official court records of an extended legal battle, and even a few poems of that period can be reconstructed for the first time the story of a series of events in the life of one black in New England. This conglomeration has come to be known collectively as "Adam Negro's Tryall."

The details are missing, but the basic story is clear. In 1694, Saffin promised to free Adam after seven years of service. In 1701, Saffin refused to honor this promise. Adam sued. His case was heard by the Superior Court in September 1701. Apparently, Saffin's defense was based upon the quality of Adam's service. Saffin's

Brief and Candid Answer quotes persons who characterize Adam as "intollerably insolent, quarrelsome and outrageous." It was charged that Adam came and went as he pleased, did his assigned tasks in his own way and at his own pace, and was not inclined to suffer maltreatment. For example, when working for Captain Clark, Adam did not perform a task to the satisfaction of Clark. In his indignation, Clark called Adam a rogue to which Adam replied that he was "no Rogue, no Rascal, no Thief."[12] Clark shoved Adam. Adam pushed him back. When Clark hit him with a stick, Adam took the stick, broke it, and attacked his assailant with a shovel. It took several men to break up the fight.

The jury decided Adam had not fulfilled his obligation and was to remain Saffin's slave. Saffin was one of the judges who heard Adam's case. Moreover, Sewall's diary for this period notes several charges that Saffin attempted to influence the testimony of witnesses and to tamper with the jury.

The decision was appealed. The case dragged on for three years. Finally, on November 2, 1703, the Superior Court, with Sewall as one of the four judges, declared "that the sd. Adam and his heirs be at peace and quiet and free with all their Chattels from the sd. John Saffin Esqr. and his heirs for Ever."

Until his death in 1710, Saffin continued his fight to regain possession of Adam. The remainder of Adam's life is unknown; however, according to Sidney Kaplan, "A few years later the name of Adam, a 'Free Negro' appears in the Boston town records as one of four blacks offering themselves as guarantors for one Madam Leblond, a black woman, to save the town from being chargeable for her 'sickness or any disaster.'"[13]

There are many gaps in Adam's story. For example, his name is given as Adam. More than Adam we do not know, for not only were first names rather haphazardly assigned, but as of yet it was not customary to grant surnames to slaves. "Negro" was a word attached to indicate race and consequently to imply social status. Nonetheless, "Adam Negro's Tryall" not only revolves around nine years in the life of a specific individual but it also reveals the determination of this person to assert his rights as a human being. The potpourri of pamphlets, court records, diaries, and events which form the story of Adam makes it the most coherent record of the experiences of a black in the first century of American literature.

With "Adam Negro's Tryall" the record of black experiences changes. No longer are there merely references to ciphers or semi-anonymous individuals. "Adam Negro's Tryall" is more than a brief mention of a court case. It is the genesis of anti- and proslavery literature in the United States. Sewall's essay was directly motivated by the experiences of blacks in this country and became the prototype for antislavery writings; but more importantly it is a literary effort which deliberately focuses upon the relations between a black person and a white person, and illustrates the irreconcilable attitudes between men of two races about the rights and responsibilities of these races in early American society.

"Adam Negro's Tryall" provides enough information that several critics have cited it as the first slave narrative. This is certainly an exaggeration of the term; however, there is enough evidence within the account to make "Adam Negro's Tryall" of great importance to the history of the development of the slave narrative. It is a precursor of the slave narratives, for it emerges as the first American writing to depict clearly the actions and circumstances under which a black slave rejected the role of chattel or permanent bondsman and asserted himself as a human being with pride, dignity, and the courage to demand respect and personal liberty. Although Adam does not narrate the story (nor do the documents of the case emphasize his version of the events), it is obvious that he played an active role in the proceedings. He refused to accept abusive language or beatings while enslaved. Rather than become a fugitive, he enlisted the aid of both prominent whites and free blacks (one of whom, Dick, paid his bail) and he sued for his freedom. Although the circumstances of "Adam Negro's Tryall" are complex, ultimately its focus is upon one black man's struggle for freedom from bondage.

The narratives of slaves which developed later were published through circumstances similar to those of "Adam Negro's Tryall." It was not a simple and sincere appreciation of individuals' attempts to come to terms with themselves, their ideals, and their circumstances that gained the first sizable audiences for slave narratives. Their recognition came as by-products of a struggle over slavery, but in which slaves had only limited influence. Antislavery literature had already become a recognizable form before any attention was given to the slave's view of the subject. It was by chance that white abolitionists discovered that a sizable market existed for such first-hand stories of slavery and thus became very active in the promulgation of what they conceived as a supplement to antislavery literature, but what evolved into a distinct classification of its own.

As with "Adam Negro's Tryall," the predilections of their intended audience first threatened to dominate the published accounts of slaves. But as the form developed, the voice of the slave himself, his assertion of manhood, and his movement from bondage to freedom became more pronounced. Differences between the white antislavery writings and the narratives of slaves became more distinct. A central difference revolved around the development in the slave narratives of a dichotomy that antislavery writings by whites lacked. Although whites condemned slavery in their writings, they rarely affirmed the complete humanness of the slaves. Slave narrators affirmed themselves as human beings with the basic qualifications necessary for membership in any human society, and they condemned the institution of slavery as antihuman.

Analysis of the seventeenth-century writings also reveals the existence of two elements which later form the basis of the slave narratives. In the records wherein the black appears as more than a cipher or anonymous being, he is inevitably a rebel struggling for some measure of freedom from his bondage, for some recognition of himself as being human. In the slave narratives, the dominant character type is the rebel, and the dominant theme is the story of bondage and freedom.

The development of the genre, however, was neither smooth nor swift. Although literary debate concerning the place of the African in the New World continued, and antislavery literature began to emerge as a definite literary form, it was thirty years after "Adam Negro's Tryall" before the personal experiences of a black enslaved in the colonies were presented as a separately published factual account. *Some Memoirs of the Life of Job* was published in London in 1734. It focused upon carefully selected episodes in the life of Ayuba Suleiman Diallo, known to the readers as Job ben Solomon. The account was recorded by Thomas Bluett, whose use of the third-person point of view emphasizes the distance between himself and the story he is relating. He prefaces his writing by saying, "I was desired by himself, a little before his departure, to draw up an account of him agreeable to the information he had given me at different times, and to the truth of the facts, which I had either been a witness to, or personally concerned in upon his account." Bluett gives his motivation for publishing the story as one way of giving public thanks to those who had befriended this black man without knowing the details of his life. He states that he will limit his narrative to "such particulars of the life and character of this African Gentleman, as I think will be most useful and entertaining." That he does not intend to be controversial is evident when he says, "I shall endeavour to make the whole as agreeable as the nature of the subject, and the limits of this pamphlet will allow."[14] The emphasis is upon some experiences of the man and his travels and not upon the issue of slavery.

The narrative begins with information concerning Diallo's family and his life before captivity, describes the circumstances of his capture and transportation to Maryland, then concentrates upon some incidents during his life as a slave in that colony. Diallo, who had been a Muslim merchant in his country, suffered from the hard work and the intolerance to his religious practices and ran away. He was jailed as an escaped slave in another town, but evidently he was not beaten or otherwise abused. He was rescued from his incarceration by Thomas Bluett, who, in spite of Diallo's inability to speak English, was somehow convinced that Diallo was an unusually well educated person. Bluett facilitated Diallo's return to the Maryland master, whereupon, we are assured, the master did not punish the runaway, but, in fact, "was much kinder to him than before; allowing him a place to pray in, and some other conveniences, in order to make his slavery as easy as possible." "Yet," Bluett reports, "slavery and confinement was by no means agreeable to Job, who had never been used to it." Therefore, Bluett commenced efforts to have Diallo liberated. With assistance from various sources, including James E. Oglethorpe, English philanthropist and founder of Georgia, he managed to arrange Diallo's passage to England. There, Bluett reports, Diallo's "mind being now perfectly easy, and being himself more known, he went chearfully among his friends to several places, both in town and country."[15]

His friends included many of the English nobility, and he was introduced to the royal family. Finally, his father received word of his whereabouts, sent a ransom, and Diallo, loaded with presents from his English sponsors, was allowed to return to Africa. Bluett's narrative concludes with information about the system of government, the habits and beliefs of the people, and a detailed description of Job's physical appearance and personality.

If one is familiar with nineteenth-century slave narratives, it is almost impossible to believe that Bluett's account is about the same institution. For example, the experiences of Solomon Northup, a freeman in the United States who was kidnapped and enslaved for twelve years while undergoing extreme deprivation (he was not even allowed to receive a sheet of paper upon which to write a plea for help), are difficult to reconcile with those related by Bluett. In reality, it is not the same institution. Slavery in the colonies of the New World in the eighteenth century was often quite different from slavery in the nineteenth century. In fact, recent studies have proved that the history of the "peculiar institution" in the United States was so peculiar that it encompassed almost every form of servitude possible as it evolved into an entity distinctly different from any other kind.

However, the differences in the narratives are not just those of two extremely different experiences. To a significant extent, they are differences in genre. Bluett's account is a biographical narrative of a black written by a white. Northup's is a slave narrative. Bluett's primary purpose was to provide information about the unusual experiences of a specific individual. He was writing to fill in the gaps for an audience which included a number of persons who had befriended Diallo at various times. Bluett's work is much like a contemporary version of the Good Samaritan parable. Diallo suffered a misfortune that left him a stranger in a strange land. He was aided by several men of goodwill and returned safely to his homeland. *Some Memoirs of the Life of Job* was intended more as a eulogy to those who had contributed to his freedom than as an exposé of the reasons for his bondage or of his response to it. His enslavement is treated as an unfortunate mistake. Slavery as an institution is not condemned. On the other hand, Solomon Northup's experience is related as one example of how freemen are deliberately kidnapped and enslaved. The focus of Northup's narrative is upon the vicious system of slavery. The fact that Northup is eventually rescued is not as important to the story as the fact that many men are not.

Between the narratives of Diallo and Northup were several years of literary experimentation by black writers. As racial discrimination and particularly the institution of slavery became increasingly significant in their lives, their writings reflected these changes. In some cases race and slavery became dominant themes. In others the fact of the narrator's racial identity and social status informed the writing, but was not the focus of the work. The slave narrative genre, of which Northup's is an example, was only one of several to evolve. The emergence of the black narrator came first.

Before the nineteenth century, it was rare that a writing was primarily concerned with relating the experiences of a particular black person. In the colonies, the characterization went from thing to humanoid to human. When the black person as statistic or subject gave way to the black person as narrator, the most common protagonist was the social degenerate. Of the approximately forty-six editions published between 1675 and 1800 which dealt with black individuals, two-thirds were about criminals.[16] These black criminal narratives encouraged stereotypical characterizations and catered to popular racial prejudices. *The Declaration and Confession of Jeffery, a Negro, who was executed at Worchester, October 17, 1745, for the murder of Mrs. Tabitha Sandford, at Mendon, the 12th of September Preceding*, appears to be the first black criminal narrative. In 1768 appeared the first title which indicates an extended autobiographical account, *The Life and Dying Speech of Arthur, A Negro Man, Who was executed at Worchester, October 20th, 1768 for a rape committed On the Body of one Deborah Metcalfe*. It is important to note that both of these narratives are concerned with crimes of violence perpetrated upon women, for there was a definite tendency in the colonial narratives to emphasize sexual crimes of blacks. Richard Slotkin demonstrates the apparent racism in the following analysis:

> Where whites were concerned, murder was the most sensational of crimes, and therefore the most commonly written-up; murder narratives constitute some 70% of all crime narrative editions. Rape

was one of the least commonly written-up, some 6% of all crime narratives; piracy and crimes against property (burglary, arson) respectively constitute 60% and 18% of the total. For narratives of black crime (some 14% of the total—higher by far than their percentage of the New England population) the proportions differ significantly: four narratives and two smaller items deal with crimes against property (12½%), but only twelve deal with murder, indicating a greater relative emphasis on this crime in narratives of black criminals; and in absolute numbers, the number of editions dealing with black rapists is three times the number dealing with whites. . . . Four narratives deal with black rebellions, in which both rape (or miscegenation) and murder figure. . . . Nor are there any narratives dealing with the most prevalent form of interracial rape, that of black or Indian women by white masters. The literature shows only white women as sexual victims, and nonwhite women as accomplices or abettors of the black rapist.

Slotkin further informs us that "the distortion is also incremental in that there is a distinct rise in the interest in sexual crimes (rape, cohabitation with whites) as the eighteenth century wears to a close."[17]

In the criminal narratives as in the slave narratives, the increasing differentiation between the narratives of whites and of blacks is apparent even in the relation of nonsexual crimes. The difference between the 1786 narrative of Johnson Green and the 1808 narrative of John Joyce is a good example. In *The Life and Confessions of Johnson Green*, Johnson Green reports that his life of crime began at age twelve, "at which time I stole four cakes of gingerbread and six biscuit, out of a horse cart." At age twenty-nine, he was condemned to death because he stole "about three shillings and three pence in money, and about nine dollars worth of clothing." Green recounts his life of crime as a warning to others. He states that "I have lived a hard life, by being obliged to keep in the woods; have suffered much by hunger, nakedness, cold, and the fears of being detected and brought to justice." Although he is proud that he "never murdered any person, nor robbed anybody on the highway," he is repentant about his "wicked and infamous conduct."[18]

The earlier black narrators such as Green seem to adhere to Puritan concepts, as they present themselves as examples to be avoided by all concerned. Their concessions to racial differences are made only in passing, but they conform to the patterns established for blacks and indicate the strength of racism in the colonies. For example, Green indicates that he is a mulatto. Following the custom identified in the Virginia census of 1624, he identifies his father not by name but by race and status: "My father was a negro, and a servant to the Hon. Timothy Edson, Esq., late of said Bridgwater, deceased." However, he identifies his mother by name and nationality and does not indicate whether she was in service or not. He states that "my mother was a widow, and her maiden name was Green. I have been called Joseph-Johnson Green." In another place, identification of his wife includes the information that she was "a mustee, who was brought up by Mr. Olney of Providence." Green also makes racial distinctions in his summary of his extramarital affairs when he states, "I have had a correspondence with many women, exclusive of my wife, among whom were several abandoned Whites, and a large number of Blacks; four of the whites were married women, three of the Blacks have had children to me." Nowhere, however, is Green's race or bondage acknowledged as an important difference between him and his audience.

Twenty-two years later, race had become a more important factor. The *Confession of John Joyce* includes "An Address to the Public, and People of Colour" by Richard Allen. After the standard sermon about the evils of murder and the need for all people to take warning from the example of John Joyce, Allen addresses the "People of Colour" by saying, "To you, the murder of Mrs. Cross speaks as with a voice of thunder. Many of you fear the living God, and walk in his commandments; but, oh, how many are slaves of Sin. . . . Be these, O man, O woman of colour, thy resolutions." Allen then gives to the blacks, in addition to the general resolutions of the first part of his sermon, special resolutions that as colored citizens they must follow. Moreover, Chief Justice Tilghman in his statements to the convicted Joyce directly refers to his race as he tells Joyce, "You have injured society in general, and the people of your own colour in particular by rendering them objects of public disgust and suspicion."[19]

The circumstances under which the autobiographical confessions were obtained and the uses to which they were directed limit their importance in the history of the slave narratives. They are helpful, however, as illustrations of the increasingly common acceptance of some techniques incorporated in the slave narratives. For example, the criminal narratives were written in the first person. This illustrates the trend toward the acceptance of a black person as narrator and indicates a willingness of a white audience to acknowledge that a black person could articulate the facts of his life from his own perspective and in a manner that entertained and instructed them.

Secondly, the criminal narratives and the slave narratives share an assertion of humanity. In both forms of narrative, the narrators take responsibility for their actions, thus indicating a sense of themselves as persons with some degree of self-determination. For example, in Green's narrative, the author says, "I, Johnson Green, having brought myself to a shameful and ignominious death by my wicked conduct, and, as I am a dying man, I leave to the world the following History of my Birth, Education, and vicious Practices, hoping that all people will take warning by my evil example and shun vice and follow virtue." There are ritualistic tones, traditional phrases, and an absolute condemnation of his life which are standard to all criminal narratives. Yet he does recite a litany that refers to himself as responsible for his actions and as an example for all people. Obviously, Green accepted himself as a human being with certain responsibilities to other human beings. Such a recognition of full humanity and such an assertion of humanness are a kind of rebellion against prevalent social attitudes. The black narrator, though condemned and accepting this condemnation for his actions, at the same time rejects the humanoid and moves toward the human. This movement continues and strengthens in the Indian captivity narratives, a form utilized by black writers in the second half of the eighteenth century.

Like the criminal narratives, the Indian captivities began as a religious literature. The earliest extant narrative of this kind written by a black man was published in 1760 for the firm of Green and Russell in Queen Street, Boston, Massachusetts. Like that of much colonial literature, the complete title of Briton Hammon's narrative provides an adequate summary of its contents. The full title of this work is *A Narrative of the Uncommon Sufferings, and*

*Surprizing Deliverance of Briton Hammon, a Negro Man,—Servant
to General Winslow, of Marshfield, in New-England: Who Returned
to Boston, after having been absent also Thirteen Years, Contain-
ing an Account of the many Hardships he underwent from the
Time of his Return to Boston,—How he was cast away in the Capes
of Florida;—the horrid Cruelty and inhuman barbarity of the
Indians in murdering the whole Ship's Crew:—the Manner of his
being carry'd by them into captivity. Also, An Account of his being
Confined Four Years and Seven Months in a close Dungeon,—and
the remarkable Manner in which he met with his good old Master
in London; who returned to New-England, a Passenger, in the same
Ship.*

Like his white contemporaries who wrote accounts of Indian
capture, Hammon claimed that he wrote "to show how great things
the Lord hath done for me."²⁰ Hammon utilized the structure of
the Indian captivity narrative, and he treats, as Richard Van der
Beets points out, "the salutary effects of the captivity, especially
in the context of redemptive suffering; the captivity as test, trial,
or punishment by God; and, finally and most demonstrably, the
captivity as evidence of Divine Providence and of God's inscrutable
wisdom."²¹ Moreover, Hammon, like other mid-eighteenth-century
narrators in the British colonies, had an obvious political bias
and used his narrative to promote England and its colonies as
countries of more noble men than those of France or Spain.

In spite of these similarities, elements that distinguish Hammon's
narrative from those by whites are apparent. As with the criminal
narratives, the differences between works by blacks and by whites
are apparent, first, in the titles. Hammon is identified as "a Negro
Man." Concern for racial differences may also be recognized when
one realizes that when Hammon lists his companions in the ship-
wreck, he gives the name, profession and/or place of residence of
all except three men. These were "Elkanah Collymore, and James
Webb, Strangers, and Moses Newmock, Molatto."²² It seems that
even though it was not necessary to present Hammon's experiences
as significantly different from those of other persons who had been
captured by Indians or imprisoned for refusing to be drafted by a
foreign army, there was some need to distinguish blacks from
nonblacks.

Another notable factor is the unusual emphasis given to Hammon's freedom to come and go, to negotiate for his services and to receive the contracted wages after each job was completed. Since in the selection of details for any narrative, the narrator chooses those which have significance, it is likely that Hammon stressed these liberties because they were unusual or a source of particular pride to him. This interpretation is strengthened by the stress given to the fact that permission to exercise these liberties was granted to Hammon by his master. In the title, Hammon is identified as "servant to General Winslow," and in the beginning of the narrative it is made clear that Hammon left for his journey with the permission of his master. At the conclusion of his adventures, the title assures us that he met "his *good old Master* in *London* [italics his]; who returned to New-England, a Passenger, in the same Ship." Hammon's attempts to escape from Cuba are carefully justified on the grounds that Cuba was a Spanish colony and not that his servitude was an unacceptable condition. Though quite similar to Indian captivity narratives, Hammon's narrative differs in ways that may be attributed to his servitude and to his race.

Another popular narrative which has been considered both an Indian captivity and a slave narrative is *A Narrative of the Lord's Wonderful Dealings with John Marrant, a Black*, first published in 1785. Although included in many bibliographies as a slave narrative, Marrant's narrative is not a slave narrative because Marrant was a freeman whose recorded adventures are directly related to his intense religious devotion and display no concern with slavery. However, consideration of Marrant's work gives increased support to the thesis that the slave narrative is a recognizable kind of narrative utilized by blacks for specific purposes because it provides a useful contrast and an example of other black narrative forms. Marrant's narrative informs us that he was born into what could be considered a middle-class black family. Marrant was educated in Florida, Georgia, and South Carolina schools before he was apprenticed to study music and dance. He soon earned recognition as an accomplished musician. At a revival meeting conducted by George Whitefield, Marrant was converted. Considered a religious fanatic by family and friends, he went to live in the forest. He survived exposure, hunger, and the danger of wild animals. He was captured by Indians and suffered other crises before he returned home. At the close of his narrative he was leaving to become a missionary in Nova Scotia.

Marrant's narrative was published in England and in the United States several times between 1785 and 1829. It appeared under at least three different titles. In none of these editions was Marrant's race or the issue of slavery given significant consideration. These omissions appear to be deliberate, for it is known that Marrant's religious fervor had not blinded him to racial injustices nor separated him from association with his fellow blacks. In fact, shortly after his narrative had been published, Marrant was made a Mason by Prince Hall at African Lodge Number 459. On June 24, 1789, as chaplain of that lodge, Marrant preached a strong antislavery sermon which was widely published for several years. His narrative illustrates one form which was popular for black writers in 1785, and serves as a contrast to the slave narratives which began to appear at this time.

Marrant's and Hammon's narratives are stories of a different sort of bondage and freedom from that dealt with in the genre identified as slave narratives. Nonetheless, they may be considered precursors to the slave narrative. Like "Adam Negro's Tryall" they dealt with stories of events in the life of colonial blacks. Like Ayuba Suleiman Diallo's story, they are structured narratives which are developed from experiences recounted by a black man. Like the criminal narratives, they are written in the first person and have their beginnings in the religious narrative tradition. But with Hammon's and Marrant's narratives, an important change occurs. Black individuals are characterized by themselves as exemplars. In the beginning they are exemplary Christians whose sufferings and deliverances are proofs of God's power and mercy. Later their symbolism becomes more specific as the black protagonists present themselves as examples of men who have faced the inhumane and anti-Christian conditions of slavery and who have escaped with humanity and Christianity intact. The focus has shifted more clearly to the black as an active individual rather than a passive object.

During the latter part of the eighteenth century, Richard Allen wrote a narrative which integrated the religious and antislavery motifs. Allen reports that he was born a slave in Philadelphia in

1760. Of his master, Allen says, "He was more like a father to his slaves than anything else," yet he reports that his good master sold Allen's mother and three of her children and that he had a continual fear of being sold also. Allen states that "I had it often impressed upon my mind that I should one day enjoy my freedom; for slavery is a bitter pill, not with standing we had a good master."[23] His master's goodness notwithstanding, Allen left as soon as he had earned enough to buy his freedom. He did manual labor and preached for several years. After an episode during which the several black members, including Allen, were ejected from St. George's Church for refusing to adhere to increasingly rigid segregation during worship, Allen devoted his efforts to organizing churches for blacks. The remainder of his narrative deals with the experiences which led to the founding of the African Methodist Episcopal Church.

With the appearance of narratives such as those by Hammon, Marrant, and Allen, the way was paved for slave narratives. The major thematic and structural elements to be found in a majority of the succeeding narratives of slaves in the United States are evident.

The black is not only the subject but is also the author of the narrative. He relates a chronological sequence of personal experiences liberally spiced with religious, philosophical, and political observations. The black narrator asserts himself as a Christian and as an individual with the right to personal liberty or at least the right to choose his own master. He judges the denial of these assertions to be unfair and rebels against such restrictions. Focus upon the struggle for freedom from bondage and identification of the protagonist as rebel has clearly begun.

The Development
of Slave Narratives

THE LITERARY HISTORY of the development of the slave narrative is similar to that of other personal narratives. Slave narrators regularly adopted the current literary conventions and made little attempt to create new forms or standards. They did not challenge the validity of current attitudes toward aesthetics, appropriate diction, or decorum. This does not mean that they were simply imitators. The conscious and consistent exploitation of the ironic potential inherent in using traditional literary techniques to tell their stories is but one example of imaginative variations that they employed. The manipulation of racist images and stereotypes promulgated by proslavery writers is another. Were circumstances different, slave narratives probably would have continued as variations rather than becoming mutants. Escalating estrangement between audience and writer and changes in the scope and urgency of slave narrators' mission compelled the divergence. By the end of the eighteenth century, the slave narrative was emerging as a distinct literary genre. This evolution is best shown by contrasting the narratives published during the latter part of the eighteenth century with those published during the ante-bellum period.

Eighteenth-century slave narratives emphasized the individual, and for the most part they reflected the Puritan theocentric society. Race was a factor in the narrator's manner and matter, but it was not at first a crucial element. Their emphasis was upon a theme more easily identified with by all heirs to a Judeo-Christian philosophy, the struggle for existence as strangers in an inhospitable land.

One reason was that most of the eighteenth-century narratives were written and published in New England or London. In both places, slavery was not as commonplace as it was in the South and in the West Indies. Thus the early slave narrators were quite frequently introducing a subject which was only vaguely known to most readers. They found it more appropriate to present slavery as a philosophical issue and to emphasize problems such as the religious and moral contradictions of permanent bondage. Often discussion centered on the evils of the slave trade. Although no evidence exists of coteries comparable to those of the 1831-65 period, a few of the more popular narrators of the latter part of the eighteenth century knew and worked with each other on various antislavery projects. It is probable, therefore, that similarities in content and form during this time were not entirely coincidental.

The structural characteristics of the eighteenth-century slave narratives are traditional and simple. The narrative is a sustained chronological account of events in an individual's life presented to create or to prolong a particular response. Its purpose is to amuse its readers while encouraging them in their humanitarian and religious efforts. The account itself is preceded by introductory remarks that include confirmation of the narrator's good moral character and the validity of the narrative's facts by a respected white person. The narrative begins with accounts of the slave's life before captivity. This serves as exposition and as contrast with the later circumstances. The complication begins with the kidnapping of an innocent being and increases as the inconveniences and abuses of slavery become more evident. The narrative climaxes with rescue from slavery and a spiritual or material reward for the hardships encountered.

The depiction of the slave is more complicated. Generally, he is a primitive being who, while undergoing various hardships, nevertheless develops some of the traits which Westerners considered civilized and thus more human.

The accounts of slaves in the eighteenth century present a series of characters who range from sinners to saints. But each of the narratives portrays an individual confronting a series of threatening incidents and having to rely quite extensively upon his courage and intelligence to survive. Sometimes this was manifest as rebellion or resistance, but at other times it was aggression. Many narrators sought out adventure as a way of achieving personal satisfaction. Olaudah Equiano, for example, encountered many of his problems because he would leave his master's sheep to buy and sell fruit, rum, and livestock for his personal gain. Richard Allen aroused the ire of persons because he refused to sit in the church balcony which was reserved for the black members. Instead, he led a group of blacks to build their own church. The protagonists of these narratives were not only reacting to situations, but they were also active participants in the situations.

Many of the narrators identified with the values of that society. This is not to say that they completely rejected the reality of their outsider status. Rather, it emphasizes the fact that their lives were not one continuous rejection of oppression and defense of manhood. Many of the early narrators display the contemporary attitudes and literary traditions of the times. Literature, they believed, could and should instruct and inform. Divine Providence controlled, but loyalty, thrift, and courage were essential.

The protagonist of the slave narratives at the end of the eighteenth century was a somewhat strange and exotic specimen, but one who was well educated or of high social status according to the standards of his primitive culture. This is evident in *Some Memoirs of the Life of Job* when the author states that Job could not only read and write but that "by his affable carriage, and the easy composure of his countenance, we could perceive he was no common slave."[1] And it was true of other eighteenth-century narrators such as Olaudah Equiano, who was the son of a chief or "Embrenche," and Venture Smith, who was the son of a prince. The savage but noble concept that was so popular in eighteenth-century racial thought could explain the eighteenth-century narratives' predilection for highborn African narrators. It gives a basis for interpreting Bluett's reference to Job as "High Priest of Boonda" and the fact that so many titles of the eighteenth-century narratives heralded the narrator as being an African of noble birth.

The protagonist's experiences include traveling to various countries where he soon acquires a satisfactory amount of westernization. He then manages to receive his freedom, almost as a reward for good behavior. In fact, the slave has usually earned the respect and admiration of all who had recognized the resourcefulness and manly bearings of this diamond in the rough. Most often his experiences have included conversion to Christianity and the adoption of a Christian name. Ayuba Suleiman Diallo became Job; Olaudah Equiano was Gustavus Vassa; and Broteer Furro became Venture Smith. Thus there was a tendency to Anglicize the protagonist and to present the plight of the eighteenth-century African slave in terms very similar to those of the wandering hero legends or the religious Pilgrim's trials. Since he seems to have experienced little more physical pain or mental anguish than any other outsider in a new situation or any other lower-class individual in a class society, and he has in the process acquired or demonstrated characteristics usually associated with the Western hero, the *"African* gentleman,"* as Bluett calls Diallo, is little more than a variation upon traditional narrative archetypes.

In the eighteenth-century narratives, slavery is presented as a loss of physical freedom. Its dehumanizing aspects are not emphasized. Physical brutalities to slaves are presented as unusual occurrences and are usually remedied by sympathetic persons who intervene on the slave's behalf or by a polite discussion between master and slave. In Britain and its colonies, the evil of the system was still being weighed against the good. Thus discussions of the religious and moral contradictions within slavery were contained in the narratives, but the institution of slavery was not totally condemned. Rather, it was the abuses of the system by certain unscrupulous persons or by misunderstandings between slave and master which caused the exposure of conflicts within the system.

A good example of the narratives written between 1760 and 1807 is *The Interesting Narrative of the Life of Olaudah Equiano, or Gustavus Vassa, the African,* first published in 1789. Equiano's narrative begins with an account of the geography and culture of his native country, Benin (part of the present-day Nigeria). He details family history, his childhood, his kidnapping, his enslavement and subsequent experiences in England, the West Indies, and the American colonies of Virginia and Georgia. Among his achievements he lists playing the French horn, reading the Bible, and hairdressing. During his varied experiences as a slave, he also learns the techniques of desalinization, navigation, and naval warfare. As a convert to Christianity, he debates with learned British Protestant ministers as well as Portuguese Catholic clergy. He eventually travels to every major area of the world, including the North Pole.

After numerous misfortunes and many instances of salvation by God's direct intervention or his own quick thinking, he earns his freedom, claims England as his home, and works actively in anti-slavery activities.

Equiano's narrative is in many ways typical of those that were published between 1760 and 1807. The narrator is a person of more than usual independence, daring, and curiosity. In the tradition of much of eighteenth-century popular literature, the focus of the narrative is upon the individual and his adventures. Slaves such as Equiano were more like Defoe's Robinson Crusoe than Defoe's characterization of the ever-faithful and servile black man, Friday. For these daring men, capture by hostile Indians, shipwrecks on deserted islands, and military combat on the high seas were occasions to demonstrate their courage and intelligence. In addition, they were usually interpreted as manifestations of God's power and grace. They reinforce the Christian idea that for those who keep the faith, good does eventually come from evil. More often than not, the slave hero not only benefits himself but also positively influences the lives of his white masters and fellow workers. Thus he earns the respect and admiration of all men of good repute and noble character, while exemplifying God's salvation, which extends to all mankind.

Olaudah Equiano relates an experience which occurred during a voyage from the West Indies to Georgia that shows both of these themes. "On the fourth of February, which was soon after we had got into our new course," says Equiano, "I dreamt the ship was wrecked amidst the surfs and rocks, and that I was the means of saving everyone on board." He had this same dream three nights in a row. Soon after this, while on watch, he actually saw the rocks. The captain did not listen to his warnings, and the ship was wrecked. Equiano states:

> And in the midst of my distress, while the dreadful surfs were dashing with unremitting fury among the rocks, I remembered the Lord, though fearful that I was undeserving of forgiveness, and I thought that as he had often delivered he might yet deliver; and, calling to mind the many mercies he had shown me in times past, they gave me some small hope that he might still help me. I then began to think

how we might be saved; and I believe no mind was ever like mine so replete with inventions, and confused with schemes, though how to escape death I knew not.

Equiano took over the management of the ship; for as he reports the captain was incapable of directing any escape attempt and most of the sailors gave up hope and proceeded to get drunk. Equiano declares:

> There were only four people that would work with me at the oars, and they consisted of three black men and a Dutch Creole sailor; and, though we went with the boat five times that day, we had no others to assist us. But, had we not worked in this matter, I really believe the people could not have been saved; for not one of the white men did anything to preserve their lives; indeed, they soon got so drunk that they were not able, but lay about the deck like swine, so that we were at last obliged to lift them into the boat, and carry them on shore by force. This want of assistance made our labor intolerably severe; insomuch, that, by going on shore so often that day, the skin was partly stript off my hands.

When all were safely on the island, he says, "I could not help thinking, that if any of these people had been lost, God would charge me with their lives; which, perhaps, was one cause of my laboring so hard for their preservation."[2]

Besides a basically episodic structure, the narratives share a peculiar impersonal tone. While the hero's physical situation is greatly affected by the outcome of these occurrences, and while his moods may vary from despair to exaltation in the narration of events, his basic psychological well-being (that is, his concept of who he is and what his relationship to society ought to be) is not seriously questioned. Often the reader is amused, intrigued, sometimes astonished by the resiliency and resourcefulness of the individual. The reader is not pulled into a journey of tears and sighs, nor is he continuously terrified by the harsh and foreboding situations that challenge and threaten the narrator. His faith in God is almost identical to that which the narrator professes, for, inevitably, the slave is a Christian convert. Consequently, the ultimate result is known, and the interest is in the ways God's will is made manifest.

The intent of many eighteenth-century narratives to justify the ways of God to man is made very clear in the preface to James Albert Ukawsaw Gronnioaw's narrative:

His long and perilous journey to the coast of Guinea, where he was sold for a slave, and so brought into a Christian land; shall we consider this as the alone effect of a curious and inquisitive disposition? Shall we, in accounting for it refer to nothing higher than the mere chance & accidental circumstances? Whatever Infidels & Deists may think, I trust the Christian reader will easily discern an all wise and omnipotent appointment in the direction of these movements. . . . God has put singular honor upon him in the exercise of his faith and patience, which, in the most distressing and pitiable trials and calamities have been found to the praise and glory of God.[3]

Equiano is predisposed to the same justification: "I had a mind in which every thing uncommon made its full impression, and every event which I considered as marvellous. Every extraordinary escape, or signal deliverance, either of myself or others I looked upon to be effected by the interposition of Providence."[4]

Another purpose was to remind the Christian reader of the sins of mankind. In the preface to *A Narrative of the Life and Adventures of Venture, a Native of Africa*, the reader is reminded that Venture's sufferings occurred in a Christian country. "And," continues the preface, "if he [the reader] shall derive no other advantage from perusing the narrative, he may experience those sensations of shame and indignation that will prove him to be not wholly destitute of every noble and generous feeling."[5]

These religious functions were not intended to neutralize the antislavery thrust, however. The narratives clearly show that there were significant differences in the experiences of these black writers and those of other writers. Unlike the Indian captives or prisoners of war, these narrators were legally chattel for life. Physical freedom was not assured after a given time of servitude or after escape from one's captors. Equiano makes it clear that even those blacks who were free could not anticipate the same respect and protection as whites. He tells the story of Joseph Clipson, who was kidnapped from a vessel, "although he showed a certificate of his being born free in St. Kitt's, and most people on board knew that he served his time to boat building, and always passed for a free man.'' Equiano adds:

> I have since often seen in Jamaica and other islands, free men, whom I have known in America, thus villainously trepanned and held in bondage. I have heard of two similar practices even in Philadelphia: and were it not for the benevolence of the quakers in that city, many of the sable race, who now breathe the air of liberty, would, I believe, be groaning indeed under some planter's chains.[6]

It is obvious in eighteenth-century slave narratives that many of the misfortunes suffered by the narrator were caused by nothing more than the condition of being black and a slave or of being black and yet not totally free. Equiano provides one of the many examples of the precariousness of the black narrators' existence:

> One Sunday night, as I was with some negroes in their master's yard, in the town of Savannah, it happened that their master, one Doctor Perkins, who was a very severe and cruel man, came in drunk; and not liking to see any strange negroes in his yard, he and a ruffian of a white man, he had in his service, beset me in an instant, and both of them struck me with the first weapons they could get hold of. I cried out as long as I could for help and mercy; but, though I gave a good account of myself, and he knew my captain, who lodged hard by him, it was to no purpose.

Equiano relates that he was left for dead. The next morning he was picked up and placed in jail. After a search, his master found him. Equiano states, ''My captain on this went to all the lawyers in the town for their advice, but they told him they could do nothing for me as I was a negro.''[7]

Even when slavery is not the direct cause of the incident, the institution of slavery permeates the narratives. The environment in which the narrator lives, the resources available to him during his crises, the humor or bitterness with which the tale is told—all are connected to the conditions of bondage and freedom and are an important part of the story.

In the narratives of the eighteenth century, there was opposition to slavery on moral, religious, economic, and social grounds, but the prime object of attack during the eighteenth century was the slave trade and not the owners of slaves or the institution itself. As the debate continued, it was generally felt that if the slave trade were abolished, the system would not survive or at least would find it necessary to institute more humanitarian procedures. Thus when the African Slave Trade Act, which prohibited the importation of slaves into the United States, was signed by Thomas Jefferson in 1807, the general public felt slavery had received its deathblow. Interest in the narratives declined and the first period was ended.

The nineteenth-century narratives were primarily a result of sociopolitical developments. With the change in economic policy occasioned by certain technological advances, it finally became apparent to the public that slavery in the United States was not only alive but was stronger than ever. When in January 1831 William Lloyd Garrison released the first issue of *The Liberator*, an antislavery periodical that would ultimately publish many slave narratives, the second period of abolitinist activity began. The slaves and exslaves had not stopped writing during the interim between 1807 and 1831, and a few had even achieved publication during that time. Yet it was not until the revived interest among whites in the abolition of slavery that the full-scale publication of these narratives began again.

Having inherited a model which was fundamentally appropriate for their concerns, the nineteenth-century narrators, much as the colonial American writers did with British forms, shaped and reshaped their structure until the end product had only a genetic resemblance to its predecessors. Among the more obvious innovations were the disappearance of the African-born freedman as narrator, the emergence of the Afro-American fugitive slave narrator, and the increasingly direct attack upon the entire slave institution. The goal of this period rapidly became the total elimination of slavery. Philosophy gave way to specific examples of physical violence and psychological abuse.

Narratives in the nineteenth century were more directly concerned with the institution of slavery in the United States and the specific sociopolitical problems that it created. When the British Parliament abolished all slavery in England and its colonies in 1833, not only were abolitionists in the United States encouraged by this victory in Britain, but the British antislavery interests then joined them in the attack upon slavery in the United States. The nineteenth-century narratives concentrated upon the struggle for freedom from bondage, a tradition created in the eighteenth century. Among other eighteenth-century traditions were the use of the narrator as a tour guide for free whites into the world of enslaved blacks and their attempt not only to inform the readers of this world of slavery but also to enlist their disapproval for these atrocities.

Nineteenth-century abolitionists recognized the potency of the earlier slave narratives and seized them as a weapon for the abolitionist cause. Eighteenth-century narratives such as Olaudah Equiano's and Venture Smith's were reissued and enjoyed brisk sales. Some works which had been written by blacks during the interim period of 1807-30 were now published. As the public interest grew, solicitation of slave narratives became greater. As these narratives made known the conditions of slavery as well as the resistance of blacks to enslavement, the public demand for the literature escalated. It reached a point where the stories of fugitives were solicited almost the moment their feet touched "free ground." The value of the narratives as abolitionist material is not sufficient to explain why the ante-bellum works were in many ways profoundly different from those of fifty years earlier.

To understand their appeal, one should remember that between the predominantly British colonies of the mid-eighteenth century and the United States of America of the mid-nineteenth century, important changes had been made. Although the nineteenth-century United States, as Russel B. Nye expresses it, "remained predominantly a religious-minded nation with an emotional, pietistic, moralistic spirit that would color its social, political, and economic thinking for generations to come," the theocentricity of the early eighteenth century had been modified to accommodate selected ideas of the Age of Reason such as an increased belief in the "perfectibility of man, the inevitability of progress and efficacy of reason."[8] The first half of the nineteenth century was a time of great optimism and social idealism. The cities were growing, the West was opening, literacy was increasing, and newspapers, magazines, and books were cheaper and more accessible than ever before.

Literature was expected to enlighten, encourage, and entertain, and it was expected to do so to a larger and more diverse audience than ever before. It was without apology a vital forum for the issues of the day. For example, temperance was never the strong national issue that slavery became; yet even this issue generated enough interest that 12 percent of all the novels published in the 1830s were temperance novels.[9] Although slavery had been a relatively unimportant issue at the beginning of the nineteenth century, with technological advances, the opening of the frontier, and the formation of a new society, the question of slavery was no longer a simple matter of a few reformists' abstract idealism. It was a national issue and a subject about which many persons realized they knew little or nothing. Their interest was augmented by the Compromise of 1850 with its strengthening of the Fugitive Slave Act, and by the Kansas-Nebraska Act of 1854. These two laws were important reasons why northerners, who had considered slavery a philosophical or religious problem located safely away in the far southern regions, suddenly realized that slavery presented economic implications of considerable importance. During the ante-bellum period, persons whose humanitarian feelings had not been touched by abolitionist appeals found their political and financial instincts awakened to a pressing need to know more about blacks and slavery. John Herbert Nelson's remark that, "By 1850 practically any writing by or about a negro [sic] was in demand, even if he had never been a slave,"[10] was not as hyperbolic as it would seem.

Coupled with the timeliness of the subject matter were the excitement and the potential romanticism of the writings. Here were stories of cruel enslavement, violence, and torture, of violated maidens and abruptly separated families. The protagonists of these stories were exotic but noble Christians who endured great misfortunes, effected dangerously desperate escapes, and then, perhaps most important, did not seek revenge but instead forgave their oppressors. These stories included all the ingredients of the then popular novels but were even better because they were true.

The social and literary conditions of the mid-nineteenth century had the expected influence upon the narratives of the second era. In the eighteenth and early nineteenth centuries, the introduction by respected citizens who affirmed the value of the work was fairly common; in the nineteenth-century narratives, the intense controversy which surrounded the subject of slavery made such introductions mandatory. Often, committees were formed to research the details of the narratives. Their reports, supported by documentation which sometimes included letters from the former masters giving their versions as well as results of interviews with eyewitnesses and inhabitants of the regions mentioned, were included in the publications. Each narrative was published with a minimum of two letters by prominent and respected white citizens—usually ministers—who certified the good character and the authenticity of the fugitive's story.

The pattern by which the actual narrative was related was still chronological, but the kinds of episodes were different from those of the eighteenth century. The kidnapping and introduction into Western society was no longer a feature, for most nineteenth-century narrators were born in the United States. Adventures on the high seas are replaced with accounts of the abolition of slavery in other regions. Most nineteenth-century slaveholders did not risk their property traveling outside the slave states.

The narratives usually begin with what is known of the facts of the exslave's birth and childhood. Often the emphasis is upon the lack of information concerning birth and parentage which is available to a slave. They progress from a description of the conditions of slavery and examples of its dehumanization for both slave and enslaver to the slave's reaching a point of desperation or his awakening to alternatives to enslavement. Then they present the process of his escape, complete with the crises and sufferings of the journey. The narratives usually end with the slave's adoption of a new Christian name and a surname and his arrival as a freeman into the promised land, which was either the northern United States, Canada, or England. A few give some hints that the new life is not entirely what was anticipated; however, the movement is from negative to positive, and the expectation of the narrator is usually that he will live happily ever after.

The physical movement in the narratives is always from South to North and from rural to urban. This is not historically accurate. Fugitives did establish maroon colonies in the swamps and mountains of the South. Others escaped to Mexico or joined Indian tribes. However, many a fugitive's pursuit of freedom in the United States was guided by the North Star, and its use in the slave narratives established the North as the metaphor for freedom.

Another formal difference was in the increased rhetorical and literary devices which began to appear within the established pattern. Some of the authors were orators on the abolitionist circuit and were used to reciting their life stories. When they were encouraged to write them, the orators simply wrote as they were used to speaking. As some had become quite accomplished in this area, devices of traditional Western oratory began to appear. An obvious example is Frederick Douglass, whose reputation as a public speaker was well known. Although he first attracted attention through his seemingly natural storytelling ability, his was not a style developed by instinct alone. In his narrative he relates that the first book he ever read was *The Columbian Orator.* Douglass's recollection of the effect of this collection of essays upon him was probably similar to the experiences of several of the narrators:

> I read them over and over again with unabated interest. They gave tongue to interesting thoughts of my own soul, which had frequently flashed through my mind, and died away for want of utterance. . . . The reading of these documents enabled me to utter my thoughts, and to meet the arguments brought forth to sustain slavery.[11]

This was a skill he began to practice before he even escaped from slavery. By the time he wrote his narrative, he had a great deal of experience in public speaking as well as in writing. When he wrote his narrative, it was heavily influenced by his training in rhetoric.

However, the pattern of *Narrative of the Life of Frederick Douglass, an American Slave. Written by Himself* is not explained only by his early exposure to oration. By 1845 Douglass was a well-read man. He knew literary traditions. He was well acquainted with *The Liberator* and had read many slave narratives. He had a sense of history and politics, and when he wrote his narrative, he chose to follow what was by this time a recognized pattern for slave narratives.

J. W. C. Pennington is another example. He prefaced his 1849 narrative as follows: "The brief narrative I here introduce to the public, consists of outline notes originally thrown together to guide my memory when lecturing on this part of the subject of slavery. This will account for its style, and will also show that the work is not full.''[12] This preface was a deliberate stylistic choice. Pennington had been a fugitive for almost twenty years by the time he wrote his narrative. During this time, he had attended Yale (but being denied regular admission to the college, he was only allowed to stand outside the doors to listen to the lectures); had written the first history of blacks (*A Text Book of the Origin and History of the Colored People*) by a black person in the new world, in 1841; and had been awarded a doctor of divinity degree by the University of Heidelberg. Obviously, Pennington was capable of writing a different kind of life story—a more finished and literary piece—if he so chose. Yet when he wrote *The Fugitive Blacksmith; or, Events in the History of James W. C. Pennington,* he wrote a story which was similar in structure, characterization, and content to other slave narratives in the United States. Nor did he choose to change even the preface in subsequent editions.

Black writers in the nineteenth century were usually aware of rhetorical convention and capable of choosing from a series of literary models. Many did just that and established themselves as essayists, poets, and novelists. Some, however, deliberately chose the pattern of American slave narratives and, consequently, contributed to the development of that genre.

This does not mean that the narratives of the nineteenth century were all conscious attempts to produce ''literature'' or to react to a ''slave narrative generic formula.'' Nor does it suggest a school of slave narrators who by common consent adhered to a defined literary code. The slave narrative tradition was not an imitation of prevailing literary modes; nor was it simply a selecting and reshaping of elements of earlier slave narratives. That there were some pressures by publishers, editors, and other sponsors to conform to standards which were tried and true is a fact, but it is also a fact that many narrators resisted such efforts.

The slave narratives grew out of those tensions and ambiguities that were common to all slaves in the United States. They were influenced by the myths and coping strategies that were perpetuated by the oral traditions of their culture. The result was a unique kind of writing—a genre called slave narratives. Some narrators were very skilled and produced writings of outstanding merit. Some narrators were less skilled, and their narratives were quite crude in style, vague in purpose, and with little to recommend them aesthetically other than that they professed to be written by slaves. Nevertheless, it is obvious that during the second era the slave narrators —whether skilled or unskilled as artists—were consciously working within a literary tradition.

As the narrators' own interests and abilities permitted, some were led to introduce various literary embellishments to their narratives. The sentimental novel had great influence upon some writers. Many narratives were full of long passages of dialogue and of discussions of the moral and spiritual dangers which assailed every slave of sensibility. Gone were the swashbuckling adventurers who took their knocks as they came, little aggravating themselves over the subtle but potent effects of the moonlight, the fog on the marsh, or one or two acts of dubious morality. Here were black Joseph Andrews and Pamelas faced with the continuous assaults upon their virtue and sensibilities.

A good example of this variation is in Harriet Brent Jacob's narrative, which was entitled *Incidents in the Life of a Slave Girl* and bore the pseudonym of Linda Brent. Linda Brent's life seems to have been mainly focused upon avoiding her master's lust and her mistress's jealousy, hiding for seven years in an attic crawl space wating for a chance to escape to freedom while enduring the mental anguish of seeing her children growing up without being able to speak to them or touch them.

The following instance will give an idea of the sentimental elements in Brent's narrative. After her master had attempted many assaults upon her virtue, Brent decided that as a female slave she would not be allowed to remain a virgin or to marry whom she chose and live as a respectable woman. Her best alternative was to submit to the sexual attentions of a white gentleman who she felt was "a man of more generosity and feeling than my master," and by whom she expected to be purchased and manumitted. She was also influenced by the idea that this man would provide better support for any children that might result—that, in fact, he would free them. She relates:

> With all these thoughts revolving in my mind, and seeing no other way of escaping the doom I so much dreaded, I made a headlong plunge. Pity me, and pardon me, O virtuous reader! You never knew

what it is to be a slave; to be entirely unprotected by law or custom; to have the laws reduce you to the condition of chattel, entirely subject to the will of another. You never exhausted your ingenuity in avoiding the snares, and eluding the power of a hated tyrant; you never shuddered at the sound of his footsteps, and trembled within hearing of his voice. I know I did wrong. No one can feel it more sensibly than I do. The painful and humiliating memory will haunt me to my dying day.[13]

Certainly no heroine of any sentimental novel of that day could have displayed more virtue or more sensibility than Brent.

Utilization of the traditional literary forms and exploitation of current sensational, sentimental, and political shibboleths was often necessary to achieve the condemnation of the slave system, a vital theme in the second period of the slave narratives. Demonstrations of philosophical and religious contradictions continued to be important; but there was also an increased emphasis upon the violence and brutality of the institution. The presentation of slavery from the perspective of the slave became even more important.

There were many reasons for these changes. The nineteenth-century black was more generally alienated from the dominant society. There were questions about his manhood which had not been raised in the eighteenth century. The black person was now three-fifths of a man for taxation purposes and not a man at all in most legal situations. Socially, the exotic savage concept still existed in white minds, but the emphasis was more often upon the savage. The whole issue had been elaborated upon in some very contradictory and unusual ways. The black slave himself was more likely to have been born in slavery and to know little of his own history, either social or familial. He had less assurance of his own identity and "nature."

The motivations for the whites' involvement in the entire situation were of course complicated, but one strong motivation was a kind of ingroup battle for power or money. Often the proslavery and the antislavery forces had the same feelings about the blacks as humans and their place in the hierarchy of man. Theirs was a family quarrel about what to do with them in this country.

The nineteenth century developed, however, to a greater extent than the eighteenth, a group of blacks whose needs and concerns led to ideas of their own about the antislavery movement, antislavery literature, and especially the slave narrative. In the second era of the slave narrative, greater tensions within the works themselves developed. Within the persona of the narrator was a conflict of self versus society which was related to the growing disagreements between the white society—including the abolitionists—and the black society represented by the narrators. The abolitionists wanted case histories. They encouraged formula expressions of stereotypical persons who often did not correspond to what the narrator felt himself to be. The narrator was often searching for his own meaning in his own experience—a quest which he often saw as a choice between appearing as a unique individual or as a nonentity. The conflict between loyalty to one's race and the possibility of being considered a common "nigger," that is, something not quite on a par with civilized man, was excruciating for many.

With the advent of the Civil War, the public interest in slavery declined. As the realities of a nation struggling for existence increased, whites had little time for theory and even less interest in "outsiders" such as blacks. Their literary interests turned to "novels about soldier life, autobiographies of Army nurses and others with unusual war experiences, biographies of military officers and heroes, journalistic narratives of campaigns, simple studies of strategy and tactics, accounts of past wars, and exuberant theories on ways to win the present war."[14] When the war was ended, slavery was legally abolished. After the war, the focus of white America was upon rebuilding a nation. It wanted to forget those elements which were considered divisive or passé now that slavery did not legally exist. When the ante-bellum period was mentioned in literature, it was with nostalgia. The sentimental legends of plantation life in an aristocratic ante-bellum South supplanted the less complimentary tales of Afro-Americans.

The American Civil War did not mark the end of slave narratives. The separately published narratives of the post-bellum period continued many of the ante-bellum traditions. Yet, as the ink on the Emancipation Proclamation began to dry, the narrators of the stories of bondage and freedom began to modify their stances. For example, in keeping with the loftiest ideals of Reconstruction, there was a definite tendency to downplay the horrors of the slave experience and to concentrate upon the contributions of the blacks to American society. Works such as Booker T. Washington's *Up From Slavery* summarize the slave years in one chapter and then proceed to argue the potential for racial progress by chronicling black versions of the Horatio Alger stories so common in early twentieth-century literature in the United States. As time passed, slavery became heritage and the slave narratives became the archetype for Afro-American autobiography.

In the history of the slave narrative, the ante-bellum period produced the most highly developed literary presentations of the experiences of blacks who had been slaves in the United States. That period was by far the most complex and productive. Paradoxically, it proved the existence of a slave narrative genre while developing the tradition in vastly important and often quite different ways.

The writings of the latter part of the eighteenth century marked the emergence of a distinctly different form of narrative in American literature; however, there are too few of them to discuss emphasis and structure in very meaningful ways. They do reveal the sources of subjects and forms which characterized the slave narrative at its zenith and provide appropriate contrasts. Both in terms of popularity and of literary achievement, it is more accurate to consider the period between 1831 and 1865 as the golden age of the slave narrative.

4

Social and Literary Influences upon Ante-bellum Slave Narratives

THE APPEARANCE OF William Lloyd Garrison's *Liberator* in 1830 is usually cited as marking the beginning of abolitionism as a national issue. Yet concerned individuals had long been noting how the 1807 act outlawing the external slave trade had treated the symptoms but failed to arrest the disease of slavery. While national attention in the earliest part of the century had turned to improving foreign relations, avoiding involvement in Europe's Napoleonic Wars, and strengthening economic independence, the slavery issue was by no means moribund. As John Hope Franklin reminds us, "Long before militant abolitionists appeared on the scene around 1830 the most convincing arguments against slavery had already been developed."[1] Garrison's activities, along with events such as the publication of David Walker's *Appeal* in 1829 and the occurrence of insurrections such as Nat Turner's in 1831, simply gave the public an increasing sense of urgency toward solving the so-called Negro problem.

From the Great Revival movement with its resultant benevolent societies and educational reform schemes to territorial expansion with the acquisition of Louisiana, Florida, Texas, and other frontier lands, the specter of slavery haunted each endeavor. Regardless of one's personal attitudes toward abolitionism, colonization, or enslavement, the future of the slave institution became an increasingly important national issue. By the fifties all other issues had become secondary. In general, the social climate into which the nineteenth-century slave narratives emerged was one wherein writings about slavery found a ready audience: Public interest, then, was one factor which brought slave narratives into a prominent position.

The changes in the American literary scene which occurred in the first three decades of the nineteenth century were less obvious but also important factors in the development of nineteenth-century slave narratives. Increased literacy resulted in larger but more diverse audiences, while increased technology made printing easier, quicker, and more economical. Literacy, cheaper prices, and circulating libraries created a potentially larger book market. Publishers began to see the value of promoting books and encouraging a closer relationship between author and reader. Many writers quickly sensed the importance of adjusting their styles to take advantage of these phenomena. There was a shift from gentleman writer to professional author. In *The Profession of Authorship in America*, William Charvat reports that by the 1820s "authors were writing so divertingly on subjects of broad interest that they broke down the barriers between reader groups and appealed to almost everyone who was literate."[2]

By the thirties, the "rising materialistic middle-class" had gained power enough to represent a serious threat to the traditional patrician guardians of culture. Charvat describes this new audience as "aggressive, materialistic, and vulgar. . . . Lacking college education, in literature they preferred novelty, brevity, sensationalism, and sentimentalism to the solid learning and stately prose of the *North American Review* and the serenity and authority of the classics."[3] Richard Altick agrees that the new audience was ill-educated and may well have "vulgarized literature," but, he admits, "it was the ill-educated mass audience with pennies in its pocket that called the tune to which writers and editors danced."[4] It was for them that the lively and often scandalous penny-a-copy newspapers replaced the "solid but dull sheets that only gentlemen had read."[5] The big circulation magazines such as *Graham's* were established to cater to their desires. Although they had a predilection for lively, even flamboyant writing styles, the new readers still expected literature to be utilitarian and moralistic. "Many Americans," says Russel Nye, "continued to believe that novels should instruct, plays draw moral lessons, satires discover and correct error, essays debate and convince, poetry please and teach."[6] Says Frank L. Mott in *Golden Multitudes: The Story of Best Sellers in the United States:*

> Among the motivations of American best sellers, from the seventeenth century to the twentieth, one of the most prominent has been the desire for self-improvement. Indeed, it may be said that, by and large, there are only three classes of readers—those who seek improvement, those who seek entertainment, and those who seek both improvement and entertainment.[7]

This was the environment in which the second major era of slave narratives appeared. Their purpose was to explain the system of slavery from the perspective of one who had been enslaved and, in most cases, to convince the reader that this system, being inherently evil, must be abolished. They were, therefore, both utilitarian and moral and, in this sense, in accordance with the expectations of most readers.

Moreover, these slave narratives appeared during the period known as the sentimental years. Contemporary literature emphasized the cultivation of sensibility, the glorification of virtue, the preservation of family life, the revival of religion, and the achievement of a utopian society. This, too, influenced the ways in which the stories of the slaves could be told. Not only did contemporary audiences demand adherence to such concepts, but also the formal education of slave narrators incorporated those traditions which produced such expectations. The literary models of the slave narrator were those same models used by the other writers in the United States. On the other hand, his racial identity, with all its connotations in the culture of the United States, gave him an additional set of references. This dual perspective at times conflicted greatly and created in the slave narratives a kind of tension peculiar to Afro-American literature. It created what W. E. B. Du Bois called "this double-consciousness, this sense of always looking at oneself through the eyes of others, of measuring one's soul by the tape of a world that looks on in amused contempt and pity."[8]

Understanding the social and literary circumstances of mainstream America, as well as the peculiar position of black writers in the nineteenth century, is vital to understanding the slave narratives. Some progress has been made, but Altick's words are as true now as in 1957 when he said, "our knowledge of the subtle relationships between literature and society is still scanty. We are beginning to understand the effect of general social conditions upon the production of literature; but the role of the reader—the consumer—had been largely neglected."[9]

Writers such as Edmund Wilson in *Patriotic Gore* have made some attempt to analyze the effects of the ante-bellum political atmosphere, educational practices, and changing patterns of leadership upon nineteenth-century literature. However, few, if any, have noted the complex and profound effects upon slave narratives, which were highly influenced by contemporary racial attitudes and literary expectations. Both the literary and social histories of their audience, which was predominantly white middle class, and of their authors, who were black and socially subordinate to their readers, determined the climate, models, and expectations that significantly determined the content and form of the writings. The black writer, because of his race and his purpose in writing, was perhaps more than any other nineteenth-century writer restricted and inhibited by the attitudes and limitations of those for whom he wrote.

Two of the more significant constraints upon slave narrators were the myths and prejudices of his readers toward the racial group which he represented and the literary precedents previously accepted for the treatment of blacks in American literature. The former presented the more complex and difficult problem, for it made what was essentially an aesthetic problem for nonblack writers a dilemma of profound social and literary impact for the slave narrator.

Nineteenth-century racial attitudes made it impossible for a black man to be accepted as a social and intellectual equal. What integration was available was based upon the degree to which an individual could divest himself of so-called Negro cultural attributes and demonstrate his acquisition of the values and skills held most dear by whites. The struggle to maintain a balance between self and the world, the subjective and the objective, which is waged by most but achieved by few autobiographical writers, became more significant for the slave narrator. The success of his narrative required that he be perceived as an example, but economic and often personal success required that he be seen as an exemplar.

A brief summary of the basic nineteenth-century racial attitudes illustrates this. The majority of whites subscribed to a theory of races that classified all mankind into several groups. Caucasians, they believed, were superior, and Negroes were most inferior. It was commonly believed that black people in the United States were an ignorant, undisciplined, and potentially dangerous group. The fugitive writer Samuel Ringgold Ward declared:

> The enemies of the Negro deny his capacity for improvement or progress; they say he is deficient in morals, manners, intellect, and character. Upon that assertion they base the American doctrine, proclaimed with all effrontery, that the Negro is neither fit for nor entitled to the rights, immunities and privileges, which the same parties say belong naturally to *all men*; indeed, some of them go so far as to deny that the Negro belongs to the human family.[10]

Whether free or enslaved, black men were victims of strong racial prejudice. Contrary to popular myth and most important for our understanding of the forces under which the slave narrator operated, this prejudice was not confined to the South. Russel Nye, in *Society and Culture in America: 1830-1860*, summarizes thus:

> Northern society believed in white supremacy and black inferiority, sanctioned social and economic discrimination, and segregated the Negro in jails, hospitals, churches, schools, parks, and public accommodations. Racial restrictions applied in burial grounds, trade and employment, and residency; the pattern of the racially-segregated city was firmly established in the North before 1850. After the opening of the aggressive phase of the abolitionist movement, there were serious anti-Negro riots in cities like Philadelphia, New York, Pittsburgh, and Cincinnati, while individual Negroes who defied custom, as Frederick Douglass and David Ruggles and Charles Remond determined to do, were beaten or humiliated.[11]

Although they often deplored the mistreatment of blacks, most white abolitionists shared the basic racial prejudices. Only the most radical advocated social and political equality among races, and the history of those abolitionist groups which were integrated is fraught with charges of racial discrimination. Rather than refute racist theories, most white abolitionists stressed slavery as a source of the degradation. In an antislavery sermon the noted Unitarian reformer James Freeman Clarke proclaimed:

> A worse evil to the slave than the cruelty he sometimes endures, is the moral degradation that results from his condition. Falsehood, theft, licentiousness, are the natural consequence of his situation. He steals, —why should he not?—he cannot, except occasionally, earn money. . . . He lies,—it is the natural weapon of weakness against tyrant strength. He goes to excess in eating and drinking and animal pleasures —for he has no access to any higher pleasures. I do not mean that there are no exceptions. There are pure, honest, and virtuous slaves. . . . But there is one evil so inherent in the system, that no care can obviate it. The slave's nature never *grows*. The slave is always a child. Slavery is the parent of vices . . . abject submission or deadly vindictiveness are now as they have always been the fruits of slavery.[12]

The very dedicated and influential abolitionist Lydia Maria Child wrote in *An Appeal in Favor of That Class of Americans Called Africans*, "From the moment the slave is kidnapped, to the last hour he draws his *miserable* breath, the white man's influence directly cherishes ignorance, fraud, licentiousness, revenge, hatred and murder. It cannot be denied that human nature thus operated upon, *must* necessarily yield, more or less to all these evils."[13]

Blacks, especially those who were free, were therefore admonished to rise above the masses and to work industriously, live frugally, and study diligently. Those who came closest to demonstrating their acquisition of what were in reality conventional attributes of the white middle class were lauded as outstanding examples of their race. The situation was such that many blacks felt their best contribution to racial progress was to divest themselves of any connection with the slave culture and to avoid as much as possible the stereotype of the undisciplined, irresponsible, primitive slave. They agreed with Samuel Ringgold Ward, who wrote in *Autobiography of a Fugitive Negro*, "I regard all the upright demeanour, gentlemanly bearing, Christian character, social progress, and material prosperity, of every coloured man, especially if he be a native of the United States, as, in its kind, anti-slavery labour."[14]

If we recall that slave narratives were meant to be personal accounts of exslaves' struggles for freedom which were also written to expose the perfidy of slavery, the tension between the depiction of the protagonist as individual and the protagonist as every slave becomes obvious. In order for the narrative to attract the largest number of readers and to focus attention upon slavery, the individual had to identify himself with the masses of slaves. If he extolled his own capabilities too much, he would be perceived as an exception. While his extraordinary talents could have some value as a defense against the charges of the natural inferiority of blacks, it was equally possible to believe that those who were naturally superior would find their own ways out of slavery, that, in fact, a slave's inability to pull himself up by his own bootstraps, so to speak, was just cause for the race remaining in bondage. Thus it was imperative that the narrator establish himself as the kind of example that William Lloyd Garrison tried to make of Frederick Douglass. After emphasizing in his preface to *The Narrative of the Life of Frederick Douglass* that Douglass had to be persuaded that he was capable of making a significant contribution, that Douglass had in fact "expressed his conviction that he was not adequate to the performance of so great a task," Garrison proclaims Douglass's superior achievements. He avoids any suggestion that such success was a result of personal talents and efforts, while he emphasizes the influence of the time and opportunities which freedom allegedly offers. "Let the calumniators of the colored race despise themselves for their baseness and illiberality of spirit, and henceforth cease to talk of the natural inferiority of those who require nothing but time and opportunity to attain to the highest point of human excellence,"[15] he says.

If, on the other hand, the exslave allowed his escape from slavery to seem too much a result of coincidence and instinct, he was degrading his own effort and achievement and risking his already slim chances for increased acceptance into American society. His petition for acceptance as a fellow citizen would be based on little more than the fact that he rejected bondage. Since discrimination was widespread in the North, the black who would be accepted as a fellowman and allowed to live and work in a given community had to prove his superior moral and intellectual talents. Maintaining a balance between the portayal of self as individual and self as type involved much more than aesthetics: It directly affected one's social and economic status as well.

The conflict between the presentation of slave narratives as an individual's account of his struggle for freedom from bondage and as documentation of a collective journey from bondage to freedom was not even-handed. On the whole, the narrators were more interested in exploiting their typicalness. For some this was because they were members of abolitionist groups and were writing their personal histories as another facet of their active involvement in antislavery movements. Austin Steward made it clear that this was his intent when he began the preface to *Twenty-two Years a Slave and Forty Years a Freeman:*

> The author does not think that any apology is necessary for this issue of his Life and History. He believes that American Slavery is now the great question before the American People: that it is not merely a political question, . . . but that its moral bearings are of such a nature that the Patriot, the Philanthropist and all good men agree that it is an evil of so much magnitude, that longer to permit it, is to wink at *sin* and to incur the righteous judgments of God. . . . The author is therefore the more willing—nay, anxious, to lay alongside of such arguments the history of his own life and experiences *as a slave,* that those who read may know what are some of the characteristics of that highly favored institution, which is sought to be preserved and perpetuated.[16]

Others were not so much interested in promotion of antislavery activities as they were in setting straight the historical record. James Mars stated in his introduction that he wrote his narrative in response to a sister's request for family history, but once it was completed, he decided it should be published because "many of the people now on the stage of life do not know that slavery ever lived in Connecticut."[17]

John Thompson candidly admits that he surveyed the other narratives before deciding that he was as qualified to write about slavery as most others who had entered the field. In the preface to *Life of John Thompson, A Fugitive Slave,* he says:

It was suggested to me about two years since, after relating to many the main facts relative to my bondage and escape to the land of freedom, that it would be a desirable thing to put these facts into permanent form. I first sought to discover what had been said by other partners in bondage once, but in freedom now. . . . I am aware that now, when public opinion makes it no martyrdom to denounce slavery, there are multitudes of men that grow bold, and wield a powerful weapon against this great evil; and even school boys daringly denounce a system, the enormity of which they cannot appreciate, surely I thought it may be permitted to one who has worn the galling yoke of bondage, to say something of its pains, and something of that freedom which, if he should not succeed in accurately defining, he can truly say he will ever admire and love.[18]

While the egotism of individual narrators may have challenged their professed goals, the greater tendency in the narratives was toward the portrayal of the slave narrator as a type. A distinguishing factor between the slave narratives and other personal narratives of this period is the rigor of the attempt deliberately to subjugate the personal courage, intelligence, and motivations which made slaves attempt and achieve freedom from bondage. Although their individuality was a part of their status as writers and of the public's interest in their writings, the slave narrators made an effort to present themselves as typical products of slavery in order to demonstrate that the problem was with the entire system, and not, as in the eighteenth-century narratives, with abuses within the system. The need for such a decision, as well as the ways in which it was manifested in the narratives, is directly related to the myths and prejudices of the readers toward the racial group to which the narrator belonged and of which he wrote.

The literary precedents for black characters in American literature was a second significant limitation. The reading public was not accustomed to heroic black characters. Prior to the Civil War, blacks were rarely portrayed in serious literature. When they did appear, it was in minor roles or as minstrels. John Herbert Nelson, in *The Negro Character in American Literature*, summarizes the early literary treatments of the black as follows:

His potential literary possibilities, at least such as made for buffoonery and humor, were clearly seen. . . . [P]ractically all the traits subsequently attributed to him we find foreshadowed in the work of our early novelists. His irrepressible spirits, his complee absorption in the present moment, his whimsicality, his irresponsibility, his intense superstitiousness, his freedom from resentment—all this was suggested, although, be it repeated, not fully or adequately treated. As a mere comic character he was discovered. Unfortunately the same cannot be said for his discovery as a serious type, as a well rounded human being.[19]

Sterling Brown in *The Negro in American Fiction* notes that black characters in early American literature included the "fabler, the loyal servant, the buffoon, the tragic octoroon, the nobel savage, and the revolter."[20] During the ante-bellum period, however, certain stereotypes became more popular than others. Ante-bellum literature featured five black character types: the wretched freedman, the clown, the contented slave, the victim, and a composite of the latter three. The contented slave is the best known. The ample-chested, bandana-headed mammy, suckling white babies, washing clothes, cooking flavorful feasts while keeping an eye on a multitude of pickaninnies who frolic by the cabin door is as well known as her woolly-headed, loyal, pious though superstitious husband. The clown is the happy-go-lucky, banjo-picking, chicken-stealing, lying but loyal slave. Childish and not too bright, he is the object of ridicule, not anger. These two characterizations preceded the ante-bellum period and have endured since, though as Sterling Brown suggests, "The assumption that Negroes are especially designed as butts for rough practical jokes is probably closer to the reality of the antebellum South than the sentimentality of more ambitious works."[21]

The wretched freedman and the victim are more accurately products of the controversy over slavery. The wretched freedman appeared in the proslavery literature. He is the poor unfortunate whose gullibility has led him to believe the Yankee abolitionist lies and to flee to the North. There, ignorant, hungry, and cold, he realizes that he has sold his birthright for a mess of pottage, that he has left family, friends and the security and benevolence of kindly white masters for the cold, cruel, and hostile North. Dejected and despised, he freezes to death in a snowstorm or returns home to the plantation as a prodigal son.

Antislavery literature presents us with the victim. This character, however, is the contented slave turned inside out. His essential characteristics are still loyalty, honesty, and Christian faith. The difference is that the situation in which he exists is not secure, but oppressive. The tragic mulatto is a special victim. The product of rape or seduction, she, or less often he, need only escape the bonds of slavery in order to live a sober, honest, and rewarding life. Interestingly, the antislavery writers did not present an alternative to the wretched freedman. Their writings usually ended with escape from bondage.

The most pervasive image was a synthesis of the clown, contented slave, and victim. Obviously, this was a characterization of much contradiction, but as Jean Fagan Yellin points out, acceptance of that contradiction "existed in American culture before there was a native literature."[22] His name was Sambo and he was a central character in both proslavery and antislavery literature. Sambo, in fact, was not considered a mere literary creation. As historians such as Stanley Elkins demonstrate, Sambo was not only considered real, but he was also believed to be "a dominant plantation type."[23] It is another historian, John Blassingame, who gives the best descriptive summary of this character. Says Blassingame, Sambo was "indolent, faithful, humorous, loyal, dishonest, superstitious, improvident, and musical . . . inevitably a clown and congenitally docile. Sambo had so much love and affection for his master that he was almost filio-pietistic; his loyalty was all-consuming and self immolating. The epitome of devotion, Sambo often fought and died heroically while trying to save his master's life."[24]

Slave narrators exploited the popularity of Sambo while trying to make him more heroic. Rather than create an entirely new character, they tried to accentuate Sambo's positive traits while either refuting as misconceptions or ignoring the negative ones.

Slave narrators demonstrated the existence of such attributes as pain, suffering, patience, faith, and loyalty, while ignoring such highly touted "traits" as rhythm and agility. Less innocent interpretations were given to his allegedly omnipresent singing, dancing, and laughter. Slave narratives proved that docility was an acquired trait and one not uniformly adopted by all. Through slave narratives the reader became aware of the disguised aggression which unjust treatment and confinement engendered in what was considered "the lady of the races." The narrator gave glimpses of the slave's attempts to maintain a family structure, achieve an education and incorporate the teachings of Christianity into his life. This presented a character which could not be dismissed as humorous and childlike. Most of all, the narratives maintained that slaves remained in captivity only because of the stringent psychological and physical manipulation by the slaveholders. Above all, they refuted the myth that slaves were content with their lot and knew little of any other life. Says Solomon Northup:

> It is a mistaken opinion that prevails in some quarters, that the slave does not understand the term—does not comprehend the idea of freedom . . . the most ignorant of them generally know full well its meaning. They understood the privileges and exemptions that belong to it—that it would bestow upon them the fruits of their own labors, and that it would secure to them the enjoyment of domestic happiness. They do not fail to observe the difference between their own condition and the meanest white man's, and to realize the injustice of the laws which place it in his power not only to appropriate the profits of their industry, but to subject them to unmerited and unprovoked punishment, without remedy, or the right to resist, or to remonstrate.[25]

Although these perspectives provided a more accurate depiction of the complexities of the slave's personality, they did not refute the basic stereotypes concerning the racial characteristics of blacks. Instead of the childish laughing and singing caricature of southern propaganda, the slave narrators presented a personage whose natural inclination was to simple and harmonious living, but in whom circumstances could create rebellion and other unsocial reactions. Rather than the impotent victim of northern propaganda, they revealed patterns of rebellion ranging from open defiance and physical confrontation to feigned loyalty and conscious sabotage. The stereotyped Sambo was given an Anglo name and most importantly was presented as a martyr, an inspirational model, a person of courage, a hero.

Because vestiges of Sambo remained and basic racial attitudes were not challenged, the slave protagonist was to the nineteenth-century reader a figure with whom sympathy was possible but empathy was out of the question. He was still, as a black man, inferior, a creature of instinct, trainable—even educable—but not one with whom most readers need fear direct competition in any realm. His long suffering, his courage in adversity, his faith, and his unshakable desire to be free made him a model worthy of emulation in these areas. The slave narratives' picture of the slave was not one of a man but of a symbol. He was a Christian, with the approved definitions of God. He also cherished home and country. His dissatisfaction was not in fact a rejection of the American Dream; it was the kind of acceptance that demanded fulfillment of its highest ideals. He was a reformist, not a revolutionary. He did not revolt singularly or collectively. He tried reason and law; if that were impossible, he fled. As William Charvat has shown us, the relationship between writer and reader has always been reciprocal in American literary history. The arrangement between the slave narrator and his reader was simple. If the slave narrator was to gain the attention of his readers, he would not demand sudden, radical attitudinal changes. Given the common notions of inferiority and given the strong legal obstacles to blacks' education, the audience was already stretching its imagination when it accepted the work as written by a black. For the narrators to demand further that they accept different literary characters and forms could break the bonds of their credulity. In light of the previously mentioned social perceptions of blacks, the slave narrators could not risk the success of their works by insisting too strongly on the complete absurdity of commonly held stereotypes. Thus slave narrators chose not to counter nineteenth-century shibboleths, sentiments, ideas, or values, but rather employed these as their own as they tried to arouse the sympathies of their readers for their causes. In the process, unfortunately, the slave narratives reinforced some racist ideas and introduced new ones.

The audience for the slave narratives was assumed to be literate, white, northern, religious, socially concerned, alien to the social context of slavery, yet not entirely without some of the same racial attitudes of the slaveholders. So the slave narratives focused their attacks on American slavery and not upon the attitudes which helped introduce and sustain the peculiar form which had evolved in the United States. Because of the audience and the more than autobiographical intentions of the narrators, they developed a style that emphasized the symbolic nature of the narrative. The protagonist became largely a unifying device, a way to give coherence and narrative immediacy to information which otherwise might have appeared (and often did) as a polemic or lecture.

To examine, expose, or condemn slavery by relating his experiences as a slave, it was necessary for the narrator to integrate the individual with the symbolic and the subjective with the objective. In addition, the narrator had always to take into account the audience's special ignorance of his topic. This influenced not only the characterization of the narrator but also the method in which he related even his most commonplace experiences. Since much of the audience had no clear knowledge of how slavery worked, the narrator had to give a crash course in what it meant to be a slave before the perfidy of that institution could be fully appreciated. He did this by having the audience develop along with the protagonist an awareness of what it meant to be a slave. The protagonist related to the reader the events which taught him what slavery was really about. He combined explicit assertions about the general pattern with his recitation of personal experiences in such a fashion that the reader saw the basic irony of the situation and began to perceive the fundamental insidiousness of the total institution.

The technique by which this was done is essentially the same for the entire narrative, but nowhere is it more successful than in the first few pages of the narrative wherein the slave's vital statistics are presented. The narrator begins by disclosing information about his birthplace, date, name, and genealogy. He uses seemingly innocuous statements to contrast the basic differences between the world of the slave and the world of the freeman.

Few narrators are as geographically precise as Frederick Douglass, who begins his narrative with the words, "I was born in Tuckahoe, near Hillsborough, and about twelve miles from Easton, in Talbot county, Maryland,"[26] but most narrators begin by identifying the state and county of birth. This information is usually followed by the name of the plantation or the person who claimed ownership of the slave. Sometimes a catalog of the master's family and its reputation is included, but fugitives frequently identify the master only by an initial and/or dash in order to prevent the master or his heirs from using the narrative as proof of ownership in the event the narrator is captured.

The quick shift from the fact of one's birth to the fact that one's birth was in a place owned by a person who claimed equally his rights to the land and to the newborn, forces the reader to recognize the differences between a freeman and a slave immediately. The slave infant is identified, like a calf or a foal, with the estate of its master. The slave babe's lineage is not an ancestry but a stock. His birthright is not hearth and homeland but perpetual servitude. Juxtaposition of birth and birthplace contrasts the traditional joy of new life with slavery's aberration, the joy of new property.

Another effect of identifying the place of birth as the place of enslavement is to make slavery a geographical phenomenon and to fix further the South as synonymous with slavery. A notable exception is the narrative of James Mars, who states:

What I have written of my own history, seems to satisfy the minds of those that read it, that the so called, favored state, the land of good morals and steady habits, was ever a slave state, and that slaves were driven through the streets tied or fastened together for market. This seems to surprise some that I meet, but it was true. I have it from reliable authority. Yet, this was done in Connecticut.[27]

Although Mars was anxious to reveal that the South was not the only location of slavery, he was quick to distinguish northern slavery as more benign than that of the South. He begins his narrative by explaining that "the treatment of slaves was different at the North from the South; at the North they were admitted to be a species of the human family."[28] Yet Mars's exploitation of the geographical uniqueness of his story was effective because the South was so firmly fixed as the scene of enslavement.

The identification of the slave's birthplace fixed the South-to-North axis of the narration and introduced the theme of the journey to the promised land. The South was described much like a wilderness of untamed land, ineffective religion, and savage brutality, while the North became the location of enlightened Christianity, harmony, and brotherhood. The journey of the freedom seeker was upward from the rural South to the urban North. The omnipresent symbol and guide to freedom was the brightest star in the heavens, the North Star.

The reader recognized the pattern immediately. Although his racism could not allow a complete identification of the black with the religious pilgrims in other literature, the structure and technique predisposed him to view the story as a moral tale and to accept the perspective of the slave as closer to that of the good Christian than was the view of the slave master.

Another piece of personal information utilized to reveal the insidiousness of slavery was the birthday or, more exactly, the absence of a birth date. While some narrators provide the day, month, and year of birth, often only the season of the approximate year is recorded. The absence of a more specific birth date becomes another example of the dehumanization of slavery. "Slaves seldom know exactly how old they are; neither they nor their masters set down the time of a birth; the slaves, because they are not allowed to write or read, and the masters, because they only care to know what slaves belong to them."[29] In this manner Moses Grandy attributed the lack of permanent recognition of a slave's birth to the attitude of the master who considers slaves as chattel and to the denial to slaves of the information with which they could calculate the anniversaries of their existence.

Frederick Douglass's discussion supplements Grandy's observation. Douglass concurs that a slave's ignorance of the circumstances of his own birth is not due to a lack of interest but is a direct result of the slave system. His personal response to the absence of such information reveals further significances of this practice:

> I have no accurate knowledge of my age, never having seen any authentic record containing it. By far the larger part of the slaves know as little of their ages as horses know of theirs, and it is the wish of most masters within my knowledge to keep their slaves thus ignorant. . . . A want of information concerning my own was a source of unhappiness to me even during childhood. The white children could tell their ages. I could not tell why I ought to be deprived of the same privilege. I was not allowed to make any inquiries to my master concerning it. He deemed all such inquiries on the part of a slave improper and impertinent, and evidence of a restless spirit.[30]

At the beginning of the slave narratives, attention is given to the parentage of the narrator. Not only is the genealogy of the slave important for all the reasons that ancestral origins are normally valued in personal narratives, but in the case of the mulatto narrator it offers an especially strong potential for the antislavery cause. In each narrative by a mulatto, the mother was a slave and the father was white. Almost without exception, these narrators used their heritage to emphasize the immorality of a system which not only allowed white men to father children by their slaves but then to own, sell, and often abuse their own children.

They report that the mulatto suffers special abuses because of his heritage. Often the abuse comes from the relatives, especially the wife of the father. Moses Roper reports:

> As soon as my father's wife heard of my birth, she sent one of my mother's sisters to see whether I was white or black, and when my aunt had seen me, she returned back as soon as she could and told her mistress that I was white, and resembled Mr. Roper very much. Mr. R's wife being not pleased with this report, she got a large club stick and knife, and hastened to the place in which my mother was confined. She went into my mother's room with full intention to murder me with her knife and club, but as she was going to stick the knife into me, my grandmother happening to come in, caught the knife and saved my life.[31]

The reaction of Roper's mistress seems extreme, but Linda Brent reports another story which illustrates the venom with which some mistresses regarded the progeny of miscegenation: "I once saw a young slave girl dying soon after birth of a child nearly white. In her agony she cried out 'O Lord, come and take me.' Her mistress stood by, and mocked at her like an incarnate fiend. 'You suffer, do you?' she exclaimed. 'I am glad of it. You deserve it all, and more too.'"[32]

More often the children and mother are removed from the area. As William Craft explains, Ellen Craft was given away: "Notwithstanding my wife being of African extraction on her mother's side, she is almost white—in fact, she is so nearly so that the tyrannical old lady to whom she first belonged became so annoyed, at finding her frequently mistaken for a child of the family, that she gave her when eleven years of age to a daughter, as a wedding present."[33] Brent's narrative also relates an incident in which a slave was severely beaten by his master for the following reason:

> The slave had quarrelled with his wife, in presence of the overseer, and had accused his master of being the father of her child. They were both black, and the child was very fair. . . . A few months afterwards Dr. Flint handed them both over to a slave-trader. The guilty man put their value into his pocket, and had the satisfaction of knowing that they were out of sight and hearing. When the mother was delivered into the trader's hands, she said, "You *promised* to treat me well." To which he replied, "You have let your tongue run too far; damn you!" She had forgotten that it was a crime for a slave to tell who was the father of her child.[34]

Frederick Douglass's description of the problems of the mulatto child summarizes the observations of several other narrators:

> Such slaves invariably suffer greater hardships, and have more to contend with, than others. They are, in the first place, a constant offence to their mistress. She is ever disposed to find fault with them; they can seldom do any thing to please her; she is never better pleased than when she sees them under the lash, especially when she suspects her husband of showing to his mulatto children favors which he withholds from his black slaves. The master is frequently compelled to sell this class of his slaves, out of deference to the feelings of his white wife; and, cruel as the deed may strike any one to be, for a man to sell his own children to human flesh-mongers, it is often the dictate of humanity for him to do so; for, unless he does this, he must not only whip them himself, but must stand by and see one white son tie up his brother, of but a few shades darker complexion than himself, and ply the gory lash to his naked back; and if he lisp one word of disapproval, it is set down to his parental partiality, and only makes a bad matter worse, both for himself and the slave whom he would protect and defend.[35]

The abuse of innocents and the division of families that illicit miscegenation imposes are presented as the results of two deadly sins, lust and greed:

The fact remains, in all its glaring odiousness, that slaveholders have ordained and by law established, that the children of slave women shall in all cases follow the condition of their mothers; and this is done too [sic] obviously to administer to their own lusts, and make a gratification of their wicked desires profitable as well as pleasurable; for by this cunning arrangement, the slave holders, in cases not a few, sustains to his slaves the double relation of master and father.[36]

With the communication of three items of personal information —the narrator's lineage, date, and place of birth—the slave narratives establish the structure which characterizes them. By indicating his name, birthplace, and parentage, the narrator supports the claim that the experiences within the narrative are those of a specific individual. As it turns out, such an introduction is only a little more personal than that of a narrative which begins "once upon a time," for immediately the individual's circumstances are put into a larger context which effectively introduces slavery as the other subject of the narrative, and the narrator's opposition to this institution is apparent.

With the presentation of vital statistics, and the assertion that the circumstances which interfere with the individual's knowledge of his own parentage and details of birth are those which also interfere with the possession of that same information by the entire group to which that person belongs, the theme of deliberately attempted psychological genocide from birth is introduced. The remainder of the narrative develops the idea that slavery is based upon unjust and immoral attempts to dehumanize an entire group of people.

The reader is introduced to the institution of slavery through a character with whom he is predisposed to sympathize. While the nineteenth-century reader might not have been greatly concerned by charges that slaves were forced to work and were not fed and clothed in the same manner as himself, he would have been angered by stories of excessive brutality, destroyed families, and violated women. He would think it extreme to deny even the recognition of one's birth into the human race.

The implication of slavery as a southern evil, the stereotypical depiction of slave personalities, and the peculiar details of the slaves' daily routines help maintain a comfortable distance between the reader and those about whom he reads. He is at once the Christian denouncing sin, the humanitarian abhorring human exploitation, and the nationalist chastising unpatriotic citizens.

In the first few pages the South-to-North, degradation-to-salvation, and tyranny-to-democracy axes are fixed. The mention of violence and miscegenation has titillated the readers' interests and at the same time reaffirmed their virtue. They are interested in and sympathetic to the cause, and probably eager to buy other slave narratives.

5

The Plot
of Ante-bellum
Slave Narratives

MORE THAN ANY other narrative element, plot remains constant. As Robert Scholes and Robert Kellogg conclude in *The Nature of Narrative:*

> Of all the aspects of narrative, plot seems to be not only the most essential but also the least variable, insofar as its general outlines are concerned. We demand variety of incident more than we demand variety of plot in our fiction. . . . When we pick up a modern picaresque tale, whether it is narrated by Felix Krull or Augie March, we know in a general way what to expect. We know our destination though we do not know specifically what scenes we shall pass by the way. . . . Plot, in the large sense, will always be *mythos* and always be traditional.[1]

"In the large sense" are key words. Although realism was most often considered the desirable form to emulate, especially in that group which we designate as didactic literature, the emphasis in the nineteenth century was upon the utilization of whatever form would best accomplish the narrator's purposes. Writers had long discovered that elements from mimesis, romance, history, and myth could be combined in ways which far exceeded the advantages offered by any one structure. The slave narrators, likewise, created a form which was an amalgam of traditional and innovative techniques. Since it was extremely important that they present a vivid depiction of slavery from the perspective of the slave, the mimetic impulse was strong.

On the other hand, it was standard for didactic writings to utilize materials of the Judeo-Christian myth. From Wigglesworth's *The Day of Doom* and Bunyan's *Pilgrim's Progress* to *A Narrative of the Captivity and Restauration of Mrs. Mary Rowlandson* and on, the American reading public was not only accustomed to literature structured in terms of this particular myth but also expected serious writings to be influenced this way.

Naturally, slave narrators, like other nineteenth-century writers, were strongly influenced by this tradition and perceived themselves and their situations in biblical terms. They often prefaced their narratives with verses from the Bible and liberally distributed biblical quotations throughout them. Allusions to themselves as contemporary children of Israel and as Christ figures, who must as Thomas Jones wrote in his account, "bear the *slave's heavy cross*,"[2] are most frequent.

It is interesting to note, however, that most slave narrators use religion primarily as a literary device. They adopted the Judeo-Christian myth structure. They alluded to Old Testament stories and prophecies. They defined good and evil by Christian standards. Slave narrators made it a point to portray themselves as Christians and to emphasize the loving, patient, forgiving quality of their lives. They were quick to identify occasional lies or thefts as "sins" and to profess repentence while trying to explain to their audiences the extenuating circumstances that necessitated such lapses. While the titles, prefaces, and appendixes of their narratives often declared they were ministers or missionaries and while they often alluded to their escapes from bondage as examples of God's mercy or power, they did not engage in extended theological discussions, nor did they chronicle their spiritual development. References to religion as a sustaining force are usually brief and infrequent. The hypocrisy of professed Christians (the slaveholders) who abused sincere Christians (the slaves) is a more favored topic. Accounts of their religious conversions were told to verify that their own Christianity was obtained by the ritual of guilt recognition, repentence of sin and salvation favored by the large fundamentalist segment of their audience. Worship practices were mentioned primarily to show the extent to which slavery attempted to thwart their salvation and to demonstrate the strength of the slave's commitment to his religion.

Their specialized use of religion in slave narratives seems a conscious choice, for cursory examination of writings that were not slave narratives by many of these same writers as well as the abundance of ante-bellum spirituals, sermons, and stories demonstrate that slaves produced religious commentary more explicit than that found in the slave narratives. Obviously, slave narrators felt that it was not appropriate to emphasize religious beliefs or experiences that were intimate, sustaining, or possibly controversial. They did recognize that demonstrations of the similarities of their essential subject matter and the basic Judeo-Christian myth could enhance the narratives' appeal to the reading public and they exploited this opportunity masterfully.

The Judeo-Christian myth, as Scholes and Kellogg demonstrate, is concerned with "the whole journey of man" which "falls between Genesis and Apocalypse." It follows a progression from innocence to the knowledge of evil, repentance and conversion, the resistance of sin, and salvation. It integrates the fertility ritual's annual cycle with a progressive concept of time. Thus it is "a linear spiral with a beginning and an end: the death-which-is-birth at the end of the spiral being the counterpart of the birth-which-is-death that begins it."[3]

The plot of the nineteenth-century slave narrative is informed by the Judeo-Christian mythological structure on both the material and the spiritual levels. The action moves from the idyllic life of a Garden of Eden into the wilderness, the struggle for survival, the providential help, and the arrival into the Promised Land. In addition, the plot of the slave narrative incorporates the parallel structure of birth into death and death into birth which also distinguishes the Judeo-Christian myth. The slave narratives are concerned with the movement from enslavement to freedom. The slave from birth is shown as being denied not only liberty and the pursuit of happiness, but also full recognition of his entrance into human society. According to the slave narratives, the ultimate aim of slavery is the negation of the slave's humanity and the transformation of a man into a thing. It is accomplished by a systematic denial of even the most commonplace elements of his birthright. The infant slave is not given a complete and permanent name, nor is the child allowed full knowledge of his lineage or the circumstances of his birth. The slave is born into a system designed to allow his physical existence but to deny the knowledge of his past or the hope for a better future. In such an environment, one can survive, but one cannot experience the fullness of life; one cannot be said to live. The account of the move from bondage to freedom is in essence the story of the move from "birth-which-is-death" to "death-which-is-birth."

In the slave narrative the mythological pattern is realized in four chronological phases. First comes the loss of innocence, which is objectified through the development of an awareness of what it means to be a slave. This can be compared to the descent from perfection or mortification. The mortification process includes purgation, for as the slave learns the meaning of slavery, he also tries to purge himself of those elements that would facilitate enslavement. Second is the realization of alternatives to bondage and the formulation of a resolve to be free. This decision begins the ascent to the ideal, or invigoration. The resolution to quit slavery is, in effect, a climax to a conversion experience. The third phase is the escape. Whether it occurs between two sentences or forms the largest portion of the narrative, it is part of the struggle to overcome evil. The interest at this point is in the details, the pitfalls and obstacles, the sufferings and moments of bravery encountered in the process of achieving freedom. Although the first attempt sometimes ends in capture, the outcome is never in doubt. The narrative, after all, was written by a freeman. The fourth phase is that of freedom obtained. It is the arrival at the City of God or the New Jerusalem and it corresponds to the jubilation period of ancient ritual.

Most of the narratives concentrate upon the mortification and purgation phase wherein the protagonist experiences the slave's role, begins to understand that role in relation to other societal roles, and decides to reject his enslavement. By far the longest and most detailed account is that which describes the material life of the slave. The emphasis is upon the plethora of degrading and brutal experiences indigenous to slavery. Although the prefatory remarks concerning his birth and childhood have been chronological and general, once the narrator begins to explain what it means to be a slave, the chronological structure is overshadowed by a series of illustrations and examples selected to emphasize his definition. Incidents and observations concerning the institution of slavery and emphasizing the brutality and exploitation of the slaves are presented at random. The direct experience of the narrator is supplemented by information he has heard or witnessed.

Often the transitions are no smoother than this one:

> During a residence of eight years in this city, numerous cases of extreme cruelty came under my own observation;—to record them all, would occupy more space than could possibly be allowed in this little volume. I shall, therefore, give but a few more, in addition to what I have already related.
> Capt. J. B. Brunt, who resided near my master, had a slave named John. . . .[4]

Or, "I must now give the account of our escape; but, before doing so, it may be well to quote a few passages from the fundamental laws of slavery; in order to give some idea of the legal as well as the social tyranny from which we fled."[5]

Usually these supplementary narratives are two or three paragraphs long, spliced into the story at various places to give the reader additional perspective by which to evaluate the protagonist's experiences. Occasionally, an extended narrative is included. Such is the case in John Brown's narrative. After three chapters he suspends his own story and devotes Chapter 4 to John Glasgow's experiences. There is no chronological reason why the narrative occurs in this place. Brown simply says:

> I must interrupt my own narrative here, to relate the story of John Glasgow. I had it from his own lips; and acting on the advice of the secretary of the *British and Foreign Anti-Slavery Society*, I have made a declaration in his presence, before a notary public, to the effect that, as given below, the narrative is substantially correct. I stated the facts to the Secretary of the Society, some time ago, and he introduced them in the *Anti-Slavery Reporter* for July 1853.[6]

The entire mortification section is a collage of experiences and observations, direct and vicarious, designed to prove the inhumanity of slavery and the impotence of the slave against that system. The audience is made aware of un-christian and inhumane practices which exist and of the social and moral changes which slavery portends for their society.

The second phase is more spiritual. This is one reason why, although crucial to the development of the narrative, it is not presented in such detailed fashion. The details of the process of contextualization, of perceiving the implications of one's situation, are more personalized, less applicable to all slaves than are descriptions of material conditions. In this phase the slave becomes aware of alternatives and of his potential for self-determination. He begins a process of analysis which results in a decision to be free. After this, the chronological structure surfaces. The revitalization and jubilation phases are swiftly completed.

In the third phase, the narrative returns to the material level. There are two ways in which the decision to be free is actualized: The slave is manumitted or he runs away. In either case his efforts are presented as a formulaic account which includes trials and tribulations, help and hinderances, failure and progress, before the goal is reached. The narrative ends soon after the slave's escape or manumission has been completed and his arrival at a place where his freedom from bondage is relatively assured. The narrative ends with the metamorphosis of a chattel into a man, with a promise of happiness for the fugitives and a remembrance of the sorrow of those yet enslaved.

The *Narrative of William Wells Brown, a Fugitive Slave* is one of the shorter narratives, but it illustrates the four phases and the proportionate emphasis given each phase. There are fourteen chapters in the original version. Each chapter is approximately three pages long. Chapters 1 and 2 cover the first thirteen or fourteen years of his life. They reveal that Brown was born in Lexington, Kentucky; that he was one of seven children, none of whom had the same father; and that his father, a relative of his master, "was connected with some of the first families in Kentucky." Brown informs us that he was a house servant and therefore received better treatment than those who worked in the fields. He did not, however, escape the sound of other slaves being flogged. The only personal incident concerning his childhood is an account of hearing his mother's screams when she was beaten. Even here, the effect is more of a witness's courtroom testimony than of one intimately concerned with the incident. He relates:

> My mother was a field hand, and one morning was ten or fifteen minutes behind the others in getting into the field. As soon as she reached the spot where they were at work, the overseer commenced whipping her. She cried, "Oh! pray—Oh! pray—Oh! pray"—these are generally the words of slaves, when imploring mercy at the hands of their oppressors. I heard her voice, and knew it, and jumped out of my bunk, and went to the door. Though the field was some distance from the house, I could hear every crack of the whip, and every groan and cry of my poor mother. I remained at the door, not daring to venture any farther. The cold chills ran over me, and I wept aloud. After giving her ten lashes, the sound of the whip ceased, and I returned to my bed, and found no consolation but in my tears. It was not yet daylight.[7]

In this account, the narrator's concern with his audience and his desire to create a particular response obviously dominate any desire to disclose a particularly significant incident in his own life. He is very detailed about the offense, the number of lashes, and his mother's pleas. His account of his own actions and emotions is remarkably vague: He felt chills and cried aloud. Brown's emphasis is upon the brutality toward slaves and the helplessness of children who must bear witness to the oppression of their elders. For example, Brown does not tell how he knows the details of his mother's infraction. According to him, he "heard her voice and knew it," and this was what aroused the six-year-old from sleep. It is, of course, entirely possible that he would have heard the details later and simply repeated this information, but the omission of details such as how he learned what he could not then have known takes the focus from him and his reactions to the plight of a slave who is late to work. The parenthetical phrase, "these are generally the words of slaves when imploring mercy at the hands of their oppressors," contributes to the interpretation of this incident as an example of the injustices of slavery instead of the personal experience of a slave child.

The remainder of the two chapters describes the farm, the overseers, and slave life. There is a long digression concerning Randall, a slave whom the master had feared to discipline, and the way in which an overseer eventually subdued Randall's spirit.

It is in Chapter 3, when Brown is about fourteen or fifteen years old, that the narrative first focuses upon his personal experiences and begins to concentrate upon his development of an awareness of what it means to be a slave, upon his loss of innocence. Phase one begins with a disruption. His master moves to St. Louis and purchases a farm near there. Brown is separated from his birthplace and from his mother, for they are each hired out to different owners in a strange town. Brown is rented by Major Freeland, "a horse-racer, cock-fighter, gambler, and withal an inveterate drunkard." Not only is he subjected to Major Freeland's capricious and violent behavior, but upon petition to his master Brown learns that "he cared nothing about it, so long as he received the money for my labor."[8] After five or six months of maltreatment, Brown runs away and hides in the woods. This escape was not the climactic event of phase three. This was another in the series of lessons of what it means to be a slave. He was fleeing from something, but it was an undirected, instinctual flight. When he is captured, jailed, flogged, "smoked," and sent back to work, Brown learns more of the slave's impotence.

After Major Freeland, Brown experiences a further series of masters, tasks, and degradations. Gradually, he becomes aware of alternatives to his situation. Phase two begins. Those same elements that contribute to his knowledge of slavery reveal the meaning of freedom. His many masters and various jobs, especially his service as valet to steamboat passengers, increase his frustration over enslavement, for, as he relates, "In passing from place to place, and seeing new faces every day, and knowing that they could go where they pleased, I soon became unhappy, and several times thought of leaving the boat at some landing place, and trying to make my escape to Canada, which I had heard much about as a place where the slave might live, be free, and be protected."[9]

Brown's orientation to slavery taught him the meaning of powerlessness. It also taught him the correlation between slavery and tyranny. As the slave of a slave trader, he witnessed the insidious depths of that institution. His narrative is replete with incidents of children torn from their mothers' arms, beautiful girls subjected to sexual abuse, and other brutal acts against the bodies and minds of black people. His realization of the moral degradation that slavery can produce in the slave is illustrated by an account of how he tricks an unsuspecting black man into a beating meant for Brown. "This incident," he says, "shows how it is that slavery makes its victims lying and mean; for which vices it afterwards reproaches them, and uses them as arguments to prove that they deserve no better fate."[10]

The first nine chapters of the narrative are concerned with the exposition of slavery's evils and a slave's reaction to enslavement. The evolution from phase one to phase two is subtle and incomplete. Along with Brown's lessons in chattel making, came his recognition of alternatives to the situation. He spent much time trying to comprehend the significance of this knowledge for himself. There are five chapters or approximately six years between Brown's flight into the woods and his attempt to flee slavery. During that time came the gradual change, one that was hindered, in part, by the fact that his desire to attain freedom meant separation from his family. Brown was especially reluctant to leave his mother enslaved in that place, for to leave her, he reasoned, "would be proving recreant to the duty which I owed her."[11]

Only when his mother and all her children are sold and the family faces permanent dissolution is he able to decide. Like a religious conversion after years of doubt, the decision is sudden and irrevocable. Brown visited his sister, who was in jail with a drove of slaves awaiting departure for Natchez. "After giving her some advice, and taking from my finger a ring and placing it on hers, I bade her farewell forever, and returned to my mother, and then and there made up my mind to leave for Canada as soon as possible."[12] The decision to leave was precipitated by a circumstance over which he had no control, but it had been building simultaneously with his realization of the implications of slavery and the meaning of freedom.

Brown convinced his mother to flee with him. They traveled 150 miles before being captured. His mother was sold away, and for William Wells Brown it seemed that "the love of liberty that had been burning in my bosom, had well nigh gone out."[13] But soon he was again plotting his escape to Canada. There are three chapters between his aborted escape and the successful one. These chapters function primarily to compile additional instances of slave oppression and to show the strength of Brown's resolution to be free. The concern over Brown's escape is only a question of when and how. The actual events are few. Brown is jailed, then sold as punishment. The new master treated him kindly, but when this owner saw a chance to realize a profit, he sold William Wells Brown. Brown masqueraded his frustration so completely that a person who purchased him in October allowed him to accompany the family on a trip to the north in December. On January 1, 1834, when the boat docked at an Ohio port, Brown walked off the boat and north to freedom.

The account of the escape is accomplished in seven pages, three of which are concerned with William Wells Brown's meeting his patron, Wells Brown, and one of which describes an incident wherein a woman refused to allow her husband to deny Brown's request for food, giving him a meal and ten cents. In effect, the narrative's purpose was accomplished with Brown's arrival into the Promised Land of the free states; therefore, the next thirteen years are summarized in four paragraphs. This was done by ignoring a marriage, three children, trips to Haiti and Cuba, several jobs, and a decade of abolitionist leadership.

The majority of slave narratives conform to the pattern just described. A few, however, have particular goals which require some variation of emphasis. The focus of some narratives, for example, is upon escape. The primary attraction of such works as *Running a Thousand Miles for Freedom* and *Narrative of Henry Box Brown* is the daring and ingenuity of the narrators' methods of leaving slavery. Consequently, the bulk of their narratives is concerned with the details of their flight. The Crafts' escape was accomplished by Ellen's exploiting her fair complexion, disguising her sex, and passing as a white master with William as her body servant. Their narrative provides the reader with such details as their solutions to the problem of signing hotel registers while illiterate, Ellen's conversations with slaveholders while riding in the white section of the railroad, and her dilemma when two young ladies, believing that their fellow passenger was indeed a man, become infatuated with her. Henry Box Brown, whose middle name was taken in tribute to his unique escape (he was mailed north in a box), includes in his narrative the kind and quantity of provisions which he carried on his journey and a copy of the "Hymn of Thanksgiving sung by Henry Box Brown after being released from his confinement in the Box, at Philadelphia." The latter item is a five-stanza poem which, the preface assures us, is a copy of "the identical words uttered by him as soon as he inhaled the fresh air of freedom, after the faintness occasioned by his journey in his temporary tomb had passed away."[14]

On the other hand, in *Slavery in the United States: A Narrative of the Life and Adventures of Charles Ball* and in *Slave Life in Georgia: A Narrative of the Life of John Brown*, the primary emphasis is upon the institution itself. Although the story of the individual's progress from bondage to freedom forms the unifying structure of the works, the narratives also include chapters on topics such as the principal crops of the South and the techniques of growing them; the differences between the treatment of slaves on cotton plantations and those on tobacco plantations; and the diets, clothing, and daily routine of slaves. In addition, they are virtual catalogs of punishment techniques, including diagrams of some of the more ingenious devices for the torture of slaves.

At the other extreme, Samuel Ringgold Ward's *Autobiography of a Fugitive Negro* disposes of the entire slave experience in 25 pages. The other 387 pages are devoted to his account of his life, his travels, and antislavery efforts. The fact that he was delivered from slavery at age three may have some bearing on this; but although Ward states that his life was affected by the tenuousness of being a fugitive, he does not dwell on that aspect either. The bulk of his work is more closely akin to a memoir or other type of autobiographical writing than most slave narratives. Ward's title, however, and the fact that all the four phases of the slave narrative's plot are included, imply that he was consciously utilizing the pattern of the slave narrative and submitting his work as an addition to that genre.

Although a few nineteenth-century narrators may have chosen to emphasize a phase of the plot different from that which was customary, they all subordinated the birth and childhood information. From the beginning, slave narrators had started chronologically with birth and childhood and thus began their narratives with an exposition of life as an innocent. Before the nineteenth century, however, the majority of the narrators were Africans (and often alleged to be of royal birth). Their foreign background could be exploited to satisfy the curiosity and romanticism of their readers. The contrast of their lives as slaves could be heightened by lavish descriptions of their native culture and land. Thus the African narrator began with descriptions of life in an Edenic setting. In the nineteenth century, most narrators were Afro-American. Not only did they lack the exoticism of being from a foreign country but also racial attitudes had nearly eliminated the noble savage aura which contributed to the popularity of the earliest slave narrators. Afro-American narrators did not try to romanticize the slave quarters, but settled for an abstract Eden, a state of mind. Although the slave narratives often begin with the relatively innocent and happy situation, a primary task of the nineteenth-century narrative was to help the reader understand what it meant to be a slave. There was little to be gained from extensive descriptions of early childhood; thus little space was devoted to this stage, and it is more appropriately considered prefatory to the mythic structure that dominates the work.

One particularly obvious reason is that the early life of most slaves was in many ways similar to, if not actually more comfortable than, the early life of most lower-class children in the nineteenth century. Not only does it seem that infants were not deliberately abused, but the slave child was usually recognized as valuable property. Consequently, he received at least the care given to any other possession.

In *The Slave Community*, John Blassingame reports that while plantation routine did not permit a lavish amount of personal attention for the slave child, the master tended to be "solicitous of the health of the new child."[15] The mother was generally allowed time off for a few days or weeks to care for the child and to recover her health. Sometimes owners established definite routines for nursing and caring for the child.

Once the postpartum period had ended, however, many children were not well supervised. Improper or irregular feeding and general neglect resulted in a high proportion of illnesses and accidents. Thus there was a certain amount of sympathy to be gained from the fact that both parents were forced to work and the child was deprived of constant individual attention. The stories of inefficient care by old women or children, and the instances of sickness and death which resulted from unattended and malnourished infants were presented in gruesome detail in many works. But on the whole, the infant slave mortality rate was not significantly different from that of other infants of the period.

Contemporary historians verify that the responsibilities of the slave child were not great. Eugene Genovese reports:

> Before the age of eight most children did little or no work apart from looking after ("nursing") those younger than themselves, although in every part of the South some masters worked the little ones unmercifully from the time they could toddle. Between eight and twelve the children graduated to such responsibilities as cleaning up the yards, digging up potatoes, many of which they appropriated for their own illicit roasting parties, shelling peas for the kitchen, or more laboriously, toting water to the field hands. Their hardest work came during the cotton-picking season, when they were sometimes called upon to help. . . . Despite a quota of abuse and danger, the slave children had a childhood; however, much misery awaited them.[16]

In fact, Genovese cautiously concludes that the physical conditions of the slave child were generally better than those of children in other societies. Although child labor was exceedingly common in the nineteenth century, according to Genovese's research, most slave children did not begin heavy field work before the age of twelve. Genovese's comparison of these findings with the conditions of peasants and workers in Britain, France, Germany, and parts of the Caribbean indicates that this was a relatively late age to assume heavy work duties.[17]

Blassingame's study of plantation life in the ante-bellum South indicates that young children were neglected and "died in droves," but he also reports:

> If he survived infancy, the slave child partook, in bountiful measure for a while, of many of the joys of childhood. . . . Slave parents, in spite of their own sufferings, lavished love on their children. Fathers regaled their children with fascinating stories and songs and won

their affections with little gifts. These were all the more important if the father lived on another plantation. The two weekly visits of the father then took on all the aspects of minor celebrations. . . .

Often assigned as playmates to their young masters, Negro children played in promiscuous equality with white children. Together they roamed the plantation or went hunting, fishing, berry picking, or raiding watermelon and potato patches. Indeed, at first, bondage weighed lightly on the shoulder of the black child.[18]

Historical evidence supports what appears to have been the contemporary attitude that, on the whole, the slave child's story was the story of the poor and the working class, and although it could contribute to the overall antislavery theme, it was not sufficiently unique to justify the abolishment of slavery, the major emphasis of the slave narratives. Slave narrators did not challenge this idea, but in fact supported it. Linda Brent says, "Though we were all slaves, I was so fondly shielded that I never dreamed I was a piece of merchandise, trusted to them for safekeeping, and liable to be demanded of them at any moment."[19] Noah Davis recalls his childhood as quite happy:

My youngest brother and I did little else than play about home, and wait upon our mother. I had several playmates, besides my brothers, and among them were the sons of Col. Thom, and the servant boys who stayed at his house. Although many years have passed away since, it gives me pleasure, even now, to recollect the happy seasons I enjoyed with the playmates of my childhood.

But this pleasant state of things was not to continue long.[20]

Josiah Henson fondly remembers his relationship with his master:

As the first negro-child ever born to him, I was his especial pet. He gave me his own Christian name, Josiah, and with that he also gave me my last name, Henson, after an uncle of his, who was an officer in the Revolutionary War. A bright spot in my childhood was my residence with him—bright, but, alas! fleeting.[21]

It is important to note that the reminiscences, though pleasant, also emphasize the impermanence of the situation. The slave child, like Adam and Eve, Joseph, Moses, or even the baby Jesus, is born into a drama which has already begun. It is only a matter of time before he is made aware of his role. Description of early childhood, then, was cursory, for the value of the author's life for the antislavery cause was limited in its usefulness as evidence of the evil of slavery. At the same time, it was not wise to omit the early childhood period, for the contrast between innocence and knowledge has its value. Consequently, the slave narratives do not attempt to deny that a slave's childhood was generally undistinguished. They depicted this period as a fairly happy time punctuated by incidents which temporarily disturbed the individual and foreshadowed for the reader the disasters to come. Such a depiction dramatized the contrast between the pleasant existence of the unsuspecting child and the horror of discovering the existence to which he was heir. Suspense had been created by the reader's knowledge that the fate of the child was sharply different from what his innocent beginnings would otherwise imply. The effect of this knowledge was further heightened by emphasizing the abruptness of the division between the protagonist's ignorance of the existence of slavery and his realization of it by direct experience.

The real value of the slave experience begins with the expulsion from Eden when the slave child, on the brink of adulthood, must confront the evil forces of slavery. Few slave narrators tell of gradual orientation to their new responsibilities. Although historical evidence suggests a series of increasing responsibilities and a social structure which provided role models for the child, in the narratives there tend to be abrupt and traumatic changes which hurl an individual from a relatively protected existence within a community to an alien and often frightening situation which he must encounter alone.

Often the death of the master precipitates this change. Upon his demise, an inventory of the estate is made and shares awarded to each claimant. Sometimes the property is converted into cash, in which case slaves are sold. However, the auction block, although a stock scene in antislavery literature, is not the usual manner in which the slave narrators were introduced to the full implications of the chattel state. The death of the owners of slave narrators usually results in the transfer of ownership of the slave to the creditors and heirs of the deceased. The procedures by which this is accomplished vary, but a typical method is vividly described by John Brown in his narrative, *Slave Life in Georgia*. He reports:

> At the appointed hour, nearly the whole of us had congregated in the great yard, under the big sycamore tree. A fourth part of the negroes on the estate, had been kept back by Betty Moore, as her share, her husband's will giving her the right of making a selection. Besides these, she had taken my brother Silas and my sister Lucy, whom she reserved on behalf of her eldest daughter, the wife of Burrell Williams. . . . All who were there stood together, facing the Executors, or Committee as they were called, who sat on chairs under the same sycamore tree I have spoken of. Burrell Williams, James Davis, and Billy Bell, held themselves aloof, and did not in any manner interfere with the proceedings of the Committee, who told us off into three lots, each lot consisting of about twenty-five or thirty, as near as I can recollect. As there was a good deal of difference in the value of the slaves, individually, some being stronger than others, or more likely, the allotments were regulated so as to equalize the value of each division. For instance, my brother Silas and my sister, Lucy, who belonged rightly to the gang of which I and my mother and other members of the family formed a part, were replaced by two of my cousin Annikie's children, a boy and a girl; the first called Henry, the other Mason, who were weak and sickly. When the lots had been told off, the names of the men, women and children composing them were written on three slips of paper, and these were put into a hat. . . . The lot in which I and my mother were, was drawn by James Davis. Each slip was then signed by the Committee, and the lot turned over to the new owner.[22]

Sometimes, the protagonist and a few other slaves or the protagonist alone is sold for financial gain. Typically, the slave has no indication that his sale is imminent. William Grimes gives this version:

> When I was ten years of age, Col. William Thornton came down from the mountains, in Culpepper County, to buy negroes, and he came to my master's house, who was his brother-in-law, and seeing me, thought me a smart boy. He asked my master what he would take for me; he replied, he thought I was worth £60. Col. Thornton immediately offered £65, and the bargain was made. The next morning I started with him for Culpepper.[23]

Although they had no voice in decisions, not all young slaves were unwilling to leave their homes. Frederick Douglass says:

> I was probably between seven and eight years old when I left Colonel Lloyd's plantation. I left it with joy. I shall never forget the ecstasy with which I received the intelligence that my old master (Anthony) had determined to let me go to Baltimore, to live with Mr. Hugh Auld, brother to my old master's son-in-law, Captain Thomas Auld. I received this information about three days before my departure. They were three of the happiest days I ever enjoyed. I spent the most part of all these three days in the creek, washing off the plantation scurf, and preparing myself for my departure.[24]

The first separation was not always the result of being sold. Several slaves learned the meaning of slavery when they were hired out, that is, rented by their owners to other persons on an annual basis. Not only was there an income to be derived from hiring slaves out, but such a practice could be manipulated for long-term benefits. J. W. C. Pennington describes the practice thus:

> The slaveholders in that state often hire the children of their slaves out to non-slaveholders, not only because they save themselves the expense of taking care of them, but in this way they get among their slaves useful trades. They put a bright slave boy with a tradesman, until he gets such a knowledge of the trade as to be able to do his own work, and then he takes him home.[25]

The slave who was most easily hired out was one who demonstrated significant potential or skill, one who was, as Pennington phrased it, "a bright slave boy." A high proportion of slave narrators "hired their own time."

Regardless of the permanence of his departure, the young protagonist leaves the relatively Eden-like scene of his childhood and sets off into the wilderness of slavery. Whatever the method, one particular scene, the separation of mother and child, recurs. Descriptions of this experience, the best-known scene of the slave narratives, do not vary substantially from that given in one of the earliest of the nineteenth-century works, Charles Ball's *Slavery in the United States:*

My poor mother, when she saw me leaving her for the last time, ran after me, took me down from the horse, clasped me in her arms, and wept loudly and bitterly over me. My master seemed to pity her, and endeavoured to soothe her distress by telling her that he would be a good master to me, and that I should not want any thing. She then, still holding me in her arms, walked along the road beside the horse as he moved slowly, and earnestly and imploringly besought my master to buy her and the rest of her children . . . the slave-driver, who had first bought her, came running in pursuit of her with a raw hide in his hand. When he overtook us he told her he was her master now, and ordered her to give that little negro to its owner, and come back with him.

My mother then turned to him and cried, "Oh, master, do not take me from my child!" Without making any reply, he gave her two or three heavy blows on the shoulders with his raw hide, snatched me from her arms, handed me to my master, and seizing her by one arm, dragged her back towards the place of sale.[26]

One reason for the preponderance of such dramatic scenes is that they emphasize the sudden and total isolation of the individual and thereby reemphasize the tragedy of his situation.

Rarely is the slave's first reaction one of overt resistance. His initial curiosity and surprise are superseded by anxiety, fear, grief, and despondency. As he begins to comprehend his situation, he is almost overpowered by the apparent omnipotence of this evil. Not only do slave narratives ignore the existence of any slave community within which a young adult slave might be accepted and by which culture that slave may be sustained, but neither do the narratives acknowledge any attempts of the new slave to gain some measure of control over his situation. Survival techniques, with which the oral literature is especially replete such as tricking the master out of additional food, hustling clothing and gifts by exploiting the prejudices of whites, and using their mother wit to avoid any number of unpleasant situations are rarely revealed. In the slave narratives the protagonist is at first a victim of almost overwhelming forces. He is alone in his struggle to survive. His energies are focused upon the essentials of life: food, rest, and the avoidance of pain.

Henry Bibb's summary of his life after leaving his mother is a good example of the image of slave life that most narratives display:

I was a wretched slave, compelled to work under the lash without wages, and often without clothes enough to hide my nakedness. I I have often worked without half enough to eat, both late and early, by day and by night. I have often laid my wearied limbs down at night to rest upon a dirt floor, or a bench, without any covering at all, because I had no where else to rest my wearied body, after having worked hard all day. I have also been compelled in early life, to go at the bidding of a tyrant, through all kinds of weather, hot or cold, wet or dry, and without shoes frequently, until the month of December, with my bare feet on the cold frosty ground, cracked open and bleeding as I walked.[27]

Abruptly thrust from the garden of innocence, the young slave enters a wilderness in which he is subjected to physical deprivation and brutality. Slave narrators were careful to include the details of food and clothing allowances, shelter construction, and daily work loads. They agreed that the amount of food was barely sufficient and the quality was poor.

Virtually every narrator declares that the basic weekly food allowance was a peck of corn per adult per week. Some report they received small amounts of fish, meat, or potatoes; however, they are quick to point out the infrequency of such supplements. Others tell of the garden plots which were used to supplement their diets. These plots were sometimes allocated by the master and sometimes appropriated by the slaves, but they were cultivated only after the plantation work was done. Narrators also reveal that for slaves hunting and fishing were not recreational pastimes, as they were for many slaveholders. For the slave, they were the means of survival.

Contrasts between the diet of slaves and that of domestic animals are frequent. Solomon Northup states that the weekly allowance of slaves was:

Three and a half pounds of bacon, and corn enought to make a peck of meal. That is all—no tea, coffee, sugar, and with the exception of a very scanty sprinkling now and then, no salt. . . . Master Epps' hogs were fed on *shelled* corn—it was thrown out to his "niggers" in the ear. The former, he thought, would fatten faster by shelling, and soaking it in the water—the latter, perhaps, if treated in the same manner, might grow too fat to labor.[28]

In a similar fashion the clothing and housing of the slave are seen as barely adequate. Exposure to the elements is played up and passages that detail the frostbite, illnesses, and general discomfort which result are frequent. Solomon Northup describes the accommodations thus:

> The softest couches in the world are not to be found in the log mansion of the slave. The one whereon I reclined year after year, was a plank twelve inches wide and ten feet long. My pillow was a stick of wood. The bedding was a coarse blanket, and not a rag or shred beside. Moss might be used, were it not that it directly breeds a swarm of fleas.
>
> The cabin is constructed of logs, without floor or window. The latter is altogether unnecessary, the crevices between the logs admitting sufficient light. In stormy weather the rain drives through them, rendering it comfortless and extremely disagreeable. The rude door hangs on great wooden hinges. In one end is constructed an awkward fire-place.[29]

Also frequent are the references to the partial nakedness and lack of privacy which results. According to John Brown:

> The clothing of the men consists of a pair of thin cotton pantaloons, and a shirt of the same material, two of each being allowed them every year. The women wear a shirt similar to the men's and a cotton petticoat. . . . They also have two suits allowed them every year. These, however, are not enough. They are made of the lowest quality of material, and get torn in the bush, so that the garments soon become useless, even for purposes of the barest decency.[30]

The slave's day begins before dawn. He must prepare breakfast and be in the fields before the whistle. He toils unceasingly under threat of a lash that is disturbingly capricious. Northup summarizes a day's work thus:

> The hands are required to be in the cotton field as soon as it is light in the morning, and, with the exception of ten or fifteen minutes, which is given them at noon to swallow their allowance of cold bacon, they are not permitted to be a moment idle until it is too dark to see, and when the moon is full, they often times labor till the middle of the night. They do not dare to stop even at dinner time, nor return

to the quarters, however late it be, until the order to halt is given by the driver.

The day's work over in the field, the baskets are "toted," or in other words, carried to the ginhouse, where the cotton is weighed. . . . After weighing, follow the whippings; and then the baskets are carried to the cotton house, and their contents stored away like hay, all hands being sent in to tramp it down. . . .

This done, the labor of the day is not yet ended, by any means. Each one must then attend to his respective chores. One feeds the mules, another the swine—another cuts the wood, and so forth; besides, the packing is all done by candle light. Finally, at a late hour, they reach the quarters, sleepy and overcome with the long day's toil. Then a fire must be kindled in the cabin, the corn ground in the small hand-mill, and supper, and dinner for the next day in the field, prepared.[31]

Slave narrators agree that there are some periods when work is not so difficult. After planting and before harvesting, during winter, and, for house servants, between social seasons are periods of routine maintenance, repair, and preparation for the next big rush. They do not, however, imply there are ever long or regular periods of rest. Even the traditional Christmas week could be eliminated without notice, as Charles Ball reports:

We were all big with hope of obtaining three or four days, at least, if not a week of holiday; but when the day at length arrived, we were sorely disappointed, for on Christmas Eve, when we had come from the field, with our cotton, the overseer fell into a furious passion, and swore at us all for our laziness, and many other bad qualities. He then told us that he had intended to give us three days, if we had worked well, but that we had been so idle, and had left so much cotton yet to be picked in the field, that he found it impossible to give us more than one day.[32]

Most narrators agree that the Christmas holidays were the most important times in the slaves' year. During that time feasting, dancing, and general merriment prevailed. Lasting from three to six days, according to the masters' pleasure, it was the time during which those separated from their families were permitted to visit. Marriages were contracted. Gifts were made and exchanged.

But some point out that these vacations were not to be construed as evidence of even a mite of humanity in the slave system. According to Frederick Douglass, the Christmas breaks were "part and parcel of the gross fraud, wrong, and inhumanity of slavery." Douglass explains:

> They do not give the slaves this time because they would not like to have their work during its continuance, but because they know it would be unsafe to deprive them of it. . . . Their object seems to be, to disgust their slaves with freedom, by plunging them into the lowest depths of dissipation. For instance, the slaveholders not only like to see the slave drink of his own accord, but will adopt various plans to make him drunk. One plan is, to make bets on their slaves, as to who can drink the most whisky without getting drunk; and in this way they succeed in getting whole multitudes to drink to excess. Thus, when the slave asks for virtuous freedom, the cunning slaveholder, knowing his ignorance, cheats him with a dose of vicious dissipation, artfully labelled with the name of liberty. The most of us used to drink it down, and the result was just what might be supposed: many of us were led to think that there was little to choose between liberty and slavery. We felt, and very properly too, that we had almost as well be slaves to man as to rum. So, when the holidays ended, we staggered up from the filth of our wallowing, took a long breath, and marched to the field,—feeling upon the whole, rather glad to go, from what our master had deceived us into a belief was freedom, back to the arms of slavery.[33]

Although slave narratives inevitably included information on the living and working environment of slaves, these subjects did not receive the major emphasis. Notwithstanding the question of the validity of comparisons of pain and deprivation, there is a strong tendency to make comparisons. In spite of the dismal picture painted in the narratives about the inadequacy of food, shelter, and clothing and about the excessively long workdays, the reading public would have been aware that such conditions did not differ significantly from those of free lower-class individuals. Comparisons, whether valid or not, could lead to conclusions that the factory workers in England, the laborers on Caribbean sugar plantations, or the poor southern white was as bad or worse off. Moreover, there were many southerners, some of whom were proslavery, who were actively working for reforms in the care of slaves, and slaveholders were quick to promulgate news of their progress.

To combat any attempts to diminish the slave's material deprivations by proving other people were similarly impoverished and to avoid the compromise efforts of moderates who would argue to continue slavery while improving the living conditions of slaves, narrators emphasized the brutal punishments and physical atrocities incurred by slaves. They then tried to show that such brutality was inherent in the slave system.

The precedent for emphasis of these particular assets is found in other antislavery writings such as Theodore Weld's *American Slavery as It Is,* which has been called "the greatest of the anti-slavery pamphlets; in all probability the most crushing indictment of any institution ever written" and for more than ten years was "the handbook of the antislavery impulse."[34] Says Weld in his prefatory remarks:

We will prove that the slaves in the United States are treated with barbarous inhumanity; that they are overworked, underfed, wretchedly clad and lodged, and have insufficient sleep; that they are often made to wear round their necks iron collars armed with prongs, to drag heavy chains and weights at their feet while working in the field, and to wear yokes, and bells, and iron horns; that they are often kept confined in the stocks day and night for weeks together, made to wear gags in their mouths for hours or days, have some of their front teeth torn out or broken off, that they may be easily detected when they run away; that they are frequently flogged with terrible severity, have red pepper rubbed into their lacerated flesh, and hot brine, spirits of turpentine, &c., poured over the gashes to increase the torture; that they are often stripped naked, their backs and limbs cut with knives, bruised and mangled by scores and hundreds of blows with the paddle, and terribly torn by the claws of cats, drawn over them by their tormentors; that they are often hunted with blood hounds and shot down like beasts, or torn in pieces by dogs. . . .

All these things, and more, and worse, we shall *prove.* Reader, we know whereof we affirm, we have weighed it well, *more and worse* WE WILL PROVE.[35]

The proportion of attention given to brutal punishments and physical atrocities in Weld's introduction to this work is indicative of the emphasis accorded this area in antislavery discourse.

It is therefore easier to understand why the protest of the slave narrators was not against punishments per se. They centered this protest instead against excessive or unjust punishments. The prevailing social attitude was that strict enforcement of laws, especially toward blacks, was necessary. Even antislavery workers complained that many free blacks were "given to Idleness, Frolicking, Drunkenness, and in some cases to Dishonesty." In 1808 the New York Manumission Society publicly regretted "the looseness and manners and depravity of conduct in many of the Persons of Colour in this city."[36] Few free states reached the extreme of Ohio by requiring blacks to post bonds insuring good behavior and self-support, but every state had its Black Codes. Most states felt so strongly that blacks required firm discipline that they enacted laws restricting the number allowed to reside within their boundaries and forbidding them the rights to possess arms or to vote. In such a climate there was little to be gained by claiming that blacks were greatly restricted or punished severely.

The slave narrator tried to prove that slavery was not *"perpetual bondage merely,* but of the *depth of degradation* that that word involves."* They concentrated upon detailed examples of the excessive cruelty and undeserved administration of punishments. They dwelled upon the practices of flogging until backs were raw then rubbing salt or hot pepper solutions into the wounds, upon the construction of unusual machines and devices to create the maximum pain for minimum offenses, and upon the punishments of pregnant women, the sick, the old, the very young, and the innocent. They emphasized the maimings and deaths that resulted and the immunity of whites to punishments for their crimes against blacks.

In an effort to support their allegations, narrators often cited instance after instance, with little attempt to integrate them into any plot structure or to elaborate upon the individual circumstances. A good example is found in Moses Roper's narrative. After several pages of detailing the numerous floggings and punishments he had received, Roper states, "My master's cruelty was not confined to me, it was his general conduct to all his slaves. I might relate many instances to substantiate this, but will confine myself to one or two." After pointing out that his master, Mr. Gooch, was a member of the Baptist Church, Roper gives, in one paragraph, three instances of the types of cruelty routinely meted out to slaves on that plantation:

> Mr. Gooch had a slave named Phil, who was a member of a Methodist church; this man was between seventy and eighty years of age: he was so feeble that he could not accomplish his tasks, for which his master used to chain him round the neck, and run him down a steep hill; this treatment he never relinquished to the time of his death. Another case was that of a slave named Peter, who, for not doing his task, he flogged nearly to death, and afterwards pulled out his pistol to shoot him, but his, (Mr. Gooch's) daughter snatched the pistol from his hand. Another mode of punishment which this man adopted was that of using iron horns, with bells, attached to the back of the slave's neck.[37]

After this, Roper describes various kinds of instruments of torture commonly used. He even provides illustrations of the horns and bells mentioned above. Having discussed the cruelties of Mr. Gooch, he then gives brief examples of assault and murder which have occurred in his area. This catalog of abuse continues for seven pages before he returns to his own activities.

In other narratives we learn of slaves suspended for hours by their hands above ground, placed in barrels into which nails had been driven and rolled down hills, branded with hot irons and disfigured by the removal of fingers, ears, and eyes. Some are described as being forced to drink injurious solutions or eat worms. Others were chained to each other or to weights and forced to do their full share of work.

An alternative to the cataloging of horrors was the detailed description of particularly gruesome experiences or particularly ominous weapons. Some narrators provided illustrations of these devices. Others painted word pictures. A favorite subject was the whip. Says Charles Ball:

The whip used by the overseers on the cotton plantations, is different from all other whips, that I have ever seen. The staff is about twenty or twenty-two inches in length, with a large and heavy head, which is often loaded with a quarter or half pound of lead, wrapped in cat-gut, and securely fastened on, so that nothing but the greatest violence can separate it from the staff. The lash is ten feet long, made of small strips of buckskin, tanned so as to be dry and hard, and plaited carefully and closely together, of the thickness, in the largest part, of a man's little finger, but quite small at each extremity. At the farthest end of this thong is attached a cracker, nine inches in length, made of strong sewing silk, twisted and knotted, until it feels as firm as the hardest twine.[38]

Although the descriptions of punishment and the capriciousness which initiates it are deemed sufficient by most narrators, a significant number find it appropriate to comment directly upon the information. Austin Steward leaves little room for misinterpretation:

Oh, who, with feelings of common humanity, could look quietly on such torture? Who could remain unmoved, to see a fellow-creature thus tied, unable to move or to raise a hand in his own defence; scourged on his bare back, with a cowhide, until the blood flows in streams from his quivering flesh? And for what? Often for the most trifling fault; and, as sometimes occurs, because a mere whim or caprice of his brutal overseer demands it.[39]

In addition to the physical abuse, punishments of slaves often resulted in personality changes. Happy slaves became sullen or despondent. Formerly brave men cringed at the approach of any white. Narrators tell of slaves whose despondence led to the ultimate surrender, suicide; however, the ultimate result for most slaves is depicted as the loss of curiosity and compassion and the desire to live. Charles Ball observed that as the cadre of slaves passed by, those who worked in the fields "did not raise their heads, to look either at the fine coaches and horses then passing, or at us; but kept their faces steadily bent towards the cotton-plants, from among which they were removing the weeds."[40] Solomon Northup tells of Mary, who "was listless and apparently indifferent. Like many of the class, she scarcely knew there was such a word as freedom. Brought up in the ignorance of a brute, she possessed but little more than a brute's intelligence. She was one of those, and there are very many, who fear nothing but their master's lash, and know no further duty than to obey his voice."[41]

Slave narrators made much of the particular problems of slave women. The treatment of pregnant women and nursing mothers is often decried. Typical are the comments of Moses Grandy:

> On the estate I am speaking of, those women who had sucking children suffered much from their breasts becoming full of milk, the infants being left at home; they therefore could not keep up with the other hands. I have seen the overseer beat them with raw hide, so that blood and milk flew mingled from their breasts. A woman who gives offence in the field, and is large in the family way, is compelled to lie down over a hole made to receive her corpulency, and is flogged with the whip, or beat with a paddle, which has holes in it; at every hole cames a blister. One of my sisters was so severely punished in this way, that labor was brought on, and the child was born in the field.[42]

William Craft specifically points out how slaveholding women contributed to the misery of slave women:

> It is a common practice in the slave States for ladies, when angry with their maids, to send them to the calybuce, sugar-house, or to some other place established for the purpose of punishing slaves, and have them severely flogged; and I am sorry it is a fact, that the villains to whom these defenceless creatures are sent, not only flog them as they are ordered, but frequently compel them to submit to the greatest indignity.[43]

It is not clear whether the "demons" to which he refers are the rapists or the mistresses who place the slave woman in these situations when he laments, "Oh! If there is any one thing under the wide canopy of heaven horrible enough to stir a man's soul, and to make his very blood boil, it is the thought of his dear wife, his unprotected sister, or his young and virtuous daughters, struggling to save themselves from falling prey to such demons!"[44]

Sexual abuse is the most frequently mentioned problem. The Victorian standards of the age made it necessary to be less graphic about sexual violations than about other subjects, but there was little doubt of the narrator's meanings when he tells of "base offers" or forced "submission to their will." Linda Brent hardly needed to be more explicit than this:

> She will become prematurely knowing of evil things. Soon she will learn to tremble when she hears her master's footfall. She will be compelled to realize that she is no longer a child. If God has bestowed beauty upon her, it will prove her greatest curse. That which commands admiration in the white woman only hastens the degradation of the female slave.[45]

According to the slave narrators, no slave woman's virtue was assured and no man could offer any security. In these works there are two basic alternatives for slave women upon whom the master has foul designs. One is to submit with or without struggle. The other is that which was chosen by Antoinette. Having been purchased by "an uneducated and drunken slave dealer" and seeing there was no other way to preserve her virtue, she jumped through an upstairs window. "Her bruised but unpolluted body was soon picked up—restoratives brought—doctor called in; but alas! it was too late: her pure and noble spirit had fled away to be at rest in those realms of endless bliss."[46]

It is usually clear that the rapes of black women were caused by the lust and greed of white males. Henry Box Brown speaks for several narrators:

> It is my candid opinion that one of the strongest motives which operate upon the slaveholders, and induce them to retain their iron grasp upon the unfortunate slave, is because it gives them unlimited control in this respect over the female slaves. The greater part of slaveholders are licentious men, and the most respectable and the kindest of masters, keep some of their slaves as mistresses. It is for their pecuniary interest to do so in several respects. Their progeny is so many dollars and cents in their pockets, instead of being a bill of expense to them, as it would be if their slaves were free; and mulatto slaves command a higher price than dark colored ones; but it is too horrid a subject to describe.[47]

Allegations of sexual abuse were prevalent not only because such situations did exist, but because the audiences were at once titillated and scandalized by such occurrences. Moreover, rape and seduction were two charges that could hardly be de-emphasized on the grounds that they were conditions regrettably common to freemen as well.

Public ire was not so easily aroused by reports of physical punishments. During the seventeenth and eighteenth centuries the lash was used to punish freemen as well as slaves. By the mid-nineteenth century public opinion considered flogging an unnecessarily cruel practice. Nonetheless, whippings of freemen were still common enough that this was not an especially effective argument against slavery. The slave narrators, then, had to demonstrate not only that slaves were punished but also that their punishments were different from those experienced outside slavery. They tried to accomplish this by showing that the punishments were overreactions to minor infractions of rules—infractions which resulted from the inability of slaves to meet unrealistic and inflexible standards or from the incompatibility of the laws of slavery with the laws of nature.

Many narrators point out that overseers were suspicious of any slave who claimed to be ill. On the plantations where Henry Bibb labored, the overseer "always pronounced a slave who said he was sick, a liar and a hypocrite; said there was nothing the matter, and he only wanted to keep from work." Bibb informs us that "his remedy was most generally strong red pepper tea boiled till it was red. This would operate on the system like salts, or castor oil. But if the slave should not be very ill, he would rather work as long as he could stand up, than to take this dreadful medicine."[48]

There is a special emphasis upon the capricious punishment of innocent persons. Says Frederick Douglass:

> It would astonish one, unaccustomed to a slaveholding life, to see with what wonderful eyes a slaveholder can find things, of which to make occasion to whip a slave. A mere look, word, or motion,—a mistake, accident, or want of power,—are all matters for which a slave may be whipped at any time. Does a slave look dissatisfied? It is said, he has the devil in him, and it must be whipped out. Does he speak loudly when spoken to by his master? Then he is getting high-minded, and should be taken down a button-hole lower. Does

he forget to pull off his hat at the approach of a white person? Then he is wanting in reverence, and should be whipped for it. Does he ever venture to vindicate his conduct, when censured for it? Then he is guilty of impudence,—one of the greatest crimes of which a slave can be guilty.⁴⁹

Another crucial difference between the harshness of physical punishments meted out to slaves and that considered routine for laborers and children is the absence of support systems which could furnish the victim some hope for the future. Henry Bibb addresses himself directly to those who would dismiss the slave's sufferings as part of the vale of tears that every man must endure during his lifetime:

That the slave is a human being, no one can deny. It is his lot to be exposed in common with other men, to the calamities of sickness, death, and the misfortunes incident to life. But unlike other men, he is denied the consolation of struggling against external difficulties, such as destroy the life, liberty, and happiness of himself and family. . . .
[A]nd his sufferings are aggravated a hundred fold, by the terrible thought, that he is not allowed to struggle against misfortune, corporeal punishment, insults and outrages committed upon himself and family; and he is not allowed to help himself, to resist or escape the blow, which he sees impending over him.
This idea of utter helplessness, in perpetual bondage, is the more distressing, as there is no period even with the remotest generation when it shall terminate.⁵⁰

The slave narrators made it clear that their objection to physical punishment was not only that it was excessive and often unmerited but also that it was especially harmful to the slaves' psyches as well.
The narrator views the period of his enslavement negatively. From the time the protagonist leaves his home, there is little recognition given to any positive influences in his life. The existence of a slave community which gives opportunity for personal and social fulfillment is barely implied. Occasionally, a description of a dance or a holiday is included in the narrative. Sometimes, the existence of semiclandestine religious services or a school is indicated. Inti-

mate relationships appear to be rare. For the most part, such positive information is not included in narratives unless it can be directly used to make a vivid contrast to a particularly odious experience or to furnish documentation on slave customs.

Courtships and marriages, for example, occur between the lines or are briefly and impersonally mentioned. The reader is entirely unaware that the young Frederick Douglass had ever had a friendship with a black woman. At the end of his narrative, after escaping to New York and before leaving that town to seek employment in New Bedford, he married. The introduction of this new and obviously significant information is achieved as follows:

> Anna*, my intended wife, came on; for I wrote to her immediately after my arrival at New York, (notwithstanding my homeless, houseless, and helpless condition), informing her of my successful flight, and wishing her to come on forthwith. In a few days after her arrival, Mr. Ruggles called in the Rev. J. W. C. Pennington, who, in the presence of Mr. Ruggles, Mrs. Michaels, and two or three others, performed the marriage ceremony.[51]

In a footnote he informs us that "She was free," but from the narrative we know nothing more of Mrs. Douglass. Even in the midst of his description of his reunion with his fiancée, Douglass seems afraid that the reader may lose sight of the deprivation of the slave and relax his sympathies; so he interjects the reminder that he does send for his fiancée despite his "homeless, houseless, and helpless condition."

Douglass is not alone in the avoidance of personal remarks in his narrative. Josiah Henson provides only a little more information about his own marriage. In Chapter 6 he announces: "When I was about twenty-two years of age, I married a very efficient, and, for a slave, a very well-taught girl, belonging to a neighboring family, reputed to be pious and kind, whom I first met at the religious meetings which I attended."[52] Precedent for some of this reluctance to divulge personal information may be found in the autobiographical writings of the times; however, the narrator's reticence in speaking about household matters or intimate feelings is not extended to his expressing his feelings about slavery nor to descriptions of white personal involvements. Henson does not give the name of his spouse nor of the twelve children he fathered. He does candidly discuss his master's marriage and personal habits, provide the names and residences of his master's kin, and reconstruct the scene, complete with dialogue, wherein his master revealed his financial crisis to him. Although the absence of many personal details about the narrator's life stems from his decision to present himself as a representative of the enslaved masses, another important factor is a decision to present every aspect of his life in as pathetic a light as possible.

One learns of a marriage in order that one can see the restrictions that slavery imposes upon a lover, but the love itself is not explored. Familial relations are discussed in stereotypical forms: mother's undying love, grief at separation, selfless devotion, soft voices and soothing hands, father's ineffectual defenses, his frustrated manhood, his climactic submission, flight or death. A slave is sick, and the medical treatment of slaves is discussed. A slave is flogged, and the lashes are counted and the treatment of his wounds detailed. Such emphasis proves that the narrator's major purpose is the exposition of slavery, not the expression of an inimitable self.

Further proof is found in the supplementary theme which permeates the slave narratives. Not only is the slave the victim, but slavery contaminates free whites also. Slave narrators, like other nineteenth-century antislavery advocates, maintained that unrestrained exploitation such as that which was inherent in slavery caused psychological and spiritual deterioration of the enslaver. Although Lewis Clarke maintains that "slaveholders have not arrived at that degree of civilization that enables them to live in tolerable peace, though united by the nearest family ties,"[53] other narrators imply that slaveholders began as typical humans but that slavery caused gradual degeneration. So degrading is the whole practice of slavery, warns Austin Steward,

> that it not only crushes and brutalizes the wretched slave, but it hardens the heart, benumbs all the fine feelings of humanity, and deteriorates from the character of the slaveholders themselves,—whether man or woman. Otherwise, how could a gentle, and in other respects, amiable woman, look on such scenes of cruelty, without a shudder of utter

abhorrence? But slaveholding ladies, cannot only look on quietly, but with approbation; and what is worse, though very common, they can and do use the lash and cowhide themselves, on the backs of their slaves, and that too on those of their own sex.[54]

Many narrators give vivid examples of the strain that slavery placed upon the slaveholders' relations. Wives accused their husbands of infidelity and quarreled with them over procedures of slave discipline and management. Young men were exposed to temptations of the flesh. Children disobeyed their parents and played in the slave quarters, pampered or abused individual slaves, and interfered with the overseer's attempts to follow instructions. The overabundance of servants encouraged sloth, greed, idleness, and many other sins, charge the slave narrators.

According to J. W. C. Pennington:

There is no one feature of slavery to which the mind recurs with more gloomy impressions, than to its disastrous influence upon the families of the masters, physically, pecuniarily, and mentally [italics his].

It seems to destroy families as by a powerful blight, large and opulent slaveholding families often vanish like a group of shadows at the third or fourth generation. . . . As far back as I can recollect, indeed, it was a remark among slaves, that every generation of slaveholders are more and more inferior. . . .

. . .

The decline is so rapid and marked, in almost every point of view, that the children of slaveholders are universally inferior to themselves, mentally, morally, physically, as well as pecuniarily.[55]

The philosophy which seems to underlie the description of adult slave life is that the nuclear family, the organized Christian church, and formal education are the basis of human survival. Slavery denies all of these to slaves. In the absence of these institutions the slave is virtually incapable of developing appropriate methods of withstanding the oppression of slavery. The impotence of the slave creates an excessive imbalance of power, so that the slaveholder has no checks upon his behavior except that of conscience. The institution of slavery, in which people are regarded as chattel, creates strong temptations to excess because of the broad authority which humans have over those they consider to be nonhumans. The result is that slaveholders lose their humanity by denying it to others. The adage that power corrupts and absolute power corrupts absolutely is taken literally. In the words of Charles Ball, "It seems to be a law of nature, that slavery is equally destructive to the master and the slave; for, whilst it stupifies the latter with fear, and reduces him below the condition of man, it brutalizes the former, by the practice of continual tyranny; and makes him prey of all the vices which render human nature loathsome."[56]

The process by which this occurs and the extent to which it has already succeeded is the major lesson of the second phase of the slave narrative plot. This goal is approached primarily through the narration of a series of experiences, observations, and tales. The unifying device is the narrator, who begins the narration as a child and ends it as an adult slave. This chronological framework is very loose, with few dates or incidents to unify the plot. Repetition of events, not progress, is the rule. The order is less important than the inclusion of a variety of examples to prove the same point. One sees instance after instance of brutality and unsatisfied needs. The slave moves from state to state and master to master. Although it is recognized that slavery in the border states seems less severe than in the Deep South and some situations are less brutal than others, the difference is presented as a mere difference in the degree of corruption.

After years in the wilderness, during which time the slave is exposed to all manner of abuse and has made only infrequent, ineffective attempts to resist the dehumanizing process, he is seemingly doomed to a life of perpetual bondage. At this point, the second phase of the narrative begins. Although the protagonist has been aware that not all persons were enslaved, the idea that freedom could be more than a dream, that it could be a lifetime, becomes an obsession. It is in this second phase that the slave decides he "must act and be free, or remain a slave forever." J. W. C. Pennington, for example, declared that after his childhood experience of seeing his father humiliated, he was in mind and spirit never again a slave; yet it was many years before he decided to attempt physical escape. He is not sure what made him decide that the hour had come. "How the impression came to be upon my mind I cannot tell,'' he says, "but there was a strange and horrifying belief, that if I did not meet the crisis that day, I should be self-doomed—that my ear would be nailed to the door post forever."[57]

The precise manner in which this point is reached varies from individual narrative to individual narrative. The general movement toward it, however, is a continuation of that begun in phase one, experience and education. While the slave was learning what it meant to be a slave, he also learned by contrast what it meant to be free.

Some had free relatives or acquaintances whose lives could be compared with their own. The contrast between their present existence and that of their childhood also helped define the differences between freedom and slavery. This was especially evident for the many slave narrators who report having played freely with their masters' children. The contrast between their current condition and that of their former playmates was easily made. Lunsford Lane is one who maintains that as a child, "I knew no difference between myself and the white children; nor did they seem to know any in turn." He discovered their difference when he reached adolescence. He explains: "When I began to work, I discovered the difference between myself and my master's white children. They began to order me about, and were told to do so by my master and mistress. I found, too, that they had learned to read, while I was not permitted to have a book in my hand." Lane, like numerous others, relates that his growing knowledge of the implications of slavery made him increasingly eager to be free: "To know, also, that I was never to consult my own will, but was, while I lived, to be entirely under the control of another, was another state of mind hard for me to bear. Indeed all things now made me *feel*, what I had before known only in words, that *I was a slave*. Deep was this feeling, and it preyed upon my heart like a never-dying worm."[58]

In the narratives, the slave's desire for freedom is presented as the natural instinct of any person, but some evidence of nineteenth-century America's political beliefs is often found in his statements. For instance, Henry Bibb says, "The circumstances in which I was then placed, gave me a longing desire to be free. It kindled a fire of liberty within my breast which has never yet been quenched. This seemed to be a part of my nature; it was just revealed to me by the inevitable laws of nature's God.'' His motivation is not merely that of nature, however, for Bibb continues, ''And I believed then, as I believe now, that every man has a right to wages for his labor; a right to his own wife and children; a right to liberty and the pursuit of happiness; and a right to worship God according to the dictates of his own conscience.''⁹ The echoes of the official human rights philosophies of the United States are obvious.

Slave narrators acknowledge an early desire to be free. They maintain that subsequent experiences merely served to kindle the spark. Their decisions to attempt to realize their dream, however, are preceded by the knowledge of the existence of a world in which slavery does not exist, and of the existence of people who believed the slave was not wrong in desiring to be a part of that free world.

For some narrators this enlightenment was experiential, often overheard in discussions about slavery or casual remarks about the North and abolitionist agents. Others, especially those that hired their time as sailors or in urban areas, traveled, came into contact with various types of people, witnessed different life-styles, and began to formulate notions of how they might assume more control over their own lives. Significantly, the narrators do not acknowledge any contact with abolitionists, or underground railway agents, or other antislavery groups before their escape deliberations began or, for that matter, before they had actually become fugitives.

Frederick Douglass remarks that his exposure to white persons who ''had been in a good degree preserved from the blighting and dehumanizing effects of slavery'' and to the life of the city slave, who ''is almost a free man, compared with a slave on the plantation,'' as well as to the variety and richness of the urban setting was the turning point in his life. However, these persons are presented as men or women of some learning, urban sophisticates, or even street-wise urchins, but they are not identified as being against slavery. It was primarily the sophistication gained from his urban environment that he credits for his ultimate freedom:

> It is possible, and even quite probable, that but for the mere circumstance of being removed from that plantation to Baltimore, I should have to-day, instead of being here seated by my own table, in the enjoyment of freedom and the happiness of home, writing this Nar-

rative, been confined in the galling chains of slavery. Going to live at
Baltimore laid the foundation, and opened the gateway, to all my
subsequent prosperity.[60]

Besides travel, a learning situation which encouraged a slave's
unrest was one which began with a fairly instinctual response. The
slave believes he is to be punished and the threat of flogging precipitates an attempt to run away. Rarely does a slave narrator achieve
more than temporary freedom from such spontaneous actions.
If the mistreatment has occurred at the hands of an overseer or new
owner, the slave often returns to his original home. Inevitably he is
sent back. Those slaves whose petitions were rejected by persons
they had believed would protect them were strengthened in their
resolve to separate themselves completely from slavery. Any vestiges
of loyalty which had survived the first part of his initiation into
slavery were destroyed. Subsequent attempts to escape would be
more deliberate.

If the slave has no reason to believe his master would or could
help him, he usually runs into the woods or follows the first road
he finds. The chances of not being caught were few; yet even if he
were not caught by search parties or persons suspicious of an un-
familiar slave without papers, hunger and fatigue often forced his
return. The treatment which he was accorded upon his return contributed substantially to his later, more deliberate escape. If he was
not punished, his sense of power was strengthened. If he was punished, he nurtured resentment. In any event, the action of running
away seems to initiate a change in attitude. Actual or imminent
intensification of misery often led to the total rejection of the chattel
role. What began as a negative situation ends up as a positive learning experience.

Others were influenced because they could read and write. Slave
narrators had great respect for literacy, and it is axiomatic in slave
narratives that a literate slave is incapable of accepting the legitimacy
of his bondage. Once he has learned to read and write, the narrator's dissatisfaction becomes intolerable. The sequence usually goes
thus: The ability to read is accompanied by an insatiable urge to
read everything available. The slave discovers that his world view
has been too narrow and that the slave master's versions are neither

accurate nor adequate. A speech or essay about liberty or democracy is discovered. The slave immediately identifies with the concept, and his mental agitation increases.

Frequently the discovery of Christianity is credited with the revival of the slave's desire to be free. Religious conversion becomes a catalyst for rebellion against slavery for several reasons. First, while the theology adopted by the slaves perceived man as entirely subject to God's will and as saved not by merit but by grace, it did not diminish the slave's self-concept. Instead, his self-esteem increased. The slave knew himself subject not to a man, but to the same God to which all men were subject. To believe that Christ died for his sins made him realize he was worth dying for. Second, his new religion provided standards by which he judged not only himself but those around him. Such evaluations often found the slave owners deficient. Some converted slaves felt pity; others felt disgust—but all realized a new sense of superiority to persons who, regardless of their socioeconomic status, were not saved or, even worse, who were hypocrites.

Another attractive aspect of Christian theology was that it promised punishment for sins. When William Craft admitted, "There is, however, great consolation in knowing that God is just, and will not let the oppressor of the weak, and the spoiler of the virtuous, escape unpunished here and hereafter,"[61] he was verbalizing the feelings of many other narrators. Exslaves frequently mention the positive effects of a belief in divine retribution for their sufferings.

The description of the agitation which precedes the decision to reject the chattel status is frequently described in terms of a religious conversion. Douglass reports that reading *The Columbian Orator* gave focus to the vague dissatisfaction he had always felt. He describes the effect of his literacy as many describe their introduction to the concept of damnation:

> As I read and contemplated the subject, behold! that very discontentment which Master Hugh had predicted would follow my learning to read had already come, to torment and sting my soul to unutterable anguish. As I writhed under it, I would at times feel that learning to read had been a curse rather than a blessing. It had given me a view of my wretched condition, without the remedy. It opened

my eyes to the horrible pit, but to no ladder upon which to get out. . . .
There was no getting rid of it. It was pressed upon me by every
object within sight or hearing, animate or inanimate. . . . Freedom
now appeared, to disappear no more forever. . . . It was ever present
to torment me with a sense of my wretched condition. I saw nothing
without seeing it, I heard nothing without hearing it, and felt nothing
without feeling it.[62]

The change in the narrator, then, occurs positively through religious or intellectual enlightenment or begins negatively with an
intensification of his misery which leads to the development of new
concepts. In any event, the slave possesses a new sense of personal
dignity. His attitudes have altered, and he can no longer tolerate
the idea of lifelong slavery.

Circumstances may require that he continue to effect the same
attitudes, and the narrators show considerable ingenuity and skill
in deceiving their masters about their intentions. William Wells
Brown is a particularly good example. In a situation reminiscent
of the black American folktale about Br'er Rabbit and the briar
patch, Brown convinced his owner that although he was a known
runaway, he no longer harbored desires for freedom. "I never like
a free state," he assured his master. His deception was so complete
that the master not only allowed Brown to accompany him on a
steamboat to Cincinnati, but to walk unguarded down the gang-
plank and disappear into the crowds. Brown must have been a
superb actor, because he admitted that "the anxiety to be a free
man would not let me rest day or night. I would think of the northern
cities that I had heard so much about; of Canada, where so many
of my acquaintances had found refuge. I would dream at night that
I was in Canada, a freeman, and on waking in the morning, weep
to find myself so sadly mistaken."[63] Although he had the reputation
of a runaway and was obsessed with the idea of escaping, no one
suspected he was discontented.

Often the slave is able to exercise patience because he considers
the decision irrevocable. The psychological escape having begun,
the actualization is simply a matter of time. Lewis Clarke made his
decision. In a manner similar to that employed by Ellen and William
Craft, he decided to exploit his light skin and to pose as the master

of another darker slave, Isaac. Isaac and Lewis actually started to implement their plan. Although they were not molested, they decided that their social inexperience and illiteracy would soon betray them, and they returned to the plantation. "Everything would have been done in such an awkward manner that a keen eye would have seen through our plot at once," explained Clarke.⁶⁴ Later, having become more sophisticated, Clarke saddled a horse, flung a grass seed sack over his shoulder, pocketed the money he had saved for this purpose, and rode boldly toward Canada.

Austin Steward reports he had long considered the possibility of obtaining his freedom. He had made many surreptitious inquiries before he discovered a way. It was the winter of 1814 and he was forced to wait until March before he could begin to execute his plan. Yet he was so firmly determined to be free that he maintains he had "a heart so light, that I could not realize that my bonds were not yet broken, nor the yoke removed from off my neck. I was already free in spirit, and I silently exulted in the bright prospect of liberty. . . . I went cheerfully back to my labor, and worked with alacrity, impatient only for March to come.⁶⁵

Once the protagonist has decided definitely that he will "be free or die," phase two has ended. Mortification has led to purgation. The ascent begins.

The final two phases are quickly recounted. A few narratives give no details of their narrator's escape. Their excuse is that such information would alert slaveholders to successful methods and thereby hinder other slaves' attempts to flee. Even those whose works focus upon their own particularly daring flight are deliberately vague in some details. Henry Box Brown, whose celebrated use of the U.S. mail is the outstanding feature of his book, mentions discarding several other plans before deciding upon the box but does not reveal the nature of these schemes. "Perhaps," he says, "it may not be best to mention what these plans were, as some unfortunate slaves may thereby be prevented from availing themselves of these methods of escape."⁶⁶

Unless the narrative was one of the small number that was written primarily to capitalize upon the notoriety of a particularly daring and innovative escape, there is little deviation in the way the physical escape is related. In the case of the fugitives, a lone slave (or, less frequently, a trembling, desperate family) steals away on a Saturday night. He travels by land in a northward direction aided only by the North Star, his faith in God, and his desire for liberty. He travels by night and hides in barns, woods, or deserted buildings by day. He suffers from exposure, fatigue, and hunger. He is threatened by wild animals, dogs, and strange men. Frequently he avoids capture by the narrowest distance, and often he is, in fact, beaten, jailed, and returned to his owner, from whence he must begin the process again.

The slave's essential isolation is emphasized, by J. W. C. Pennington, for example: "Having passed through the town without being recognised, I now found myself under cover of night, a solitary wanderer from home and friends; my only guide was the *north star*, by this I knew my general course northward, but at what point I should strike Penn, or when and where I should find a friend, I knew not."[67] If he is traveling with a group, as in the case of Josiah Henson, or as one of a pair such as Ellen and William Craft, the narratives do not indicate mutual encouragement and shared responsibilities. Instead, there is one person who is responsible and upon whom the others rely. The pressure upon the individual is intensified, and his desperation is even more evident.

Besides his loneliness, the narratives exploit the naïveté of the fugitive. He has little knowledge of geography, and he is ignorant of routine procedures concerning the schedule and use of trains, stagecoaches, ferries, and ships. Most frequently the fugitive is unable to read road signs he may encounter or passes that he may possess. He knows and trusts no one. Whatever help he does receive is spontaneous and brief, or the result of his ability to invent stories and excuses. There is no reference to aid from any group until the fugitive has at least reached the Philadelphia area or crossed the Ohio River.

The escape, then, follows as much a formula as a contemporary Western. Many obstacles may be encountered. The fugitive may be captured several times before his escape is successful, but he does become a freeman.

For those who purchased their freedom the process was also fairly standard. The slave worked unceasingly, lived frugally, and saved his money. His progress was often retarded by providing living expenses for himself or his family, by unexpected emergencies, robbery, and forced loans to whites who failed to repay. Frequently, having obtained the agreed-upon amount to buy his freedom, the slave found his master had raised the price, changed his mind about selling, or accepted the money but did not grant him freedom. Moses Grandy, for example, paid for himself three times before being officially manumitted. Sometimes there were legal obstacles such as restrictions upon manumissions, judicial procedures, or court fees to circumvent. Lunsford Lane found it relatively easy to buy his freedom and to begin the purchase of his wife and children on the installment plan. His success was abruptly threatened when a few townspeople decided to invoke a state law that required all free persons of color to leave the state within twenty days after official notification of eviction. Lane's court appeal was denied, and he was forced to leave his family. He traveled throughout the northern states and eventually raised enough money to purchase his family and to bring them north.

The arrival in the Promised Land is a time of intense emotion. Josiah Henson tells of the feelings that gripped him as he boarded the ship for Canada:

I was praising God in my soul. Three hearty cheers welcomed us as we reached the schooner, and never till my dying day shall I forget the shout of the captain—he was a Scotchman—"Coom up on deck, and clop your wings and craw like rooster; you're a free nigger as sure as the devil." Round went the vessel, the wind plunged into her sails as though innoculated with the common feeling—the water seethed and hissed passed her sides. Man and nature, and, more than all, I felt the God of man and nature, who breathes love into the heart and maketh the winds his ministers, were with us. My happiness, that night, rose at times to positive pain. Unnerved by so sudden a change from destitution and danger to such kindness and blessed security, I wept like a child.[68]

The narrator often indulges in humor as he acknowledges his compulsions to "Clop your wings and craw like a rooster." One of the most amusing descriptions was of Cyrus Clarke upon crossing the Ohio River. His brother, Lewis, reports:

> When we were fairly landed upon the northern bank, and had gone
> a few steps, Cyrus stopped suddenly, on seeing the water gush out
> at the side of the hill. Said he, "Lewis, give me that tin cup." "What
> in the world do you want of a tin cup now? We have not time to stop."
> The cup he would have. Then he went up to the spring, dipped and
> drank, and dipped and drank; then he would look round, and drink
> again. "What in the world," said I, "are you fooling there for?"
> "O," said he, "this is the first time I ever had a chance to drink water
> that ran out of the *free* dirt." Then we went on a little further, and
> he sat down on a log. I urged him forward. "O," said he, "I must
> sit on this free timber a little while."
>   . . . In going up the hill, Cyrus would stop, and lay down and roll
> over. "What in the world are you about, Cyrus? Don't you see Ken-
> tucky is over there?" He still continued to roll and kiss the ground.
> . . . "First time," he said, "he ever rolled on *free* grass."[69]

The relation of the slave's metamorphosis into a freeman to that
of the traditional Judeo-Christian spiritual conversion is explicit
in Lunsford Lane's description of his feelings upon having his
manumission recorded:

> I cannot describe it, only it seemed as though I was in heaven. I used
> to lie awake whole nights thinking of it. . . . He who has passed from
> spiritual death to life, and received the witness within his soul that his
> sins are forgiven, may possibly form some distant idea, like the ray
> of the setting sun from the far off mountain top, of the emotions of
> an emancipated slave. That opens heaven. To break the bonds of
> slavery, opens up at once both earth and heaven. Neither can be truly
> seen by us while we are slaves.[70]

Once the protagonist achieves his freedom, the nineteenth-century
slave narrative terminates. A few paragraphs may summarize the
intervening years between freedom and the writing of the narrative,
but for all practical purposes the exslave's account of his struggle
for freedom from bondage ends with his arrival in the Promised
Land. This abrupt close does not necessarily weaken the work, for
its definition of freedom has been essentially restricted to escape
for the body and liberation for the soul. Thus there is no structural
need for analysis, description, or evaluation of the life of free blacks.

It is also appropriate that the narrative end here, for to continue
the adventures of a black in the so-called free states or countries

would be to expose the overwhelming prejudice and discrimination which existed therein. The problem would be revealed as more complex and pervasive than would be to the advantage of most narrators to expose, for it would necessarily indict those from whom their narratives sought sympathy and aid.

From the summaries, prefaces, and introductions, expecially those of the "revised or enlarged" versions of the narratives, one learns, however, that freedom usually did not result in an easier life. More often than not, the narrator has had to move frequently or even leave the United States to avoid recapture. Other times, his itinerancy was necessitated by unemployment. One of the more detailed descriptions of an exslave's immigration to the North is provided by Thomas Jones:

> The Sabbath after my arrival in Brooklyn, I preached in the morning in the Bethel; I then came on to Hartford. A gentleman kindly paid my passage to that place, and sent me an introduction to a true-hearted friend. I staid [sic] in Hartford twenty-four hours; but finding I was pursued, and being informed that I should be safer in Massachusetts than in Connecticut, I came to Springfield, and from thence to Boston, where I arrived penniless and friendless, the 7th of October. A generous friend took me, though a stranger, in, and fed and cheered me. He loaned me five dollars to get my dear family in Boston. He helped me to get a chance to lecture in May Street Church, where I received a contribution of $2.58, also, in the Sion Church, where I obtained $2.33; and in the Bethel Church, where they gave me $3.53. And so I was enabled to get my family to Boston. Entirely destitute, without employment, I now met with a kind friend who took me with him to Danvers.[71]

The narrative ends with Jones still an itinerant preacher, grubbing out his existence from the donations of sympathetic listeners. Jones's case was by no means an exception. The vast majority of jobs available to blacks were those of unskilled, menial, or domestic labor. Educated or skilled persons found that "such was the strength of prejudice against color" that their special talents were rarely of benefit and they had to take whatever job they could get.

Often the preface indicates that an auxiliary purpose of the narrative is to raise money for the support of the narrator or for the purpose of his relatives. Lunsford Lane discreetly admits he wrote at the behest of friends and for the aid of all slaves but "also that I may realize something from the sale of my work towards the support of a numerous family."[72]

William Grimes is much more straightforward about his desire for financial profit when he says, "I hope some will buy my books from charity; but I am no beggar. I am now entirely destitute of property;where and how I shall live I don't know; where and how I shall die I don't know; but I hope I may be prepared."[73]

Grimes offers an even more revealing glimpse into the life of exslaves in his revised edition. Written thirty years after the original publication of his narrative, this work was also presented "for the purpose, in the first place, of raising, if possible, a small amount of money." The second edition consists of the first narrative plus a "conclusion" of approximately 2,500 words in which he lists several calamities which have befallen him and provides a copy of a poem written about him entitled "Old Grimes' Son." Grimes summarizes his life as a freeman thus:

> I have now been in New Haven more than thirty years, and have always meant to be an honest man and deal justly with all. I have always tried to pay my debts and kept out of jail; but I have been in jail twice in New Haven—once because I didn't pay Mr. Bradley for breaking his carriage—amounting to twenty dollars, and once because I hadn't the money to pay two or three dollars for rent.
>
> . . .
>
> And now, as I have brought my narrative to a close, I wish only to add a few lines to say that I hope all my friends and acquaintances will purchase a copy of my book, and thus help "Old Grimes" to pay the printer, and have a small amount left to carry him safely through the coming year. As before remarked, I am now an old man, and am almost wholly dependent on my acquaintances for the means of support.[74]

Many slave narrators suffered greatly from their poverty. Many reported disillusionment with the North and intense loneliness for loved ones left behind. None, however, indicated a desire to return to the South.

Racial Myths
in Slave Narratives

ALTHOUGH THE NINETEENTH-CENTURY slave narratives were intended to promote the welfare of the American slave by providing real and accurate accounts of his life, they contributed heavily to the development of racial distortions and myths. In their attempts to synthesize art and history, to create general concepts from specific events, and to cater to the demands of less hostile whites in order to gain their help in controlling more hostile whites, the slave narrators perpetrated and perpetuated images and ideas which were not entirely accurate but which gained increased respectability from their inclusion in the slave narratives.

Their focus upon the institution of slavery as the evil and the South as the location of that evil tended to diminish the role of racism, one of the basic reasons for slavery and a trait which existed in the North as well as in the South. In setting the physical axis as South to North and identifying that journey with the thematic movement of chattel to man, sin to salvation, and in ending most narratives with the safe arrival in free territories which offered the promise of just rewards for honest labor, the slaves narratives provided additional ammunition for the antisouthern forces without challenging or identifying the racist assumptions which both anti- and prosouthern forces shared.

Whether the identification of the South as the one site of slave evil was an intentional device of the slave narrators is debatable. By the 1830s, when the nineteenth-century slave narratives began to be popular, the South was the only place where slavery was a recognized and legal institution. Consequently, any but the most abstract discussions of slavery had to identify the southern United

States as the location of that evil. On the other hand, many of the narrators expressed great love for the South and that section's natural beauties and would have preferred to remain there among their friends had they been free. Another reason to doubt the willful slander of the region was that many of the abolitionists who encouraged the writing of slave narratives were extremely concerned with preventing unnecessary antagonisms between the sections of the country. In Emphraim Peabody's article, "Narratives of the Fugitive Slaves,"[1] for example, the author objects to what he perceives as biased portrayals of slaveholders and of the South. He reminds his readers that not all southerners are slaveholders, nor do they all approve of the institution. He warns that antisouthern sentiments can alienate not only all those who reside in the South, but those northerners who have southern friends, relatives, and business acquaintances. He maintains that, in the final analysis, slavery can be abolished or ameliorated only by the persons of sensibility and good conscience who live in the South. Peabody's argument typifies one school of abolitionist thought.

Other abolitionists were not so concerned about increasing sectional animosities and gleefully pointed to slavery as a southern evil. Gilbert Hobbs Barnes, in *The Antislavery Impulse: 1830-1844*, maintains that not only were abolitionists unconcerned about arousing possible antisouthern feelings, but that the abolitionist movement itself had its origins in the religious reform fervor of the 1830s, focused upon antislavery temporarily, "then broadened into a sectional crusade against the South."[2]

Of greater importance than the extraneous uses to which the majority of the slave narratives could be directed are the pervasive but basically false and destructive depictions that they reinforced. One of the most dramatic and tantalizing stereotypes which the slave narratives developed was that of the mulatto. The mulatto was a manifestation of the most evil results of slavery. He embodied the defilement of womanhood and the violation of marital sacraments. In addition, he was the living proof that the sins of the father are visited upon his sons. Not only was he a product of evil, but evil was visited upon him because his complexion was a constant reminder of his origins.

The tragic mulatto theme so captivated the antislavery imaginations that many believed the southern black population was predominantly mulatto. This misconception was strengthened by the high percentage of slave narratives by racially mixed authors. The group included some of the best-known and most articulate spokesmen, such as Frederick Douglass, William Wells Brown, and Josiah Henson, as well as Ellen Craft and Moses Roper, who had used their color to effect the most dramatic of escapes. In their narratives, the mulattoes emphasized the commonplaceness of miscegenation as well as the turmoil this caused in family life. Not everyone was misled into believing that dark-complexioned people were a minority in the slave population, but the number of mulattoes who wrote slave narratives encouraged considerable speculation about the impact of racial mixing upon society.

The number of mulatto narrators could be explained as the result of extraordinary pressures upon that group. If mulattoes were, as many narrators have said, singled out for particularly harsh treatment, it would be easy to assume that fewer members of that group could adjust to slavery and consequently that a higher percentage of them would try to escape. Their color, it could be argued, which was a disadvantage in slavery, could be easily used to facilitate their escape, and there are several popular narratives which show how the mulatto protagonist passed for white or Indian as he openly traveled out of slave territory.

This theory is countered by the fact that while a substantial number of narrators were mulattoes, the majority of the writers were not, and relatively few of the mulatto narrators who could pass chose to try that method of escape. Obviously, it was not simply a case of mulatto enslavement being so much more oppressive and the escape avenues being more available that created their substantial representation in the works.

The best reasons can be deduced from facts about the antislavery movement itself. Two basic tenets of the nineteenth-century abolitionists were that slavery prevented normal family relationships and that the kind of absolute authority that slave owners legally possessed over slaves encouraged atrocities. These ideas are easily combined in the concept of miscegenation (which to the abolitionist meant the sexual exploitation of women slaves by white men). Antislavery movements often pictured such exploitation as epidemic and as threatening, at least in the South, some of the fundamental institutions of civilization. The mulatto character had great value as a symbol of the sins fostered by slavery. In addition, such characters catered to the predilections of nineteenth-century audiences for sensationalism.

Historians, as well as blacks other than authors of slave narratives, have indicated that the mulatto was not always the tragic and omnipresent figure the slave narratives depict. Fogel and Engleman, for example, provide evidence that in the twenty-three decades of black and white contact in this country between 1620 and 1850, only 7.7 percent of the slave population was mulatto (though by 1860 that figure had risen to 10.4 percent). These figures include the unions between mulatto and black as well as between mulatto or black and white.[3] Though cliometricians such as Fogel and Engleman are often criticized for their quantitatively based views, it is important to note that this percentage is approximately the same as the estimate offered by social historian John Hope Franklin. According to Franklin, "By 1850 there were 246,000 [7.7 percent] mulatto slaves out of a total slave population of 3.2 million. By 1860 there were 411,000 [10.5 percent] mulatto slaves out of a total slave population of 3.9 million."[4] The number seems to have increased extremely rapidly between 1850 and 1860, but this does not necessarily mean a higher percentage of rapes or illicit unions because the children of mulattoes were naturally also counted as mulattoes.

Although many mulattoes were abused because of their heritage, as the slave narratives indicate, still others were given significantly better treatment for the same reason. Such advantages included social prestige and material awards. Franklin reminds us that while some men "felt nothing" for their black children, other men developed "a great fondness for their Negro children and emancipated them and provided for them."[5] Evidence that the "high yellow" individuals were often awarded greater social status among blacks is also abundant.

The emphasis which slave narratives gave to the mulatto and the interest which the readers manifested in that figure were disproportionate; furthermore, the narratives did not challenge assumptions of racial inferiority. The ante-bellum racial attitude held that an increased percentage of Caucasian blood made a more intelligent and aggressive person, one who was less likely to accept enslavement. Based on the proportion of mulatto narrators and the ways in which mulattoes were depicted, the slave narratives did not discourage such ideas.

The greatest disadvantage of the slave narratives' emphasis upon the mulatto was that he became a symbol of the absence of a viable black family structure and in the process contributed to the further degradation of the black woman's image. The designation of a slave as a mulatto meant the union of a white man and a black woman. Although evidence shows that interracial sexual relationships were not confined to that arrangement, social and legal sanctions prevented any possible misinterpretation of that relationship. Slave narratives did not challenge this idea, but presented the slave woman as the unwilling and distraught victim. Emphasis upon the mulatto encouraged, therefore, the popular notion that sexual exploitation was frequent in slave quarters.

Writing in 1843, Stephen S. Foster exemplifies the popular image of slave women when he declares:

> By converting woman into a commodity, to be bought and sold, and used by her claimant as his avarice or lust may dictate, he totally annihilates the marriage institution; and transforms the wife into what he very significantly terms a "BREEDER," and her children into "STOCK."
>
> This change in woman's condition from a free moral agent to a chattel, places her domestic relations entirely beyond her own control, and makes her a mere instrument for the gratification of another's desires. The master claims her body as his property, and of course employs it for such purposes as best suit his inclinations—demanding free access to her bed; nor can she resist his demands, but at the peril of her life. Thus is her chastity left entirely unprotected, and she is made the lawful prey of every pale-faced libertine, who may choose to prostitute her!![6]

As a result of such depictions, the black woman became closely identified with illicit sex. If the "negress" were not a hot-blooded, exotic whore, she was a cringing, terrified victim. Either way she was not pure and thus not a model of womanhood. Moreover, her ability to survive sexual degradation was her downfall. As victim she became the assailant, since her submission to repeated violations was not in line with the values of sentimental heroines who died rather than be abused. Her survival of these ordeals and continued participation in other aspects of slave life seemed to connote, if not outright licentiousness, at least a less sensitive and abused spirit than that of white heroines.

Her portrayal as a victim of rape and an object of barter left little room for other, more positive, images. What may have been advanced as a more positive portrayal turned out to be another negative picture: that of the slave mother, the center of a weak and impermanent family structure, performing both the masculine and feminine roles. The image of the matriarch did not eliminate the lusty, animalistic image or the insensitive and impure one, nor did it help establish the black woman as sister to the white female.

The reasons for the failure of either depiction are understood when the general attitudes of the ante-bellum era toward women are considered. Less fragile than her grandmother seemed to be, the mid-nineteenth-century lady emerged as the superintendent of "the arts, social deportment, and domestic standards." She was considered physically inferior to men, but morally superior. She was pure, sensitive both to the beauties and to the horrors of the world. According to James D. Hart, it was publicly acknowledged that the "leading features of the American woman were domestic fidelity, social cheerfulness, unostentatious hospitality, and moral and religious benevolence." Although a few radicals had called the first Women's Rights Convention in 1848, most women seemed to consider the home as their rightful domain. Hart points out that "anyone outside this sphere was either more or less than a woman."[7] A female slave, with the emphasis upon her physical exploitation and her lack of masculine protection, home, and family, suffered from the contrast.

With the attitude that miscegenation was rampant came the notion that slave marriages were frequent and casual and that children received only intermittent and cursory family support. The stereotype of the slave family as reinforced in the slave narratives was that it was at best a weak and impermanent unit. The image of the matriarch not only prevented unquestioning acceptance of the black woman as woman, but it also provided the stereotype for what kind of family unit could exist under slavery.

The broken-family motif appears even when the protagonist is the legitimate offspring of a slave couple. Narrators emphasize the division of the family by reminders that marriage among slaves was not recognized by law and thus any slave marriage was subject to the will of the master and could be dissolved at any time. They also emphasized the law that slave children belong to the owners of the mothers.

In slave narratives the dominant image of the slave family unit is a fatherless home. Often he has been sold to a distant place. Sometimes he has been killed or has even run away. Usually, he is identified as the property of a neighboring slaveholder. The father lives in one place, while his wife and children reside on her master's property.

Two notable exceptions are the narratives of Linda Brent and Samuel Ringgold Ward. In both cases the narrators had parents who "hired their time"; that is, the parent paid his master for the privilege of finding his own employment, paying for his own room and board, and consequently enjoying more control over his everyday activities. Brent's father was a carpenter of considerable reputation. He paid $200 a year for the right to support his mother-in-law, wife, and two children. Even such a modified nuclear family unit as this is not presented as intact for any period of time. When Brent was six, her mother died and the family was divided up. Brent and her brother went to live with her mother's mistress, but her grandmother and father were nearby and visits were frequent. Even this arrangement did not last long, for Brent's father soon died. Her grandmother became the center of the family and did what little she could to protect and nurture her. Her grandmother proved powerless to prevent Brent's exploitation, but Brent pays tribute to her attempts:

On my various errands I passed by grandmother's house, where there was always something to spare for me. I was frequently threatened with punishment if I stopped there; and my grandmother, to avoid detaining me, often stood at the gate with something for my breakfast or dinner. I was indebted to *her* for all my comforts, spiritual or temporal. It was *her* labor that supplied my scanty wardrobe.[1]

Samuel Ringgold Ward describes his father as descended from an African prince and "of good figure, cheerful disposition, bland manners, slow in deciding, firm when once decided, generous and unselfish to a fault."[9] Yet his father cannot protect himself from beatings nor his outspoken wife from being sold. Ward's family remains together only because they chose the terrifying and almost impossible alternative of a group escape rather than family division. In this account, the woman again emerges as the dominant figure. Ward reports that his mother's master wished to sell her, but because he was a frail, sickly baby, the master decided to postpone the separation until the infant slave was stronger and could survive without the mother. When he began to improve, the mother chose to flee rather than accept the inevitable separation. She forced her husband to accompany her. Such a solution is rare in slave narratives, and Ward emphasizes the extreme daring of such a plan as he reconstructs the events leading to the decision:

> The more certain these poor slaves became that their child would soon be well, the nearer approached the time of my mother's sale. Motherlike, she pondered all manner of schemes and plans to postpone that dreaded day. . . . "William," said she to my father, "we must take this child and run away." She said it with energy; my father felt it. He hesitated; he was not a mother. She was decided; and when decided, *she was decided* with all consequences, conditions, and contingencies accepted. As in the case in other families where the wife leads, my father followed my mother in her decision, and accompanied her in—I almost said, her *hegira.*[10]

Most narrators did not have mothers who tried to escape with them; yet the devotion of the mother to her child is a common theme. Moses Grandy's mother's desperate attempts to save her children is one of many similar incidents:

> I remember well my mother often hid us all in the woods, to prevent master selling us. When we wanted water, she sought for it in any hole or puddle formed by falling trees or otherwise. . . . For food, she gathered berries in the woods, got potatoes, raw corn, &c. After a time, the master would send word to her to come in, promising he would not sell us. But, at length, persons came who agreed to

give the prices he set on us. His wife, with much to be done, prevailed on him not to sell me; but he sold my brother, who was a little boy. My mother, frantic with grief, resisted their taking her child away. She was beaten, and held down; she fainted; and, when she came to herself, her boy was gone. She made much outcry, for which the master tied her up to a peach-tree in the yard, and flogged her.[11]

While the mulatto and the ineffective, matriarchal family helped support the concept of the helpless black slave, they did not create it. As mentioned earlier, the entire structure of the narratives was based on the image of the lonely wayfarer. The idea of a strong family unit was incompatible with such a foundation. The viability of the slave family had to be denied to increase the pathos of the homeless victim. Such pathos is also encouraged in the romanticized reports of the rare and brief instances of a nuclear family relationship in slave naratives. The narrator's depiction of such families is simplistic and highly idealistic. The narrators imply that loving, harmonious familial relations are the natural impulse of blacks by emphasizing the strong love and devotion among kith and kin. They attribute all problems to slavery, which, they assert, is antithetical to the existence of a viable black family.

The slave narratives portray the black family as industrious, pious, and eager to acquire an education. Noah Davis lived with his family until he was fourteen years old. He says both of his parents were

pious members of a Baptist church, and from their godly example, I formed a determination, before I had reached my twelfth year, that if I was spared to become a man, I would try to be as good as my parents. My father could read a little, and make figures, but could scarcely write at all. His custom, on those Sabbaths when we remained at home, was to spend his time in instructing his children, or the neighboring servants, out of a New Testament, sent him from Fredericksburg by one of his older sons. I fancy I can see him now, sitting under his bush arbor, reading that precious book to many attentive hearers around him.[12]

The fathers and mothers were faithful to each other and most solicitous about their offspring. In his narrative Thomas Jones reports:

Father and mother tried to make it a happy place for their dear children. *They* worked late into the night many and many a time to get a little simple furniture for their home and the home of their children; and they spent many hours of willing toil to stop up the chinks between the logs of their poor hut, that they and their children might be protected from the storm and the cold. . . . My dear parents were conscious of the desperate and incurable woe of their position and destiny, and of the lot of inevitable suffering in store for their beloved children. They talked about our coming misery, and they lifted up their voices and wept aloud, as they spoke of our being torn from them and sold off to the dreaded slave-trader, perhaps never again to see them or hear from them a word of fond love. I have heard them speak of their willingness to bear their own sorrows without complaint, if only we, their dear children, could be safe from the wretchedness before us. And I remember, and *now* fully understand, as I did not *then*, the sad and tearful look they would fix upon us when we were gathered round them and running on with our foolish prattle.[13]

Few narrators rhapsodize as much as Jones, but they display the same attitudes. For them a major tragedy of slavery was that it denied the tranquillity and security of the family fireside. Every narrator emphasized the strains that slavery placed upon the family unit and the inevitable division of families that were enslaved. They emphasized those situations, the instances wherein a husband could not protect the chastity of his wife or the parents could neither plan for their children's futures nor protect an infant from harm.

Henry Bibb creates a heartbreaking scene when he describes his and his wife's inability to care for their child:

There was no one to take care of poor little Frances while her mother was toiling in the field. She was left at the house to creep under the feet of an unmerciful old mistress, whom I have known to slap with her hand the face of little Frances, for crying after her mother, until her little face was left black and blue. I recollect that Malinda and myself came from the field one summer's day at noon, and poor little Frances came creeping to her mother smiling, but with large tear drops standing in her dear little eyes, sobbing and trying to tell her mother that she had been abused, but was not able to utter a word. Her little face was bruised black with the whole print of Mrs. Gatewood's hand. This print was plainly to be seen for eight days after it was done. But oh! this darling child was a slave; born of a slave mother. Who can imagine what could be the feeling of a father and mother, when looking upon their infant child whipped and tortured with impunity, and then placed in a situation where they could afford it no protection.[14]

Slave narratives do not mention interfamilial bickering or delinquencies among children. Instead, they focus upon the many individuals who were sold, beaten, or murdered for trying to protect their spouses or children. They describe the heartbreak of persons who chose not to marry or bear children because they would be powerless to protect them. They confess that many ran away rather than be forced to observe the humiliation of their loved ones. The obvious message of the narratives was that the family ties were strong among slaves and that left to themselves, they could work hard and peacefully. A fair summation of their argument would be: Slavery and family, no! Freedom and family, yes!

The extent to which slavery destroys the inherent bond between mother and child is reported by Frederick Douglass. He states that his sole contact with his mother consisted of four or five occasions when, after completing a full day's work, she would walk the twelve miles between plantations to see him. During these brief nocturnal reunions, his mother would lie with him until he slept. When Douglass awoke at dawn, she would have returned to her owner's plantation. He reports that "never having enjoyed, to any considerable extent, her soothing presence, her tender and watchful care, I received the tidings of her death with much the same emotions I should have probably felt at the death of a stranger."[15]

J. W. C. Pennington maintains that slavery deprived the slave not only of family but of society:

About this time, I began to feel another evil of slavery—I mean the want of parental care and attention. My parents were not able to give any attention to their children during the day. I often suffered much from *hunger* and other similar causes. To estimate the sad state of a slave child, you must look at it as a helpless human being thrown upon the world without the benefit of its natural guardians. It is thrown into the world without a social circle to flee to for hope, shelter, comfort, or instruction. The social circle, with all its heaven-ordained blessings, is of the utmost importance to the *tender child*; but of this, the slave child, however tender and delicate is robbed.[16]

The effect of such comments in the narratives was to maintain that slavery seriously weakened or virtually destroyed the family and social structure of the black, and that it in turn contributed to the dehumanization of the slave. Therein lie the beginnings of the idea of the black matriarchal family and the broken family which Moynihan and others have asserted to this day. What it does not acknowledge is that alternative family structures may have arisen among slaves which, although not apparently of the nuclear mode of white middle-class Americans, could fulfill and satisfy the needs of the slaves in ways which the nuclear model could not.

There is a contradiction in the narrators' presentation of the family structure: They depict heroic struggles of slaves to maintain the purity of a family relationship the existence of which was considered impossible. Familial attachments were so great, in fact, that upon obtaining his own freedom, the exslave's next actions were to rescue his relatives and any other victim of bondage. Many fugitives risked their own freedom to return to the slave states in efforts to find and rescue their families. Some were captured several times because they returned to help others. William Craft, Henry Bibb, Noah Davis, Moses Grandy, Lewis Clarke, William Hayden, and Lunsford Lane are a few of the better-known narrators who chronicled their attempts to free their kinsmen. The narratives do not provide plausible sources of such fidelity and strength that would compel so many slaves to protect their loved ones at the risk of being beaten or sold. Nor do they help explain why exslaves would risk their hard-gained freedom and their lives to help others become free if, in fact, slavery had so devastated the black family and its culture.

Recent research makes such a paradox even more interesting, for scholars have presented evidence that not only did slaves have strong family ties, but the family unit was considered an asset by the slaveholders and worth much effort to keep families together. Historians such as Herbert G. Gutman and Eugene Genovese admit that good intentions were not always actualized and more families were separated than the owners may have wished, but their research shows that while the fear of separation was strong, that fear was not usually realized. Scholars also challenge the assumptions that the slave family was an impermanent and ineffective unit. From private correspondence between slaves, personal interviews, census records, and other kinds of public documents many historians are increasingly agreeing with Genovese, who says, "[T]he average plantation slave lived in a family setting, developed strong family ties, and held the nuclear family as the proper social norm."[17]

Not only does he maintain that the nuclear family unit was the most common environment for slaves, but Genovese maintains that the male's role was strong and the relationship within the black family had its bad and good times:

> Both masters and ex-slaves tell us about some plantations on which certain women were not easily or often punished because it was readily understood that, to punish the woman, it would be necessary to kill her man first. These cases were the exception, but they tell us at the start that the man felt a duty to protect his woman. . . . Beyond that, the man of the house did do various things. He trapped and hunted animals to supplement the diet in the quarters, and in his small but important and symbolic way he was a breadwinner. He organized the garden plot and presided over the division of labor with his wife. He disciplined his children—or divided that function with his wife as people in other circumstances do—and generally was the source of authority in the cabin. This relationship within the family was not always idyllic. In many instances, his authority over both wife and children was imposed by force. Masters forbade men to hit their wives and children and whipped them for it; but they did it anyway and often. And there is not much evidence that women readily ran to the master to ask that her husband be whipped for striking her. The evidence on these matters is fragmentary, but it suggests that the men asserted their authority as best they could; the women expected to have to defer to their husbands in certain matters; and that both tried hard to keep the master out of their lives.[18]

Other historians of American slavery, such as George P. Rawick, support the idea that the slaves had a strong family structure, but argue that it was not a nuclear structure. Rawick maintains that the slaves created a family system that was more appropriate and consequently more beneficial than the nuclear family:

The slave community acted like a generalized extended kinship system in which all adults looked after all children and there was little division between "my children for whom I'm responsible" and "your children for whom you're responsible." . . . There was always some older person who would, with relative ease, take over the role of absent parents. . . . Indeed, the activity of the slave in creating patterns of family life that were functionally integrative did more than merely prevent the destruction of personality that often occurs when individuals struggle unsuccessfully to attain the unattainable. It was part and parcel, as we shall see, of the social process out of which came black pride, black identity, black culture, the black community, and black rebellion in America.[19]

John Blassingame in *The Slave Community* makes a highly revealing statement, but fails to pursue its implications: "In spite of the fact that probably a majority of the planters tried to prevent family separations in order to maintain plantation discipline, practically all of the black autobiographers were touched by the tragedy."[20] Although Blassingame does not elaborate upon this idea, it is obvious that the slave narrator group included a disproportionate number of mulattoes, and that many of the narrators came from broken homes as well. Although it is possible that slave narrators were not a random sample of the population and consequently gave accounts that were valid for only one segment of the slave population, it is more probable that the traditions of the slave narrative genre determined the selection of details and emphases.

The content, structure, and communicative context of the slave narratives made them create a particular kind of literature, to shape and reveal their realities in ways most beneficial to their needs. That this is so can be seen as much from what was said and how as from what was not said and why. For example, the slave narratives tend to diminish the cultural value of Afro-American folktales and songs. Douglass mentions that singing slaves were not necessarily happy slaves and that their "sorrow songs" were full of meaning to the slaves that were singing them, but does not admit any real significance for him other than "opening his eyes to the overwhelming oppression of slavery in a very transcendental experience." Henry Bibb wryly admits an early faith in conjuration and witchcraft. Several narratives indicate the solace and inspiration of secret worship services. Few deal extensively with these early experiences or acknowledge them as vital influences. Although the majority of Afro-American folktales celebrate the wit and imagination of the weaker individual over the stronger, in the slave narratives the trickster image is subordinated. The dominant figure is the innocent victim, and the emphasis after freedom is upon the attainment of literacy, Christianity, and white middle-class values. This is true in spite of the fact that scholars such as Sterling Stuckey have made a strong case for the existence and strength of a viable black culture. "Slaves," says Stuckey, "were able to fashion a life style and a set of values—an ethos—which prevented them from becoming imprisoned altogether by the definitions which the larger society sought to impose. . . . The process of dehumanization was not so pervasive. . . . A very large number of slaves, guided by this ethos, were able to maintain their essential humanity."[21]

The evidence of other kinds of slave literature and the recorded testimony of hundreds of exslaves also provide eivdence of a more complex and positively functional environment than that offered by the nineteenth-century slave narrators. Although the slave narratives are guilty of perpetuating racist illusions and of perpetrating some inaccurate and potentially damaging stereotypes of their own, their ultimate significance is not damaged by this. If one attempts to study them in the context of their time, it becomes apparent why many of these seeming weaknesses exist. These same documents then become even more important for what their "negative" as well as "positive" aspects reveal. What is important is the influence that the slave narrators had upon their society and ultimately upon ours.

7

Post-bellum Influence

SLAVE NARRATIVES HAD a great impact upon the attitudes of their readers. As their writers intended, their slave reminiscences further encouraged those whose consciences were uneasy about the enslavement of men or the use of labor without compensation. Their sensationalism attracted many readers who at a later time might mull over the lists of cruelties and abuses and develop a greater sympathy for the plight of the slaves. At the very least, they provided a different perspective on slavery. Says Ephraim Peabody, "These biographies of fugitive slaves are calculated to exert a very wide influence on public opinion. We have always been familiar with slavery, as seen from the side of the master. These narratives show how it looks as seen from the side of the slaves. They contain the *victim's* account of the workings of this great institution."[1]

The abolitionists were well aware of the potential value of slave narratives for influencing persons to the antislavery cause. They were especially fond of fugitive tales and encouraged their publication at every opportunity. A letter from Angelina Grimké to Theodore Weld, both well-known abolitionists, exemplifies such enthusiasm:

> We rejoiced to hear of the fugitives' escape from bondage, tho' some of the pleasure was abridged by the caution to keep these things close. Let us know when the brother is off. Yes—publish his tale of woe, such narratives are greatly needed, let it come burning from his own lips in England and publish it here; it must do good. Names, dates and facts will give additional credibility to it. Many and many a tale of romantic horror can the slaves tell.[2]

The popularity of the slave narratives cannot be attributed simply to their antislavery content, however. Several commentaries recognize their appeal to those with traditional inclinations toward tales of romanticism and heroic struggle. Ephraim Peabody's abolitionist enthusiasm did not blind him to the importance of the romantic appeal of narratives:

> In the declamations and exhibitions of school-boys, the freedom and the wrongs of Greece and Poland and Ireland are almost superseded by those of the Southern slaves. Nothing seems to have such power as descriptions of their conditions to set into a flame the minds of the young. If this shows nothing else, it shows that the slave who endeavours to recover his freedom is associating with himself no small part of the romance of the time.[3]

A writer for *Putnam's* places the slave narratives in the context of Western literary tradition:

> Our English literature has recorded many an example of genius struggling against adversity,—of the poor Ferguson, for instance, making himself an astronomer, of Burns becoming a poet, of Hugh Miller finding his geology in a stone quarry, and a thousand similar cases— yet none of these are so impressive as the case of the solitary slave, in a remote district, surrounded by none but enemies, conceiving the project of his escape, teaching himself to read and write to facilitate it, accomplishing it at last, and subsequently raising himself to a leadership in a great movement in behalf of his brethren.[4]

The nineteenth-century slave narratives had something for everybody. An advertisement for Charles Ball's narrative touted its versatility in no uncertain terms: "To those residing in States where slavery is prohibited, or only known in its mildest forms," the ad promises, "it will convey a knowledge of the state of society amongst the Planters of the South, and of the effects resulting from the practice of slavery in that region." For the southerner the narrative would provide "a faithful view of the opinions and feelings of the colored population. . . . He will here see portrayed in the language of truth, by an eye witness and a slave, the sufferings, the hardships, and the evils which are inflicted upon the millions of human beings." The publishers and distributors of the works did not hesitate to appeal directly to the sensationalists and thrill seekers: "To those who take delight in lonely and desperate undertakings, pursued with patient and unflinching courage, we recommend the flight and journey from Georgia to Maryland, which exhibits the curious spectacle of a man wandering six months in the United States without speaking to a human creature."[5]

The hyperbole of Lincoln's much-quoted comment upon meeting Harriet Beecher Stowe, that she was the little lady who started the great big Civil War, is obvious. But within that exaggeration is recognition of the influence of literature upon society in general and specifically of the effect which nineteenth-century pro- and antislavery writers had in the United States. If, indeed, Lincoln attributed such strength to secondhand, imitative, and fictionalized works, it is easy to imagine what this implies about the effect of literature which was presented as firsthand, original, and true.

The impact of nineteenth-century slave narratives was not limited to societal attitudes. Writers of all statures were impressed and influenced by these works. Some became amanuenses and editors for the slaves. Among the more famous are John Greenleaf Whittier, Joseph Lovejoy, Wendell Phillips, Edmund Quincy, and Lydia Maria Child. Others produced imitation slave narratives, sometimes passing them off as authentic and other times submitting them as novels. Included in this group are Richard Hildreth's *The Slave; or, Memoirs of Archy Moore* (1836), Mattie Griffith's *Autobiography of a Female Slave* (1857), and Harriet Beecher Stowe's *Uncle Tom's Cabin* (1852).

The extent to which the slave narratives captured the imaginations of contemporary writers and readers is revealed in a bitter essay published in *Graham's*. The writer is especially vexed by the enthusiasm of women writers:

> Our female agitators have abandoned Bloomers in despair, and are just now bestride a new hobby—an intense love of black folks, in *fashionable novels*! . . . We have a regular incursion of the blacks. The shelves of booksellers groan under the weight of Sambo's woes, done up in covers! What a dose we have had and are having! The populations of readers has gone a wool-gathering! Our "Helots of the West" are apparently at a premium with the publishers just now; and we have Northern folks as anxious to make money of them, as the Southrons [sic] can be, for their lives. . . . Let us go back to our Mexican brigands, our fresh Texans, with their big bears and unerring

"Beeswings," our Prairie heroines, and all that wonderful adventure which is only sunburnt, at the deepest. . . . We are weary of preaching negroes, and "Mas'r" and " 'spects Ise wicked," and "that yer old man," and "dat ar nigger." We want something refreshing.[6]

Not only did slave narratives provide, as John Herbert Nelson phrases it, "the material out of which many a secondhand account of Southern life was elaborated,"[7] but the many slave narratives were increasingly influenced by the secondhand accounts. Their popularity encouraged profiteering persons of both races to capitalize upon the current vogue; and this in turn encouraged occasional exaggerations of the truth in some works and even produced some completely fraudulent works. Some creative black writers became aware of the potential value of novels patterned after the narratives but presented quite frankly as fiction. In both cases the development of the slave narrative was following traditional literary techniques and forms coupled with the unique and particular realities and needs of its writers and their society. The slave narratives themselves developed variants in the course of the next sixty years. The literary tradition remained relatively stable; what changed noticeably was the communicative context of the slave narratives.

Partly because of their deliberate decisions to subordinate their personalities in order to emphasize their typicality and partly because it is the fate of many writers of popular literature to be overshadowed by their creations, few individuals gained prominence on the basis of their writing of slave narratives. Slave narrators were valuable as informants, and their contributions were cherished because they could give new and exciting information or corroborate the accounts of other narrators, but the identities of the particular writers were less important than the context and effect of their work.

The fate of the author of a slave narrative is strikingly similar to that of his protagonist. Once the protagonist achieves his freedom from bondage, the plot is finished. Once his narrative is published, the narrator's literary career is ended. During the height of their popularity, it was common for slave narratives to be reprinted and even revised. These reprints and revisions, however, rarely differed significantly from the originals. Additional prefaces or appendixes may indicate a writer's pleasure at the narrative's reception or may provide additional proofs of authenticity. A few writers attempted to bring their readers up to date concerning their experiences since the last publication, but it was essentially the same work. The slave narratives were, for most exslaves, their only literary endeavor and they marked the end of their lives as public figures.

There were exceptions. A few became successful ministers, teachers, and businessmen; and some were able to become professional exslaves. Among those who "made a career of their unique status" were William and Ellen Craft, Henry Bibb, Josiah Henson, Anthony Burns, Lewis and Milton Clarke, Samuel Ringgold Ward, Henry "Box" Brown, William Wells Brown, and Frederick Douglass. They capitalized upon their experiences in many ways, but few attempted a second book. Consequently, their fame as writers is based upon a brief, even accidental, experiment. As the interests and appetites of their readers varied, so did the form of the narratives. The ways in which the slave narratives gradually developed into other genres are well exemplified by the works of three slave narrators who did develop literary careers.

Josiah Henson's first account, *Life of Josiah Henson, formerly a Slave, Now an Inhabitant of Canada. Narrated by Himself*, was published in 1849. It received only moderate attention. However, when Harriet Beecher Stowe announced in *The Key to Uncle Tom's Cabin* that, "A last instance parallel with that of Uncle Tom is to be found in the published memoirs of the venerable Josiah Henson, now, as we have said, a clergyman in Canada,"[8] it was a golden moment for the enterprising author. A second narrative, *Truth Stranger than Fiction: Father Henson's Story of His Own Life*, was released in 1858, and Mrs. Stowe wrote the preface. As the popularity of *Uncle Tom's Cabin* increased, interest in Henson's narratives did also. In 1877 a third version entitled *"Uncle Tom's Story of His Life": An Autobiography of the Rev. Josiah Henson (Mrs. Harriet Beecher Stowe's "Uncle Tom"), from 1789-1876* appeared. Introductory notes by Wendell Phillips and John Greenleaf Whittier were added to Stowe's preface in 1879. The publishers stated 100,000 copies had been sold prior to this edition. Another version was issued in 1881, and seven years after his death a final edition, *The Autobiography of the Rev. Josiah Henson ("Uncle Tom") from 1789-1833*, was published.

The publications in this series were not simple revisions of the same text. Each edition dealt with the same basic subject, but the content and style were revised in so many ways that many of them should be considered as completely new works. In his essay "Josiah Henson and Uncle Tom," Robin Winks states:

> The first version of his autobiography, published in 1849, is without guile, straight-forward, dramatic in its simplicity. But this fugitive from Kentucky, clearly intelligent and hard-working, also shared the normal desire to collect a few of the merit badges that life might offer, and when he found himself thrust into fame in a role that just might fit, he hugged his new role to himself until his death. . . . Those versions of his autobiography which appeared after the publication of *Uncle Tom's Cabin* in 1852 showed substantial alterations, extensions, and fabrications.[9]

The number of inaccuracies or exaggerations that appear in subsequent public statements by both Mrs. Stowe and Henson concerning the relationship of their works reveals that they found their association profitable. Such evidence is almost convincing enough to argue that Henson should be accepted both as a slave narrator and a novelist.

There is some doubt concerning the extent to which the series of publications attributed to Henson were the personal efforts of Henson and the extent to which they reflect the creative imaginations and abilities of his two editors, Samuel A. Eliot and John Lobb. There exists no such doubt about another prolific author, Frederick Douglass; the Boston Anti-Slavery Office published his *Narrative of the Life of Frederick Douglass* in 1845. "Written by Himself," this work consisted of 125 pages and sold for 50 cents a copy. Its introductions were by William Lloyd Garrison and Wendell Phillips. It was written to stifle rumors that Douglass was not really a fugitive slave and to "do something toward throwing light on the American slave system, and hastening the glad day of deliverance to the millions of my brethren in bonds."[10] This brief volume sold 30,000 copies in five years. By January 1848 it had had nine editions in England alone.

In 1855, Douglass wrote *My Bondage and My Freedom*, a narrative three times as long as his first. The size alone would indicate this was not simply a revision of his first work, but there are several other significant differences to validate it as a separate work. Although he did not change or refute previous statements, Douglass gave more details about the incidents and facts recorded in his first work. More importantly, he provided additional and more elaborate accounts of his life as an exslave and as a freeman. He described his work as an abolitionist, his flight to England and subsequent purchase for $700, and his founding of the paper *The North Star*. *My Bondage and My Freedom* went beyond the traditional slave narrative not only in its extensive depiction of life outside slavery but also in its thematic concerns. This work not only strongly exposes the evil of slavery but also attacks northern discrimination and American racism. *My Bondage and My Freedom* was not introduced by whites, as was the case with the first work; a prominent black New York medical practitioner, Dr. J. McCune Smith, provided the introduction. Instead of an apology for his seemingly antireligious statements in the narrative, the appendix of his second narrative consisted of extracts from seven of Douglass's speeches and the now-famous letter to his ex-master, Thomas Auld.

In 1881 Douglass published a third book, *The Life and Times of Frederick Douglass*. In this work, his life as a slave is briefly told, but the major emphasis is upon his abolitionist activities and his Civil War and Reconstruction experiences. *The Life and Times of Frederick Douglass* is more in the traditional autobiography genre then any of his previous works. By this time, the era of the slave narrative had passed and Douglass was writing in the mode of other contemporary black writers. His extended literary efforts were limited to autobiographical works, but with these three publications Douglass established himself as an important American writer.

William Wells Brown published extensively in several genres and achieved his prominence by his prolific and diverse contributions. In 1847 the *Narrative of William W. Brown, a Fugitive Slave. Written by Himself* appeared. It was one of the more popular narratives and sold 8,000 copies within two years. The quality of his writing can be seen from an incident related by his biographer, William Edward Farrison. Farrison reports that Brown submitted his manuscript to Edmund Quincy for criticism, but Quincy apparently was not enthusiastic about reviewing another slave narrative. He kept

Brown's manuscript for a fortnight before he even opened its cover. Finally, on the morning of July 1, he decided to review the manuscript. Quincy reports, "I thought I would glance over a few pages to see what it was like. But it was so good that I could not lay it down until dinnertime." He judged it "a much more striking story than Douglass' & was well told." He noted, "quite correctly," says Farrison, "no attempt at fine writing, but only a minute account of scenes & things he saw & suffered, told with a good deal of skill & great propriety & delicacy."[11]

There were at least eight editions of this first work. Although Brown continued his autobiographical endeavors and published a number of such works, his subsequent experiments in two other areas were logical extensions of his slave narrative interests. On one hand, he chose to expand the expositional aspects of slave narratives by creating a series of textbooks on the history of the black man. Included in this group are *The Black Man, His Antecedents, His Genius, and His Achievements* (1863) and *The Rising Son; or, the Antecedents and Advancement of the Colored Race* (1873).

On the other hand, he utilized the dramatic potential of slave narratives by publishing a play and three novels, all of which combined the form and content of traditional slave narratives with Brown's imagination. His first attempt at fiction was published in 1853 as *Clotel; or, The President's Daughter: A Narrative of Slave Life in the United States. With a Sketch of the Author's Life.* It is generally considered to be the first novel by an Afro-American. From the example of Brown, the impact of slave narratives upon Afro-American literature becomes more evident.

The literary achievements of Henson, Douglass, and Brown reveal specific ways in which the slave narrative evolved. The relationship between Stowe and Henson exemplifies the effect of slave narratives upon abolitionist literature. From the history of Douglass's publications, the relationship between slave narratives and autobiography becomes apparent. From the example of Brown, the impact of slave narratives upon Afro-American literature becomes more evident. Such examples validate the assertion that slave narratives as popular literature served to bridge the gap between societal segments and made lasting contributions to the development of literature in the United States. Most slave narrators, however, like most Indian captivity narrators, Revolutionary War narrators, and other writers of specific and immediate interests, disappeared with their cause or at least with their readers' interest in their cause. Their obscurity, and the differences in theme and technique of those who continued to publish, reflect the loss of public interest and the narrators' revision of priorities. The most obvious reason for the slave narratives was the Civil War. After the grim reality of the American Civil War, the emancipation of the slaves and Reconstruction, the primary concerns of slave narratives had only historical value. The slavery issue, in the opinion of the reading public, had been settled, and the wounds were too fresh for objective contemplation.

From the Reconstruction period on, a number of autobiographical writings by exslaves were published. These works, however, did not dwell upon the horrors of their writers' past conditions of servitude but were instead cheerleading exercises to urge continued opportunities for integration of blacks into American society or to depict black contributions to the Horatio Alger tradition. Their descriptions of slavery were mild and offered as "historical" evidence only. Says Louis Hughes in his preface to *Thirty Years a Slave. From Bondage to Freedom: The Institution of Slavery As Seen on the Plantation and In the Home of the Planter* (1897):

> The institution of human slavery, as it existed in this country, has long been dead; and, happily for all the sacred interests which it assailed, there is for it no resurrection. It may, therefore, be asked to what purpose is the story which follows, of the experiences of one person under that dead and accursed institution? . . . As the enlightenment of each generation depends upon the thoughtful study of the history of those that have gone before, everything which tends to fullness and accuracy in that history is of value, even though it be not presented with the adjuncts of literary adornment, or thrilling scenic effects.[12]

The titles of these postwar accounts reflect this change. Elizabeth Keckley in 1868 called her work *Behind the Scenes: Thirty Years a Slave and Four Years in the White House.* In 1885 Issac Williams offered *Sunshine and Shadow of Slave Life, Reminiscences Told to*

William Ferguson Goldie by Isaac Williams. In 1894 appeared John
Mercer Langston's *From Plantation to Congress.* And the greatest
success story of them all appeared in 1900 under the label, *Up From
Slavery: An Autobiography.* Booker T. Washington's decision to
entitle his book *Up From Slavery* is a fine example of the sagacity
that characterized his remarkable career. His title reveals the book's
basic theme of educational and economic progress; yet its similarity
to the titles of slave narratives is obvious. The title's allusion is
reinforced immediately with Washington's opening words: "I was
born a slave on a plantation in Franklin County, Virginia. I am not
quite sure of the exact place or exact date of my birth."[13] Washington was encouraging his readers to place his work in the slave narrative tradition. It was not a slave narrative, however. Washington
was born about five years before the Emancipation Proclamation
and admits little personal knowledge about slavery. "So far as I
can recall," he says, "the first knowledge that I got of the fact that
we were slaves . . . was early one morning before day, when I was
awakened by my mother kneeling over her children and fervently
praying that Lincoln and his armies might be successful."[14] His
narrative discusses slavery experiences in terms of the poverty, the
difficulty of cultivating good table manners, and the enduring
loyalty of slaves to their masters. Chapter 2 begins with freedom
and its effects upon the former slaves and specifically his own family.
    In her perceptive work, *Where I'm Bound: Patterns of Slavery
and Freedom in Black American Autobiography,* Sidonie Smith
describes the general movement of these postslave narrative works:

> From a lowly beginning on the fringes of society, the hard-working
> and virtuous individual rises slowly yet steadily to success and social
> prominence: self-realization is fulfilled by social arrival. In this tradi-
> tional myth of American identity, the individual's relationship to
> society is fluid, and his possibilities are unlimited. For the black
> American, this pattern becomes especially expressive and often pain-
> fully ironic since he begins on the furthest fringe of the social scale
> (the fluidity of his movement is problematic) and the odds against
> him are greater (his unlimited possibilities are in fact narrowly limited).
> In reenacting the successful struggle with his background and his
> society, he reinforces and reaffirms the "American" side of his dual

identity. Freedom becomes synonymous with the ability to participate in the American myth of democratic possibility.[15]

Exslaves' accounts of their progress from bondage to freedom continued to filter through the presses from the end of the nineteenth century and into the twentieth. As legalized slavery became a thing of the past, they acquired more of a historical and anthropological flavor. As the personal accounts by witnesses of a bygone era, they were regarded as curiosities, testimonies, or romances. Their functional significance changed from hard-hitting exposés or passionate appeals for action to data with which to create or re-create an era or a depth from which to chart one's progress.

The influence of the slave narratives continues to the present day. Scholars of black autobiography, such as Sidonie Smith, identify the slave narratives as a direct and vital source:

> The autobiography of the black American has continued to be a form of slave narrative. The two patterns inherent in the slave narrative, however, tend to separate. On the one hand, there is the story of a successful BREAK INTO the community, a reenactment of America's secular drama of selfhood. This autobiographical tradition reflects, through the story of a social calling, the slave narrative's focus on the achievement of place within northern society. On the other hand, there is the story of the BREAK AWAY from the imprisoning community, a reenactment of the sacred quest for selfhood. Hence, this tradition reflects more the initial direction of the slave narrative and the latter illusory nature of the achievement of freedom.[16]

Mary W. Burger recognizes the slave narratives as cultural works that create and re-create the archetypal patterns of black experience:

> Relying on the oral tales passed among slaves as well as his own memory and experience, the slave narrator gives literary form to primordial rites, myths and values recurrent among blacks. They express seminal images of the forces and techniques through which blacks have survived in America, and dramatize through various characters, the mistaken values and motives that have hindered their people as well as those hopes and ideals that have pushed them on-

ward. In so doing, they call into play the repeated experience of the black American in particular, and of man oppressed or imprisoned in general.[17]

The study of the slave narratives leads us from American colonial literature, which was more national than racial, to the emergence of Afro-American prose literary expression to the fictional works of such black writers as Richard Wright, Ralph Ellison, James Baldwin, Claude Brown, and even Cecil Brown. It provides a context within which to deal with such contemporary treatments of slavery as *Black Thunder*, by Arna Bontemps; *The Autobiography of Miss Jane Pittman*, by Ernest Gaines; *Jubilee*, by Margaret Walker; and *Roots*, by Alex Haley.

In "That Same Pain, That Same Pleasure," Ralph Ellison states that people must realize that sociological conditions are not the only factors that determine values, and they must recognize that "art is a celebration of life even when life extends into death." If these concepts are not learned, Ellison says, "I see a period when Negroes are going to be wandering around because, you see, we have had this thing thrown at us for so long that we haven't had a chance to discover what in our own background is really worth preserving."[18]

The slave narratives serve as excellent sources for contemporary writers who wish to avoid the prophecy of Ellison. Margaret Walker gives evidence of this when she says in *How I Wrote* Jubilee:

When I was not working in the Nelson Tift papers I was reading slave narratives. . . . These slave narratives only further corroborated the most valuable slave narrative of all, the living account of my great-grandmother which had been transmitted to me by her own daughter. I knew then that I had a precious, almost priceless, living document of my own. There are hundreds of these stories, most of them not written, but many of them are recorded for posterity. These written accounts tell of the brutalizing and dehumanizing practices of human slavery. They recount such atrocities as branding, whipping, killing, and mutilating slaves. They are sometimes written in the form of letters to former masters, sometimes as autobiographical sketches, and some—like that of Frederick Douglass—have become classics. But all of them contain crucial information on slavery from the mouth of the slave.[19]

The personal accounts of slaves and exslaves concerning their struggles from bondage to freedom are indeed a legacy of great value. Not only are they important as sources of information concerning the slave's view of slavery, not only are they significant as historical relics—examples of nineteenth-century America's taste, culture, and issues—not only did they play an influential role in the history of the United States, but they were also perhaps the single most important development in Afro-American literature, and they continue to this moment to provide insights into the history from which America was created, the history to which we must turn in order to begin to learn who we are and what our relation is to the world.

Notes

CHAPTER 1

1. James D. Hart, *The Popular Book: A History of America's Literary Taste* (New York: Oxford University Press, 1950), p. 14.

2. Winthrop D. Jordan, *White Over Black: American Attitudes Toward the Negro, 1550-1812* (Chapel Hill: University of North Carolina Press, 1968), p. 44.

3. "The Voyage Made by M. John Hawkins . . . to the Coast of Guinea and the Indies of Nova Hispania . . .," in Jordan, *White Over Black*, p. 4.

4. "The First Voyage of Robert Baker to Guinie," in Richard Hakluyt, *The Principall Navigations, Voiages and Discoveries of the English Nation . . .* (London, 1589), p. 132.

5. Philip D. Curtin, *The Image of Africa: British Ideas and Action, 1780-1850* (Madison: University of Wisconsin Press, 1964), 1:34-35.

6. Morgan Godwin, *The Negro's and Indians' Advocate . . . in our Plantations* (London: Printed for the Author by F. D., 1680), pp. 3, 13.

7. Thomas Jefferson, "Notes on Virginia," in *The Life and Selected Writings of Thomas Jefferson*, edited by Adrienne Koch and William Peden (New York: Random House, 1944), pp. 261-62.

8. Benjamin Banneker, *Copy of a Letter from Benjamin Banneker to the Secretary of State, with His Answer* (Philadelphia: Daniel Lawrence, 1792), pp. 3-4.

9. Ibid., p. 11.

10. George M. Fredrickson, *The Black Image in the White Mind: The Debate on Afro-American Character and Destiny, 1817-1914* (New York: Harper & Row, 1971), p. 91.

11. Olaudah Equiano, *The Interesting Narrative of the Life of Olaudah Equiano, or Gustavus Vassa, the African*, 1st American ed. (New York: W. Durell, 1791), 1:75, 36.

12. Venture Smith, *A Narrative of the Life and Adventures of Venture, a Native of Africa* (New London, Conn.: C. Holt, 1798), p. 30.

13. Henry Bibb, *Narrative of the Life and Adventures of Henry Bibb, an American Slave* (New York: Published by the Author, 1849), p. 14.

14. Charles Ball, *Slavery in the United States: A Narrative of the Life and Adventures of Charles Ball, a Black Man* (New York: John S. Taylor, 1837), pp. 21-22.

15. John Hope Franklin, *From Slavery to Freedom: A History of Negro Americans,* 4th ed. (New York: Knopf, 1974), p. 50.

16. Austin Steward, *Twenty-two Years a Slave, and Forty Years a Freeman* (Rochester, N.Y.: William Alling, 1857), p. 34.

17. James W. C. Pennington, *The Fugitive Blacksmith; or, Events in the History of James W. C. Pennington,* 2nd ed. (London: Charles Gilpin, 1849), pp. xii, 2.

18. Bibb, *Narrative,* p. 204.

19. Ephraim Peabody, "Narratives of Fugitive Slaves," *Christian Examiner* 37 (July 1849):62, 68.

20. Equiano, *Narrative,* 1:94; 2:52.

21. Ibid., 2:138.

22. William Craft and Ellen Craft, *Running a Thousand Miles for Freedom; or, The Escape of William and Ellen Craft from Slavery* (London: William Tweedie, 1860), p. 93.

23. Ibid., p. 94.

24. Lewis Clarke and Milton Clarke, *Narratives of the Sufferings of Lewis and Milton Clarke* (Boston: Bela Marsh, 1846), p. 40.

25. Ibid., p. 40.

26. Equiano, *Narrative,* 1:3-4.

27. Pennington, *Fugitive Blacksmith,* pp. iv-v.

28. Quoted in *Five Hundred Thousand Strokes for Freedom,* edited by Wilson Armistead, Leeds Anti-Slavery Series, no. 34 (London: W. & F. Cash, 1853), p. 12.

29. Robin Winks, ed., *Four Fugitive Slave Narratives* (Reading, Mass.: Addison-Wesley, 1969), p. vi.

30. John Herbert Nelson, *The Negro Character in American Literature* (Lawrence, Kansas: Department of Journalism Press, 1926), p. 61.

31. Arna Bontemps, "The Slave Narratives: An American Genre," in *Great Slave Narratives* (Boston: Beacon Press, 1969), p. xviii.

32. Charles H. Nichols, *Many Thousands Gone: The Ex-slaves' Account of their Bondage and Freedom* (Leiden, Netherlands: E. J. Brill, 1963), p. xii.

33. Marion Starling, "The Slave Narrative: Its Place in American Literary History" (Dissertation, New York University, 1946), p. 313.

34. For publication statistics I am indebted to Bontemps, "The Slave Narratives," pp. xiv-xvii; Nichols, *Many Thousands Gone,* pp. xiv-xv; and Starling, "The Slave Narrative," pp. 47-51.

35. Hart, *Popular Book,* p. 92.

CHAPTER 2

1. Susan Myra Kingsbury, ed., *The Records of the Virginia Company of London* (Washington, D.C.: Government Printing Office, 1933), 3:243. Fragments, such as the Rolfe notations, have been frequently quoted in studies of early Afro-American culture. Few have bothered to analyze their significance. Among those whose analyses are particularly helpful are Winthrop D. Jordan, *White Over Black: American Attitudes Toward the Negro, 1550-1812* (Chapel Hill: University of North Carolina Press, 1968); Alden T. Vaughan, "Blacks in Virginia: A Note on the First Decade," *William and Mary Quarterly* 29 (1972); and Warren M. Billings, "The Cases of Fernando and Elizabeth Key: A Note on the Status of Blacks in Seventeenth-Century Virginia," *William and Mary Quarterly* 30 (1973).

2. Edward Arber, ed., *Travels and Works of Captain John Smith* (Edinburgh: J. Grant, 1910), II, p. 541.

3. Vaughan, "Blacks in Virginia," p. 472.

4. John Winthrop, *Winthrop's Journal: History of New England, 1630-1649*, edited by James Kendall Hosmer (New York: Scribner's, 1908), 1:260.

5. "Decisions of the General Court," *Virginia Magazine of History and Biography* 5 (1898): 236.

6. William Waller Hening, ed., *The Statutes at Large Being a Collection of All the Laws of Virginia* (Richmond, New York: R. & W. & G. Bartow, 1810-1823), 2:267.

7. Billings, "Fernando and Elizabeth Key," p. 467.

8. Hening, *Statutes at Large*, 2:260.

9. *Collections of the Massachusetts Historical Society: The Diary of Samuel Sewall 1699-1700-1714*, 5th series (Boston: Massachusetts Historical Society, 1879), 6:16.

10. Ibid.

11. Sidney Kaplan, "Samuel Sewall and the Iniquity of Slavery," *The Selling of Joseph: A Memorial* (Amherst: University of Massachusetts Press, 1969), p. 43.

12. *A Brief and Candid Answer to a Late Printed Sheet, Entituled, The Selling of Joseph* (1701; reprint ed., in *Publications of the Colonial Society of Massachusetts* [Boston, 1895]), 1:112.

13. Kaplan, "Iniquity of Slavery," pp. 44-45.

14. Thomas Bluett, *Some Memoirs of the Life of Job*, in *Africa Remembered*, edited by Philip D. Curtin (Madison: University of Wisconsin Press, 1967), pp. 34-35.

15. Ibid., pp. 43, 46.

16. Richard Slotkin, "Narratives of Negro Crime in New England, 1675-1800," *American Quarterly* 25 (March 1973):16.

17. Ibid., pp. 16, 18.

18. Joseph Johnson Green, *The Life and Confession of Johnson Green, Who is to be Executed this Day, August 17th, 1786, for the Atrocious Crime of Burglary; together with his Dying Words. A Broadside* (Worchester, Mass.: Printing Office, 1786).

19. John Joyce, *Confession of John Joyce, alias Davis, who was Executed on Monday, the 14th of March, 1808, for the Murder of Mrs. Sarah Cross; with an Address to the Public, and People of Colour* (Philadelphia: Printed for Bethel Church, 1808), pp. 5, 29.

20. Briton Hammon, *A Narrative of the Uncommon Sufferings, and Surprizing Deliverance of Briton Hammon, a Negro Man* (Boston: Green & Russell, 1760), p. 14.

21. Richard Van der Beets, *Held Captive by Indians: Selected Narratives 1642-1836* (Knoxville: University of Tennessee Press, 1973), p. xiii.

22. Hammon, *Narrative*, p. 6.

23. Richard Allen, *The Life, Experience, and Gospel Labors of the Rt. Rev. Richard Allen* (Philadelphia: Lee and Yeocum, 1837), pp. 6, 8.

CHAPTER 3

1. Thomas Bluett, *Some Memoirs of the Life of Job*, in *Africa Remembered*, edited by Philip D. Curtin (Madison: University of Wisconsin Press, 1967), p. 42.

2. Olaudah Equiano, *The Interesting Narrative of the Life of Olaudah Equiano, or Gustavus Vassa, the African*, 1st American ed. (New York: W. Durell, 1791), 2:29, 32, 34-35, 36.

3. James Albert Ukawsaw Gronniosaw, *A Narrative of the Most Remarkable Particulars in the Life of James Albert Ukawsaw Gronniosaw, an African Prince* (Newport, R. I.: S. Southwick, 1774), p. 4.

4. Equiano, *Narrative*, 1:109.

5. Venture Smith, *A Narrative of the Life and Adventures of Venture, a Native of Africa* (New London, Conn.: C. Holt, 1798), p. iii.

6. Equiano, *Narrative*, 1:177-78.

7. Ibid., pp. 193-94.

8. Russel B. Nye, *American Literary History: 1607-1830* (New York: Knopf, 1970), p. 191.

9. James D. Hart, *The Popular Book: A History of America's Literary Taste* (New York: Oxford University Press, 1950), p. 108.

10. John Herbert Nelson, *The Negro Character in American Literature* (Lawrence, Kansas: Department of Journalism Press, 1926), p. 61.

11. Frederick Douglass, *Narrative of the Life of Frederick Douglass, an American Slave* (Boston: Anti-Slavery Office, 1845), pp. 39-40.

12. James W. C. Pennington, *The Fugitive Blacksmith; or, Events in the History of James W. C. Pennington,* 2nd ed. (London: Charles Gilpin, 1849), p. iv.

13. Harriet Brent Jacobs [Linda Brent], *Incidents in the Life of a Slave Girl* (Boston: Published for the Author, 1861), pp. 85-86.

14. Hart, *Popular Book*, pp. 113-14.

CHAPTER 4

1. John Hope Franklin, *From Slavery to Freedom: A History of Negro Americans*, 4th ed. (New York: Knopf, 1974), p. 188.

2. William Charvat, *The Profession of Authorship in America, 1800-1870*, edited by Matthew J. Bruccoli (Columbus: Ohio State University Press, 1968), p. 30.

3. Ibid., p. 65.

4. Richard Altick, *The English Common Reader: A Social History of the Mass Reading Public, 1800-1900* (Chicago: University of Chicago Press, 1957), p. 5.

5. Charvat, *Profession of Authorship*, p. 65.

6. Russel B. Nye, *American Literary History: 1607-1830* (New York: Knopf, 1970), pp. 212-13.

7. Frank Luther Mott, *Golden Multitudes: The Story of the Best Sellers in the United States* (New York: Macmillan, 1947), p. 88.

8. W. E. B. DuBois, *The Souls of Black Folk: Essays and Sketches* (Chicago: A. C. McClurg & Co., 1903), p. 3.

9. Altick, *Common Reader*, p. 8.

10. Samuel Ringgold Ward, *Autobiography of a Fugitive Negro* (London: John Snow, 1855), pp. 37-38.

11. Russel B. Nye, *Society and Culture in America: 1830-1860* (New York: Harper & Row, 1974), p. 219.

12. James Freeman Clarke, *Slavery in the United States: A Sermon Delivered in Armory Hall on Thanksgiving Day, November 24, 1842* (Boston: Benjamin H. Greene, 1846), pp. 8-9.

13. Lydia Maria Child, *An Appeal in Favor of That Class of Americans Called Africans* (New York: John S. Taylor, 1836), p. 16.

14. Ward, *Fugitive Negro*, p. 37.

15. William Lloyd Garrison, *Narrative of the Life of Frederick Douglass*, Preface (Boston: Anti-Slavery Office, 1845), p. vi.

16. Austin Steward, *Twenty-two Years a Slave, and Forty Years a Freeman* (Rochester, N.Y.: William Alling, 1857), p. xi.

17. James Mars, *Life of James Mars, a Slave Born and Sold in Connecticut* (Hartford, Conn.: Case, Lockwood & Co., 1864), p. 3.

18. John Thompson, *The Life of John Thompson, a Fugitive Slave* (Worcester, Mass.: Printed for Author, 1856), pp. v-vi.

19. John Herbert Nelson, *The Negro Character in American Literature* (Lawrence, Kansas: Department of Journalism Press, 1926), p. 23.

20. Sterling Brown, *The Negro in American Fiction* (Washington, D.C.: The Associates in Negro Folk Education, 1937), p. 15.

21. Ibid., p. 14.

22. Jean Fagan Yellin, *The Intricate Knot: Black Figures in American Literature, 1776-1863* (New York: New York University Press, 1971), p. 17.

23. Stanley Elkins, *Slavery: A Problem in American Institutional and Intellectual Life* (Chicago: University of Chicago Press, 1959), p. 82.

24. John W. Blassingame, *The Slave Community: Plantation Life in the Ante-bellum South* (New York: Oxford University Press, 1972), p. 134.

25. Solomon Northup, *Twelve Years a Slave: Narrative of Solomon Northup* (New York: Miller, Orton & Mulligan, 1855), pp. 259-60.

26. Frederick Douglass, *Narrative of the Life of Frederick Douglass, an American Slave* (Boston: Anti-Slavery Office, 1845), p. 1.

27. Mars, *Life*, p. 57.

28. Ibid., p. 38.

29. Moses Grandy, *Narrative of the Life of Moses Grandy, Late a Slave in the United States of America,* 1st American ed. (Boston: Oliver Johnson, 1844), p. 5.

30. Douglass, *Narrative*, p. 1.

31. Moses Roper, *A Narrative of the Adventures and Escape of Moses Roper from American Slavery,* 5th ed. (London: Harvey and Darton, 1843), pp. 9-10.

32. Harriet Brent Jacobs [Linda Brent], *Incidents in the Life of a Slave Girl* (Boston: Published for Author, 1861), p. 24.

33. William Craft and Ellen Craft, *Running a Thousand Miles for Freedom; or, the Escape of William and Ellen Craft from Slavery* (London: William Tweedie, 1860), p. 2.

34. Jacobs, *Incidents*, pp. 23-24.

35. Douglass, *Narrative*, p. 4.

36. Ibid., pp. 3-4.

CHAPTER 5

1. Robert Scholes and Robert Kellogg, *The Nature of Narrative* (New York: Oxford University Press, 1966), p. 238.

2. Thomas H. Jones, *The Experience of Thomas H. Jones, Who was a*

Slave for Forty-three Years (Worcester, Massachusetts: Henry J. Howland, 1857).

3. Scholes and Kellogg, *Nature of Narrative*, p. 224.

4. William Wells Brown, *Narrative of William Wells Brown, a Fugitive Slave. Written by Himself* (Boston: Anti-Slavery Office, 1847), p. 28.

5. William Craft and Ellen Craft, *Running a Thousand Miles for Freedom; or, the Escape of William and Ellen Craft from Slavery* (London: William Tweedie, 1860), p. 13.

6. John Brown, *Slave Life in Georgia: A Narrative of the Life of John Brown, a Fugitive Slave*, edited by L. A. Chamerovzow (London: British and Foreign Anti-Slavery Society, 1855), p. 31.

7. W. W. Brown, *Narrative*, pp. 13, 15-16.

8. Ibid., pp. 21, 22.

9. Ibid., p. 31.

10. Ibid., p. 57.

11. Ibid., p. 32.

12. Ibid., p. 66.

13. Ibid., p. 8.

14. Henry Box Brown, *Narrative of Henry Box Brown* (Boston: Brown and Stearns, 1849), p. ix.

15. John W. Blassingame, *The Slave Community: Plantation Life in the Ante-bellum South* (New York: Oxford University Press, 1972), p. 94.

16. Eugene Genovese, *Roll, Jordan, Roll: The World the Slaves Made* (New York: Random House, 1974), pp. 502-3.

17. Ibid., pp. 503-4.

18. Blassingame, *Slave Community*, pp. 94-95.

19. Harriet Brent Jacobs [Linda Brent], *Incidents in the Life of a Slave Girl* (Boston: Published for the Author, 1861), pp. 11-12.

20. Noah Davis, *A Narrative of the Life of Rev. Noah Davis, a Colored Man* (Baltimore: John F. Weishampel, Jr., 1859), p. 11.

21. Josiah Henson, *Truth Stranger than Fiction: Father Henson's Story of His Own Life* (Boston: John J. Jewett, 1858), pp. 8-9.

22. John Brown, *Life*, pp. 6-8.

23. William Grimes, *Life of William Grimes, the Runaway Slave, Brought Down to the Present Time* (New Haven, Conn.: Published for the Author, 1855), p. 8.

24. Frederick Douglass, *Narrative of the Life of Frederick Douglass, an American Slave* (Boston: Anti-Slavery Office, 1845), p. 27.

25. James W. C. Pennington, *The Fugitive Blacksmith; or, Events in the Life of James W. C. Pennington* (London: Charles Gilpin, 1849), p. 4.

26. Charles Ball, *Slavery in the United States: A Narrative of the Life and Adventures of Charles Ball, a Black Man* (New York: John S. Taylor, 1837), p. 17.

27. Henry Bibb, *Narrative of the Life and Adventures of Henry Bibb, an American Slave* (New York: Published by the Author, 1849), pp. 14-15.

28. Solomon Northup, *Twelve Years a Slave: Narrative of Solomon Northup* (New York: Miller, Orton & Mulligan, 1855), pp. 168-69.

29. Ibid., pp. 170-71.

30. John Brown, *Life*, pp. 4-5.

31. Northup, *Twelve Years*, pp. 167-68.

32. Ball, *Slavery*, pp. 268-69.

33. Douglass, *Narrative*, pp. 75-76.

34. Gilbert Hobbs Barnes, *The Antislavery Impulse: 1830-1844* (New York: Appleton, 1933), p. 139.

35. Theodore Weld, *American Slavery as It Is: Testimony of a Thousand Witnesses* (New York: Anti-Slavery Society, 1839), p. 9.

36. Quoted in Arthur Zilversmit, *The First Emancipation: The Abolition of Slavery in the North* (Chicago: University of Chicago Press, 1967), pp. 223-24.

37. Moses Roper, *A Narrative of the Adventures and Escape of Moses Roper from American Slavery*, 5th ed. (London: Harvey and Darton, 1843), pp. 25, 26-27.

38. Ball, *Slavery*, p. 161.

39. Austin Steward, *Twenty-two Years a Slave, and Forty Years a Freeman* (Rochester, N.Y.: William Alling, 1857), p. 17.

40. Ball, *Slavery*, p. 82.

41. Northup, *Twelve Years*, p. 62.

42. Moses Grandy, *Narrative of the Life of Moses Grandy, Late a Slave in the United States of America*, 1st American ed. (Boston: Oliver Johnson, 1844), p. 18.

43. Craft and Craft, *Running*, p. 8.

44. Ibid.

45. Jacobs, *Incidents*, pp. 45-46.

46. Craft and Craft, *Running*, p. 21.

47. H. B. Brown, *Narrative*, p. 23.

48. Bibb, *Narrative*, pp. 117-18.

49. Douglass, *Narrative*, pp. 78-79.

50. Bibb, *Narrative*, p. 18.

51. Douglass, *Narrative*, p. 110.

52. Henson, *Truth*, p. 42.

53. Lewis Clarke and Milton Clarke, *Narratives of the Sufferings of Lewis and Milton Clarke* (Boston: Bela Marsh, 1846), p. 9.

54. Steward, *Twenty-two Years*, p. 26.

55. Pennington, *Fugitive Blacksmith*, pp. 69-73.

56. Ball, *Slavery*, pp. 14-15.

57. Pennington, *Fugitive Blacksmith*, p. 13.

58. Lunsford Lane, *The Narrative of Lunsford Lane*, 2nd ed. (Boston: J. E. Torrey, 1842), pp. 6, 7, 8.

59. Bibb, *Narrative*, p. 17.

60. Douglass, *Narrative*, pp. 32, 34, 30-31.

61. Craft and Craft, *Running*, pp. 8-9.

62. Douglass, *Narrative*, pp. 40-41.

63. W. W. Brown, *Narrative*, p. 84.

64. Clarke and Clarke, *Narrative*, p. 32.

65. Steward, *Twenty-two Years*, p. 110.

66. H. B. Brown, *Narrative*, p. 59.

67. Pennington, *Fugitive Blacksmith*, p. 15.

68. Henson, *Truth*, p. 125.

69. Clarke and Clarke, *Narrative*, p. 57.

70. Lane, *Narrative*, pp. 17-18.

71. Jones, *Experience*, pp. 47-48.

72. Lane, *Narrative*, p. iii.

73. Grimes, *Life*, p. 82.

74. Ibid., pp. 84, 91-92.

CHAPTER 6

1. Ephraim Peabody, "Narratives of the Fugitive Slaves," *Christian Examiner* 37 (July 1849): 61-93.

2. Gilbert Hobbs Barnes, *The Antislavery Impulse: 1830-1844* (New York: Appleton, 1933), p. vii.

3. Robert William Fogel and Stanley L. Engerman, *Time on the Cross: The Economics of American Negro Slavery* (Boston: Little, Brown, 1974), p. 132.

4. John Hope Franklin, *From Slavery to Freedom: A History of Negro Americans*, 4th ed. (New York: Knopf, 1974), p. 155.

5. Ibid., p. 153.

6. Stephen Symonds Foster, *The Brotherhood of Thieves, or A True Picture of the American Church and Clergy* (New London, Conn.: William Bolles, 1843), pp. 9-10.

7. James D. Hart, *The Popular Book: A History of America's Literary Taste* (New York: Oxford University Press, 1950), p. 87.

8. Harriet Brent Jacobs [Linda Brent], *Incidents in the Life of a Slave Girl* (Boston: Published for the Author, 1861), pp. 19-20.

9. Samuel. Ringgold Ward, *Autobiography of a Fugitive Negro* (London: John Snow, 1855), p. 5.

10. Ibid., pp. 19-20.

11. Moses Grandy, *Narrative of the Life of Moses Grandy, Late a Slave in the United States of America*, 1st American ed. (Boston: Oliver Johnson, 1844), pp. 5-6.

12. Noah Davis, *A Narrative of the Life of Rev. Noah Davis, a Colored Man* (Baltimore: John F. Weishampel, Jr., 1859), pp. 9-10.

13. Thomas H. Jones, *The Experience of Thomas H. Jones, Who was a Slave for Forty-three Years* (Worcester, Mass.: Henry J. Howland, 1857), pp. 5-6.

14. Henry Bibb, *Narrative of the Life and Adventures of Henry Bibb, an American Slave* (New York: Published by the Author, 1849), pp. 42-43.

15. Frederick Douglass, *Narrative of the Life of Frederick Douglass, an American Slave* (Boston: Anti-Slavery Office, 1845), p. 3.

16. James W. C. Pennington, *The Fugitive Blacksmith; or, Events in the History of James W. C. Pennington*, 2nd ed. (London: Charles Gilpin, 1849), p. 2.

17. Eugene D. Genovese, "American Slaves and Their History," *The New York Review of Books* 15 (December 3, 1970): 36.

18. Ibid., pp. 37-38.

19. George P. Rawick, *From Sundown to Sunup: The Making of the Black Community* (Westport, Conn.: Greenwood, 1972), p. 93.

20. John W. Blassingame, *The Slave Community: Plantation Life in the Ante-bellum South* (New York: Oxford University Press, 1972), p. 89.

21. Sterling Stuckey, "Through the Prism of Folklore: The Black Ethos in Slavery," *The Massachusetts Review* 9 (Summer 1968): 418-19.

CHAPTER 7

1. Ephraim Peabody, "Narratives of Fugitive Slaves," *Christian Examiner* 37 (July 1849): 64.

2. *Letters of Theodore Dwight Weld, Angelina Grimké Weld and Sarah Grimké: 1822-1844*, edited by Gilbert H. Barnes and Dwight L. Dumond (New York: Appleton, 1934), 2:523.

3. Peabody, "Narratives," p. 63.

4. "Editorial Notes—Literature," *Putnam's Monthly* 35 (November 1855):547.

5. "Prospectus of a New York, Entitled *Slavery in the United States: A Narrative of the Life and Adventures of Charles Ball, a Black Man*," *Liberator* 29 (August 1835)):140.

6. "Black Letters; or Uncle Tom-Foolery in Literature," *Graham's Magazine* 42 (February 1853): 209.

7. John Herbert Nelson, *The Negro Character in American Literature* (Lawrence, Kansas: Department of Journalism Press, 1926), p. 69.

8. Harriet Beecher Stowe, *The Key to Uncle Tom's Cabin* (Boston: John P. Jewett & Co., 1853), p. 26.

9. Robin Winks, "Josiah Henson and Uncle Tom," in *Four Fugitive Slave Narratives* (Reading, Mass.: Addison-Wesley, 1969), p. vi.

10. Frederick Douglass, *Narrative of the Life of Frederick Douglass, an American Slave* (Boston: Anti-Slavery Office, 1845), p. 125.

11. William Edward Farrison, *William Wells Brown, Author and Reformer* (Chicago: University of Chicago Press, 1969), pp. 112-13.

12. Louis Hughes, *Thirty Years a Slave: From Bondage to Freedom* (Milwaukee: South Side Printing Co., 1897), p. 4.

13. Booker T. Washington, *Up From Slavery: An Autobiography* (New York: Doubleday, Page & Co., 1902), p. 1.

14. Washington, *Up From Slavery*, p. 7.

15. Sidonie Smith, *Where I'm Bound: Patterns of Slavery and Freedom in Black American Autobiography* (Westport, Conn.: Greenwood, 1974), p. 30.

16. Ibid., p. 29.

17. Mary W. Burger, "Black Autobiography—A Literature of Celebration" (Dissertation, Washington University, 1973), p. 47.

18. Ralph Ellison, *Shadow and Act* (New York: Random House, 1964), p. 22.

19. Margaret Walker, *How I Wrote* Jubilee (Chicago: Third World Press, 1972), p. 18.

Selected Bibliography

Significant collections of slave narratives are found in the libraries of Brown, Cornell, Harvard, Howard, Oberlin, and Hampton Institute universities. The Boston Public Library and the Providence Public Library own several narratives; however, the largest group of narratives is found in the Shomburg Collection of the New York Public Library. Although several reprints and collections of slave narratives have been published during the last decade, it is difficult to determine which would be most accessible. I have, therefore, whenever possible cited the original work. A review of standard sources such as *Books in Print* and *Reprints in Print* would be helpful to those interested. In addition, many microform series—including the Sabin, Early American Reprint, and Shomburg—contain copies of the original works. Generally, though, the writings are not grouped together or otherwise identified as slave narratives, and thus it is necessary to know the author or year of publication before easily locating these works within the microform series.

Several bibliographies include slave narratives. Among the most helpful are the following: Dwight Lowell Dumond, *A Bibliography of Antislavery in America* (Ann Arbor: University of Michigan Press, 1967); Geraldine O. Matthews, *Black American Writers, 1773-1949: A Bibliography and Union List* (Boston: G. K. Hall, 1974); and Dorothy B. Porter, "Early American Negro Writings: A Bibliographical Study," *The Papers of the Bibliographical Society of America* 39 (1945): 192-268.

There are few studies devoted to slave narratives. Two of the best are unpublished American doctoral dissertations: Marion Starling, "The Slave Narrative: Its Place in American Literary History" (New York University, 1946), and Margaret Young Jackson, "An Investigation of Biographies and Autobiographies of American Slaves Published Between 1840 and 1860: Based upon the Cornell Special Slavery Collection" (Cornell University, 1954). A third important work is Charles Nichols, *Many Thousands Gone: The Ex-slaves' Account of Their Bondage and Freedom* (Bloomington: Indiana University Press, 1969).

Allen, Richard. *The Life, Experience, and Gospel Labors of the Rt. Rev. Richard Allen.* Philadelphia: Lee & Yeocum, 1837.

Altick, Richard. *The English Common Reader: A Social History of the Mass Reading Public, 1800-1900.* Chicago: University of Chicago Press, 1957.

Armistead, Wilson, ed. *Five Hundred Thousand Strokes for Freedom.* London: W. & F. Cash, 1853.

Arthur. *The Life and Dying Speech of Arthur. A Broadside.* Boston: Printed and sold in Milk Street, 1768.

Baker, Houston A., Jr. "Balancing the Perspective: A Look at Early Black American Literary Artistry." *Negro American Literature Forum* 6 (1972): 65-70.

Ball, Charles. *Slavery in the United States: A Narrative of the Life and Adventures of Charles Ball, a Black Man, Who Lived Forty Years in Maryland, South Carolina, and Georgia as a Slave.* New York: John S. Taylor, 1837.

Banneker, Benjamin. *Copy of a Letter from Benjamin Banneker to the Secretary of State, with His Answer.* Philadelphia: Daniel Lawrence, 1792.

Barnes, Gilbert Hobbs. *The Antislavery Impulse: 1830-1844.* New York: Appleton, 1933.

Barnes, Gilbert H., and Dwight L. Dumond, eds. *Letters of Theodore Dwight Weld, Angelina Grimké Weld and Sarah Grimké: 1822-1844.* 2 vols. New York: Appleton, 1934.

Bayliss, John F., ed. *Black Slave Narratives.* New York: Macmillan, 1970.

Bibb, Henry. *Narrative of the Life and Adventures of Henry Bibb, an American Slave.* New York: Published by the Author, 1849.

Billings, Warren M. "The Cases of Fernando and Elizabeth Key: A Note on the Status of Blacks in Seventeenth Century Virginia." *William and Mary Quarterly* 30 (July 1973):467-74.

"Black Letters; or Uncle Tom-Foolery in Literature." *Graham's Magazine* 42 (February 1853):209-15.

Blassingame, John W. *The Slave Community: Plantation Life in the Antebellum South.* New York: Oxford University Press, 1972.

———. "Black Autobiographies as History and Literature." *Black Scholar* 5 (December 1973-January 1974): 2-9.

———. *Slave Testimony: Two Centuries of Letters, Speeches, Interviews, and Autobiographies.* Baton Rouge: Louisiana State University Press, 1977.

Bluett, Thomas. *Some Memoirs of the Life of Job.* London: Printed for R. Ford, 1734.

Bontemps, Arna, ed. *Great Slave Narratives.* Boston: Beacon Press, 1969.

Botkin, B. A. "The Slave as His Own Interpreter." *Library of Congress Quarterly Journal of Current Acquisitions* 2 (1944):37-63.

————, ed. *Lay My Burden Down: A Folk History of Slavery.* Chicago: University of Chicago Press, 1969.

Branch, E. Douglas. *The Sentimental Years: 1836-1860.* New York: Appleton, 1934.

Brawley, Benjamin. *Early Negro American Writers: Selections with Biographical and Critical Introductions.* Chapel Hill: University of North Carolina Press, 1935.

Brown, Henry Box. *Narrative of Henry Box Brown.* Boston: Brown and Stearns, 1849.

Brown, Herbert Ross. *The Sentimental Novel in America, 1789-1860.* New York: Pageant, 1959.

Brown, John. *Slave Life in Georgia: A Narrative of the Life of John Brown, a Fugitive Slave.* Edited by L. A. Chamerovzow. London: British and Foreign Anti-Slavery Society, 1855.

Brown, Sterling. *The Negro in American Fiction.* Washington, D.C.: The Associates in Negro Folk Education, 1937.

Brown, William Wells. *Narrative of William Wells Brown, a Fugitive Slave. Written by Himself.* Boston: Anti-Slavery Office, 1847.

Burger, Mary W. "Black Autobiography—a Literature of Celebration." Dissertation, Washington University, 1973.

Butcher, Margaret Just. *The Negro in American Culture.* New York: Knopf, 1956.

Butterfield, Stephen. *Black Autobiography in America.* Amherst: University of Massachusetts Press, 1974.

Callcott, George H. "Omar Ibn Seid, a Slave Who Wrote an Autobiography in Arabic." *Journal of Negro History* 30 (January 1954):58-63.

Canaday, Nicholas. "The Antislavery Novel Prior to 1852 and Hildreth's 'The Slave' (1836)." *CLA Journal* 17 (December 1973):175-91.

Carleton, Phillips D. "The Indian Captivity." *American Literature* 15 (May 1943):169-80.

Charvat, William. *The Profession of Authorship in America, 1800-1870: The Papers of William Charvat.* Edited by Matthew J. Bruccoli. Columbus: Ohio State University Press, 1968.

Child, Lydia Maria. *An Appeal in Favor of That Class of Americans Called Africans.* New York: John S. Taylor, 1836.

Clarke, James Freeman. *Slavery in the United States: A Sermon Delivered in Armory Hall on Thanksgiving Day, November 24, 1842.* Boston: Benjamin H. Greene, 1846.

Clarke, Lewis, and Milton Clarke. *Narratives of the Sufferings of Lewis and Milton Clarke.* Boston: Bela Marsh, 1846.

Collections of the Massachusetts Historical Society: The Diary of Samuel Sewall 1699-1700-1714. 5th series. Boston: Massachusetts Historical Society, 1879.

Craft, William, and Ellen Craft. *Running a Thousand Miles for Freedom; or, The Escape of William and Ellen Craft from Slavery.* London: William Tweedie, 1860.

Curtin, Philip D. *The Image of Africa: British Ideas and Action, 1780-1850.* 2 vols. Madison: University of Wisconsin Press, 1964.

———, ed. *Africa Remembered: Narratives by West Africans from the Era of the Slave Trade.* Madison: University of Wisconsin Press, 1967.

Dathorne, Oscar R. "African Writers in the Eighteenth Century." *Black Orpheus* 18 (October 1965): 50-53.

Davis, Noah. *A Narrative of the Life of Rev. Noah Davis, a Colored Man.* Baltimore: John F. Weishampel, Jr., 1859.

"Decisions of the General Court." *Virginia Magazine of History and Biography* 5 (1898).

Douglass, Frederick. *Narrative of the Life of Frederick Douglass, an American Slave. Written by Himself.* Boston: Anti-Slavery Office, 1845.

Drew, Benjamin. *A North-Side View of Slavery.* Boston: J. P. Jewett & Co., 1856.

Duberman, Martin, ed. *The Antislavery Vanguard: New Essays on the Abolitionists.* Princeton, N.J.: Princeton University Press, 1965.

DuBois, W. E. B. *The Souls of Black Folk. Essays and Sketches.* Chicago: A. C. McClurg & Co., 1903.

"Editorial Notes—Literature." *Putnam's Monthly* 35 (November 1855): 547.

Elkins, Stanley. *Slavery: A Problem in American Institutional and Intellectual Life.* Chicago: University of Chicago Press, 1959.

Ellison, Ralph. *Shadow and Act.* New York: Random House, 1964.

Equiano, Olaudah. *The Interesting Narrative of the Life of Olaudah Equiano, or Gustavus Vassa, the African.* 1st American ed. 2 vols. New York: W. Durell, 1791.

Fanon, Franz. *Black Skin White Masks: The Experiences of a Black Man in a White World.* New York: Grove, 1967.

Farrison, William Edward. *William Wells Brown, Author and Reformer.* Chicago: University of Chicago Press, 1969.

Feldstein, Stanley, ed. *Once a Slave: The Slaves' View of Slavery.* New York: Morrow, 1971.

Fogel, Robert William, and Stanley L. Engerman. *Time on the Cross: The Economics of American Negro Slavery.* Boston: Little, Brown, 1974.

Foner, Laura, and Eugene D. Genovese. *Slavery in the New World: A Reader in Comparative History.* Englewood Cliffs, N.J.: Prentice-Hall, 1969.

Foster, Stephen Symonds. *The Brotherhood of Thieves, or A true Picture of the American Church and Clergy.* New London, Conn.: William Bolles, 1843.

Franklin, H. Bruce. *The Victim as Criminal and Artist: Literature from the American Prison.* New York: Oxford University Press, 1978.

Franklin, John Hope. *From Slavery to Freedom: A History of Negro Americans.* 4th ed. New York: Knopf, 1974.

Fredrickson, George M. *The Black Image in the White Mind: The Debate on Afro-American Character and Destiny, 1817-1914.* New York: Harper & Row, 1971.

Gara, Larry. "The Professional Fugitive in the Abolition Movement." *Wisconsin Magazine of History* (Spring 1965):196-203.

Genovese, Eugene D. *The World the Slaveholders Made: Two Essays in Interpretation.* New York: Vintage, 1969.

———. *Roll, Jordan, Roll: The World the Slaves Made.* New York: Random House, 1974.

Godwin, Morgan. *The Negro's and Indians' Advocate, Shewing for their Admission into the Church: Or a Persuasive to the Instructing and Baptizing of the Negro's and Indians' in our Plantations.* London: Printed for the author by F.D., 1680.

Gohdes, Clarence. *American Literature in Nineteenth-Century England.* New York: Columbia University Press, 1944.

Grandy, Moses. *Narrative of the Life of Moses Grandy, Late a Slave in the United States of America.* 1st American ed. Boston: Oliver Johnson, 1844.

Green, Joseph Johnson. *The Life and Confession of Johnson Green, Who Is to be Executed this Day, August 17th 1786, for the Atrocious Crime of Burglary; together with his Dying Words. A Broadside.* Worcester, Mass.: Printing Office, 1786.

Green, Lorenzo Johnston. *The Negro in Colonial New England.* New York: Atheneum, 1969.

Grimes, William. *Life of William Grimes, the Runaway Slave Brought Down to the Present Time.* New Haven, Conn.: Published for the Author, 1855.

Gronniosaw, James Albert Ukawsaw. *A Narrative of the Most Remarkable Particulars in the Life of James Albert Ukawsaw Gronniosaw, an*

African Prince. Newport, R.I.: S. Southwick, 1774.

Hammon, Briton. *A Narrative of the Uncommon Sufferings, and Surprizing Deliverance of Briton Hammon, a Negro Man*. Boston: Green & Russell, 1760.

Hart, James D. *The Popular Book: A History of America's Literary Taste*. New York: Oxford University Press, 1950.

Hayden, William. *Narrative of William Hayden*. Cincinnati: Published for the Author, 1846.

Henson, Josiah. *Truth Stranger than Fiction: Father Henson's Story of His Own Life*. Boston: John J. Jewett, 1858.

Herring, Maben Dixon. "The Defined Self in Black Autobiography." Dissertation, University of Notre Dame, 1974.

Hughes, Louis. *Thirty Years a Slave: From Bondage to Freedom: The Institution of Slavery As Seen on the Plantation and In the Home of the Planter*. Milwaukee: South Side Printing Co., 1897.

Jackson, Bruce. *The Negro and His Folklore in Nineteenth-Century Periodicals*. Austin: University of Texas Press, 1967.

Jacobs, Harriet Brent [Linda Brent]. *Incidents in the Life of a Slave Girl*. Boston: Published for the Author, 1861.

Jefferson, Isaac. *Memories of a Monticello Slave*. Edited by Rayford W. Logan. Charlottesville: University of Virginia Press, 1951.

Jeffery. *Declaration and Confession of Jeffery, a Negro*. Boston: T. Fleet, 1745.

Johnson, Clifton H., ed. *God Struck Me Dead: Religious Conversion Experiences and Autobiographies of Ex-slaves*. Philadelphia: Pilgrim, 1969.

Johnson, Paul. "Goodby to Sambo: The Contribution of Slave Narratives to the Abolition Movement." *Negro American Literature Forum* 6 (1972):79-84.

Jones, Thomas H. *The Experience of Thomas H. Jones, Who Was a Slave for Forty-three Years*. Worcester, Massachusetts: Henry J. Howland, 1857.

Jordan, Winthrop D. *White Over Black: American Attitudes Toward the Negro, 1550-1812*. Chapel Hill: University of North Carolina Press, 1968.

Joyce, John. *Confession of John Joyce, alias Davis, who was Executed on Monday, the 14th of March, 1808, for the Murder of Mrs. Sarah Cross; with an Address to the Public, and People of Colour*. Philadelphia: Printed for Bethel Church, 1808.

Kaplan, Sidney, *The Selling of Joseph: A Memorial*. Amherst: University of Massachusetts Press, 1969.

Katz, William Loren, ed. *Five Slave Narratives: A Compendium.* New York: Arno, 1968.

Keckley, Elizabeth. *Behind the Scenes, or, Thirty Years a Slave, and Four Years in the White House.* New York: G. W. Carleton & Co., 1868.

Koch, Adrienne, and William Peden, eds. *The Life and Selected Writings of Thomas Jefferson.* New York: Random House, 1944.

Kraditor, Aileen S. *Means and Ends in American Abolition: Garrison and His Critics on Strategy and Tactics, 1834-1850.* New York: Vintage, 1967.

Lane, Lunsford. *The Narrative of Lunsford Lane.* 2nd ed. Boston: J. E. Torrey, 1842.

Lester, Julius, ed. *To Be a Slave.* New York: Dell, 1973.

Levy, David W. "Racial Stereotypes in Anti-slavery Fiction." *Phylon,* Fall 1970, pp. 265-79.

Loggins, Vernon. *The Negro Author: His Development in America to 1900.* New York: Columbia University Press, 1931.

Loguen, Jermain W. *The Rev. J. W. Loguen, as a Slave and as a Freeman.* Syracuse, New York: J. G. K. Truair & Co., 1859.

McDougall, Marion Gleason. *Fugitive Slaves 1619-1865.* Boston: Ginn & Company, 1891.

Margolies, Edward. "Ante-bellum Slave Narratives: Their Place in American Literary History." *Studies in Black Literature,* 4 (Autumn 1973): 1-8.

Mars, James. *Life of James Mars, a Slave Born and Sold in Connecticut.* Hartford, Conn.: Case Lockwood and Co., 1864, reprinted in *Five Black Lives,* edited by Arna Bontemps. Middletown, Conn.: Wesleyan University Press, 1971.

Mellon, Matthew T. *Early American Views on Negro Slavery: From the Letters and Papers of the Founders of the Republic.* Boston: Meador Publishing Company, 1934.

Montejo, Esteban. *The Autobiography of a Runaway Slave.* Edited by Miguel Barnet. Translated by Jocasta Innes. New York: Pantheon, 1968.

Mott, Frank Luther. *Golden Multitudes: The Story of Best Sellers in the United States.* New York: Macmillan, 1947.

Murray, Alexander L. "The Provincial Freeman: A New Source for the History of the Negro in Canada and the United States." *Journal of Negro History* 44 (April 1959):123-35.

Musgrave, Marian E. "Patterns of Violence and Non-violence in Pro-slavery and Anti-slavery Fiction." *CLA Journal* 16 (June 1973): 426-37.

Nelson, John Herbert. *The Negro Character in American Literature.*

Lawrence, Kansas: Department of Journalism Press, 1926.

Nichols, Charles H. "Slave Narratives and the Plantation Legend." *Phylon* 10 (Third Quarter, 1949):201-10.

———. "Who Read the Slave Narratives?" *Phylon* 20 (Summer 1959): 149-62.

———, ed. *Black Men in Chains: Narratives by Escaped Slaves.* New York: Lawrence Hill, 1972.

Northup, Solomon. *Twelve Years a Slave: Narrative of Solomon Northup.* New York: Miller, Orton & Mulligan, 1855.

Nye, Russel B. *American Literary History: 1607-1830.* New York: Knopf, 1970.

———. *Society and Culture in America: 1830-1860.* New York: Harper & Row, 1974.

Offley, G. W. *Narrative of the Life and Labors of the Reverend G. W. Offley, a Colored Man, and Local Preacher.* Hartford, Conn.: n.p., 1860.

Osofsky, Gilbert, ed. *Puttin' On Ole Massa.* New York: Harper & Row, 1969.

Pascal, Roy. *Design and Truth in Autobiography.* Cambridge, Mass.: Harvard University Press, 1960.

Pattee, Fred Lewis. *The First Century of American Literature 1770-1870.* New York: Cooper Square, 1966.

Peabody, Ephraim. "Narratives of Fugitive Slaves." *Christian Examiner* 37 (July 1849):61-93.

Pearce, Roy Harvey. "The Significances of the Captivity Narrative." *American Literature* 19 (March 1947):1-20.

———. *Historicism Once More: Problems and Occasions for the American Scholar.* Princeton, N.J.: Princeton University Press, 1969.

———. *Savagism and Civilization. A Study of the Indian and the American Mind.* Baltimore: Johns Hopkins Press, 1971.

Pease, Jane H., and William H. Pease. *They Who Would Be Free: Blacks' Search for Freedom, 1830-1861.* New York: Atheneum, 1974.

———, eds. *The Antislavery Argument.* Indianapolis, Ind.: Bobbs-Merrill, 1965.

Pennington, James W. C. *The Fugitive Blacksmith; or, Events in the History of James W. C. Pennington.* 2nd ed. London: Charles Gilpin, 1849.

Porter, Dorothy. *Early Negro Writing: 1760-1837.* Boston: Beacon, 1971.

Quarles, Benjamin. *Black Abolitionists.* New York: Oxford University Press, 1969.

Rawick, George P. *From Sundown to Sunup: The Making of the Black Community.* Westport, Conn.: Greenwood, 1972.

———, ed. *The American Slave: A Composite Autobiography.* 12 vols. Westport, Conn.: Greenwood, 1972.

The Records of the Virginia Company of London. Vol. 3. Edited by Susan Myra Kingsbury. Washington, D.C.: Government Printing Office, 1933.

Robinson, William H., Jr. *Early Black American Prose: Selections with Biographical Introductions.* Dubuque, Iowa: Brown, 1971.

Roper, Moses. *A Narrative of the Adventures and Escape of Moses Roper from American Slavery.* 5th ed. London: Harvey and Darton, 1843.

Saffin, John. *A Brief and Candid Answer to a Late Printed Sheet, Entituled, The Selling of Joseph.* Boston: n.p., 1701.

Scholes, Robert, and Robert Kellogg. *The Nature of Narrative.* New York: Oxford University Press, 1966.

Slotkin, Richard. "Narratives of Negro Crime in New England, 1675-1800." *American Quarterly* 25 (March 1973):3-31.

Smith, John. *Travels and Works of Captain John Smith.* Edited by Edward Arber. Edinburgh: J. Grant, 1910.

Smith, Sidonie. *Where I'm Bound: Patterns of Slavery and Freedom in Black American Autobiography.* Westport, Conn.: Greenwood, 1974.

Smith, Venture. *A Narrative of the Life and Adventures of Venture, a Native of Africa.* New London, Conn.: C. Holt, 1798.

Stark, Catherine J. *Black Portraiture in American Fiction: Stock Characters, Archetypes, and Individuals.* New York: Basic Books, 1971.

Starobin, Robert S. *Blacks in Bondage: Letters of American Slaves.* New York: New Viewpoints, 1974.

The Statutes at Large Being a Collection of All the Laws of Virginia. 13 vols. Edited by William Waller Hening. Richmond, N.Y.: R. & W. & G. Bartow, 1810-23.

Steward, Austin. *Twenty-two Years a Slave, and Forty Years a Freeman.* Rochester, N.Y.: William Alling, 1857.

Stone, Albert E. "Identity and Art in Frederick Douglass's 'Narrative.'" *CLA Journal* 17 (December 1973): 192-97.

Stowe, Harriet Beecher. *Uncle Tom's Cabin.* Boston: John P. Jewett & Co., 1852.

———. *The Key to Uncle Tom's Cabin.* Boston: John P. Jewett & Co., 1853.

Thompson, John. *The Life of John Thompson, a Fugitive Slave.* Worcester, Mass.: Printed for the Author, 1856.

Thompson, William Fletcher, Jr. "Pictorial Images of the Negro During the Civil War." *Wisconsin Mazagine of History* (Summer 1965): 282-94.

Turner, Lorenzo Dow. *Anti-slavery Sentiment in American Literature Prior to 1865.* 2nd ed. Washington, D.C. Associated Publishers Inc., 1929.

Van der Beets, Richard. "The Indian Captivity Narrative as Ritual." *American Literature* 43 (January 1972):548-62.

————. *Held Captive by Indians: Selected Narratives 1642-1836.* Knoxville: University of Tennessee Press, 1973.

Vaughan, Alden T. "Blacks in Virginia: A Note on the First Decade." *William and Mary Quarterly* 29 (1972):469-78.

Walker, Margaret. *How I Wrote* Jubilee. Chicago: Third World Press, 1972.

Ward, Samuel Ringgold. *Autobiography of a Fugitive Negro.* London: John Snow, 1855.

Washington, Booker T. *Up From Slavery: An Autobiography.* New York: Doubleday, Page & Co., 1902.

Wax, Darold D. "Preferences for Slaves in Colonial America." *Journal of Negro History* 58 (October 1973): 371-401.

Weinstein, Allen, and Frank Otto Gatell. *American Negro Slavery: A Modern Reader.* 2nd ed. New York: Oxford University Press, 1973.

Weld, Theodore. *American Slavery as It Is: Testimony of a Thousand Witnesses.* New York: Anti-Slavery Society, 1839.

Williams, Kenny J. *They Also Spoke: An Essay on Negro Literature in America, 1797-1930.* Nashville, Tenn.: Townsend, 1970.

Wilson, Edmund. *Patriotic Gore: Studies in the Literature of the American Civil War.* New York: Oxford University Press, 1962.

Winks, Robin, ed. *Four Fugitive Slave Narratives.* Reading, Mass.: Addison-Wesley, 1969.

Winthrop, John. *Winthrop's Journal: "History of New England," 1634-1649.* Edited by James K. Hosmer. New York: Scribner's, 1908.

Woodson, Carter G., ed. *The Mind of the Negro as Reflected in Letters Written During the Crisis 1800-1860.* Washington, D.C.: The Association for the Study of Negro Life and History, Inc., 1926.

Yellin, Jean Fagan. *The Intricate Knot: Black Figures in American Literature 1776-1863.* New York: New York University Press, 1971.

Yetman, Norman R. "The Background of the Slave Narrative Collection." *American Quarterly* 19 (Fall 1967):534-53.

Zilversmit, Arthur. *The First Emancipation: The Abolition of Slavery in the North.* Chicago: University of Chicago Press, 1967.

Supplementary Bibliography
1979–1992

THIS BIBLIOGRAPHY IS NOT intended to be definitive. Since the 1970s, the number of articles, books, and dissertations that discuss slave narratives as a literary genre has expanded dramatically. From all indications, interest in this genre will continue for some time, and additional publications will appear before this list does. Moreover, locating all the studies about slave narratives can be quite difficult. Data searches under that rubric generally yield very disappointing results. Whether one uses the card catalog, microform indexes, or computer searches, keeping up with slave narrative scholarship requires imagination and endurance. Descriptors that have proven helpful include "Slave Narrative"; "Slave Narratives"; "Slaves—United States—Biography"; "Slavery and Slaves in Literature"; "Fugitive Slaves—United States—Biography"; "Slavery: Personal Narratives"; "Afro-Americans—Biography"; "Biographies and Autobiographies of Afro-Americans: Slave Narratives"; "Literature—Blacks"; "African American Women Writers"; "Autobiography"; "Personal Narratives"; "Narrative Technique;" "American Literature 1800–1899;" and "Slaves—United States—History." However, while I have often become exhausted looking, I do not claim this to be an exhaustive list.[1]

In compiling this bibliography, I did not attempt to catalog the introductions and afterwords to reprinted narratives, even though many are analytical or scholarly. Although interest from scholars in Germany, France, Italy, Japan, Latin America, and the Caribbean seems to be increasing, and although several studies of the genre as it developed in the United States and elsewhere are valuable, I have limited this bibliography to works written in English that focus in a substantial way upon narratives about slavery in the United States and that were published before 1865 as discrete texts. I do include a section on the

1. Off and on over the years many individuals have brought works to my attention. I thank them all, and especially Maggie Sale, my research assistant, whose imagination and persistence added many entries I would have overlooked entirely.

results of a subject search on individual narrators because it highlights another aspect of the state of slave narrative research. Currently, Frederick Douglass and Harriet Jacobs are receiving the overwhelming majority of scholarly attention. While a list of all the references to these two narrators that I found would be a very graphic illustration of the disproportionate attention given to a few texts and the enormous number of slave narratives yet to be seriously studied, I have chosen to limit their citations to eleven—arbitrary—examples. There are many, many other authors whose works not only deserve attention but who also influenced and were influenced by these two. I hope that the "Individual Author" section will be read as an indication of where the scholarly hoards have gathered and will stimulate interest in other narratives and in new approaches to the more popular ones.

Individual Narratives

My original "Selected Bibliography" includes those texts that formed the basis for my study of separately published ante-bellum slave narratives. In the "Bibliographies" section are other, more inclusive lists. We will probably never know of all the extant individually published slave narratives, and scholars will inevitably find it difficult to locate particular works. Several first editions, though, are now available on microfilm in most research libraries. Many have been reprinted and may be found in school, college, and neighborhood libraries. Anthologies of individual narratives and editions with helpful introductions are currently available in paperback. Among the more useful editions published since 1979 in paperback are: *Incidents in the Life of a Slave Girl, Written by Herself*, edited by Jean Fagan Yellin (Cambridge: Harvard University Press, 1987); *The Classic Slave Narratives*, edited by Henry Louis Gates, Jr. (New York: New American Library, 1987); *Six Women's Slave Narratives*, edited by William L. Andrews (New York: Oxford University Press, 1988); and *Early African-American Classics*, edited by Anthony Appiah (New York: Bantam, 1990).

Bibliographies of Slave Narratives

Austin, Allan. "Narratives of African Muslims in Antebellum America." *The Slave's Narrative*. Edited by Charles T. Davis and Henry Louis Gates, Jr. New York: Oxford University Press, 1985. 328-30.

Davis, Charles T., and Henry Louis Gates, Jr. "A Selected Bibliography: Black Narratives, 1760-1865." *The Slave's Narrative*. New York: Oxford University Press, 1985. 319-27.

Sojka, Gregory S. "Appendix Two: Black Slave Narratives—a Selected Checklist of Criticism." *The Art of the Slave Narrative: Original Essays in Criticism and Theory.* Edited by John Sekora and Darwin T. Turner. Macomb: Western Illinois University, 1982. 135–47.

Starling, Marion Wilson. "Separately Published Slave Narratives." *The Slave Narrative: Its Place in American History.* Boston: G. K. Hall, 1982. 339–50

Articles, Books and Dissertations
About Ante-bellum Slave Narratives

Alonzo, Andrea Starr. "A Study of Two Women's Slave Narratives: *Incidents in the Life of a Slave Girl* and *The History of Mary Prince. Women's Studies Quarterly* 17 (1989): 118–22.

"American Slave Narratives." *Nineteenth-Century Literature Criticism.* Edited by Janet Mullane and Robert Thomas Wilson. Detroit: Gale, 1989. 1–91.

Bailey, David Thomas. "A Divided Prism: Two Sources of Black Testimony on Slavery." *The Journal of Southern History* 46 (1980): 381–404.

Banes, Ruth A. "Antebellum Slave Narratives as Social History: Self and Community in the Struggle against Slavery." *Journal of American Culture* 5 (1982): 62–70.

Bartholomaus, Craig W. " 'Of One Blood': The Nineteenth Century African American Literary Response to Racial Stereotyping." Dissertation, University of Colorado, Boulder, 1991.

Bodziock, Joseph. "The Weight of Sambo's Woes." *Journal of American Culture* 12 (1989): 89–97.

_____. "What I Am About: Creating the Self in the Ante-Bellum Slave Narratives." Dissertation, University of Minnesota, 1988.

Braxton, Joanne M. "Harriet Jacobs' *Incidents in the Life of a Slave Girl:* The Re-Definition of the Slave Narrative Genre." *Massachusetts Review* 27 (1986): 379–87.

Byerman, Keith. "We Wear the Mask: Deceit as Theme and Style in Slave Narratives." *The Art of the Slave Narrative.* Edited by John Sekora and Darwin T. Turner. Macomb: Western Illinois University, 1982. 70–82.

Cobb, Martha K. "The Slave Narrative and the Black Literary Tradition." *The Art of the Slave Narrative.* Edited by John Sekora and Darwin T. Turner. Macomb: Western Illinois University, 1982. 36–44.

Diedrich, Maria. "The Characterization of Native Americans in the Antebellum Slave Narrative." *College Language Association Journal* 31 (1988): 412–35.

————. " 'My Love is Black as Yours is Fair': Premarital Love and Sexuality in the Antebellum Slave Narrative." *Phylon* 47 (1986): 238–47.

Dixon, Melvin. "Singing Swords: The Literary Legacy of Slavery." *The Slave's Narrative.* Edited by Charles T. Davis and Henry Louis Gates, Jr. New York: Oxford University Press, 1985. 298–317.

Dobkins, Rebecca Jane. " 'Who Can Blame Slaves for Being Cunning?': Strategies of Concealment and Exposure in the Narratives of Harriet Jacobs, Louisa Picquet, and Lucy Delaney." Dissertation, University of California, Berkeley, 1990.

Doyle, Mary Ellen, S.C.N. "The Slave Narratives as Rhetorical Art." *The Art of the Slave Narrative.* Edited by John Sekora and Darwin T. Turner. Macomb: Western Illinois University, 1982. 83–95.

Dudley, David Lewis. " 'The Trouble I've Seen': Visions and Revisions of Bondage, Flight, and Freedom in Black American Autobiography." Dissertation, Louisiana State University, 1988.

Early, Gerald Lyn. " 'A Servant of Servants Shall He Be—': Paternalism and Millennialism in American Slavery Literature, 1850–1859." Dissertation, Cornell University, 1982.

Foster, Frances Smith. " 'In Respect to Females . . .': Differences in the Portrayals of Women by Male and Female Narrators." *Black American Literature Forum* 15 (1981): 66–70.

————. "Slave Testimony." *Dictionary of American Slavery.* Edited by Randall M. Miller and John David Smith. Westport: Greenwood, 1988. 722–25.

————. *Witnessing Slavery: The Development of Ante-bellum Slave Narratives.* Westport: Greenwood, 1979.

Furman, Marva J. "The Slave Narrative: Prototype of the Early Afro-American Novel." Dissertation, Florida State University, 1979.

————. "The Slave Narrative: Prototype of the Early Afro-American Novel." *The Art of the Slave Narrative.* Edited by John Sekora and Darwin T. Turner. Macomb: Western Illinois University, 1982. 120–26.

Gray, James L. "Culture, Gender, and the Slave Narrative." *Proteus* 7 (1990): 37–42.

Gwin, Minrose C. "Green-Eyed Monsters of the Slavocracy: Jealous Mistresses in Two Slave Narratives." *Conjuring: Black Women, Fiction and Literary Tradition.* Edited by Marjorie Pryse and Hortense Spillers. Bloomington: Indiana University Press, 1986. 39–52.

Harris, Sharon M. "Early American Slave Narratives and the Reconfiguration of Place." *Journal of the American Studies Association of Texas* 21 (1990): 15–23.

Hedin, Raymond. "The American Slave Narrative: The Justification of the Picaro." *American Literature* 53 (1982): 630–45.

———. "Muffled Voices: The American Slave Narrative." *Clio* 10 (1981): 129–42.

———. "Paternal At Last: Booker T. Washington and the Slave Narrative Tradition." *Callaloo* 2 (1979): 95–102.

———. "Strategies of Form in the American Slave Narrative." *The Art of Slave Narrative.* Edited by John Sekora and Darwin T. Turner. Macomb: Western Illinois University, 1982. 25–35.

Jordan, Millicent Dobbs. "Literature of Race and Culture: Looking at the Narrative." *Phylon* 43 (1982): 92–94.

Knighton, Mary Alice. " 'Live Burial' in an American Gothic Mode: Harriet Jacobs's *Incidents in the Life of a Slave Girl.* " Dissertation, University of California, Berkeley, 1991.

Lowance, Mason, Jr. "Slave Narratives." *Black Women in America: An Historical Encyclopedia.* Edited by Darlene Clark Hine. Brooklyn: Carlson, 1993. 1043–45.

———. "The Slave Narrative in American Literature." *African American Writers.* Edited by Valerie Smith. New York: Scribners, 1991.

Mackethan, Lucinda H. *"Black Boy* and *Ex-Colored Man:* Version and Inversion of the Slave Narrator's Quest for Voice." *College Language Association Journal* 32 (1988): 123–47.

———. "Huck Finn and the Slave Narratives: Lighting Out as Design." *The Southern Review* 20 (1984): 247–64.

———. "Metaphors of Mastery in the Slave Narratives." *The Art of the Slave Narrative.* Edited by John Sekora and Darwin T. Turner. Macomb: Western Illinois University, 1982. 55–69.

Moody, Joycelyn K. "Ripping Away the Veil of Slavery: Literacy, Communal Love, and Self-Esteem in Three Slave Women's Narratives." *Black America Literature Forum* 24 (1990); 633–48.

Mullen, Harryette Romell. "Gender and the Subjugated Body: Readings of Race, Subjectivity, and Difference in the Construction of Slave Narratives." Dissertation, University of California, Santa Cruz, 1990.

Nichols, Charles H. "The Slave Narrators and the Picaresque Mode: Archetypes for Modern Black Personae." *The Slave's Narrative.* Edited by Charles T. Davis and Henry Louis Gates, Jr. New York: Oxford University Press, 1985. 283–98.

Niemtzow, Annette. "The Problematic Self in Autobiography: The Example of the Slave Narrative." *The Art of the Slave Narrative.* Edited by John Sekora and Darwin T. Turner. Macomb: Western Illinois University, 1982. 96–109.

Olney, James. "The Founding Fathers: Frederick Douglass and Booker T. Washington; or, The Idea of Democracy and a Tradition of Afro-American Autobiography." *Amerikastudien/American Studies* 35 (1990): 281–96.

————. " 'I Was Born': Slave Narratives, Their Status as Autobiography and as Literature.'' *Callaloo* 7 (1984): 46–73.

Sekora, John. "Black Message/White Envelope: Genre, Authenticity, and Authority in the Antebellum Slave Narrative." *Callaloo* 10 (1987): 482–515.

Sekora, John, and Darwin T. Turner, eds. *The Art of Slave Narratives: Original Essays in Criticism and Theory.* Macomb: Western Illinois University, 1982.

Starling, Marion Wilson. *The Slave Narrative: Its Place in American History.* Boston: G. K. Hall, 1982.

Tanner, Laura E. "Self-Conscious Representation in the Slave Narrative." *Black American Literature Forum* 21 (1987): 415–24.

Turner, Patricia Ann. "Tampered Truths: A Rhetorical Analysis of Antebellum Slave Narratives." Dissertation, University of California, Berkeley, 1985.

Waters, Carver Wendell. "Voice in the Slave Narratives of Olaudah Equiano, Frederick Douglass, and Solomon Northrup." Dissertation, University of Southwestern Louisiana, 1988.

Wesling, Donald. "Writing as Power in the Slave Narrative of the Early Republic." *Michigan Quarterly Review* 26 (1987): 459–72.

Wilson, Charles Edgar, Jr. "The Antebellum Slave Narrative and American Literature." Dissertation, University of Georgia, 1988.

Winter, Kari Joy. "Subjects of Slavery, Agents of History: Women and Power in Female Gothic Novels and Slave Narratives." Dissertation, University of Minnesota, 1990.

————. *Subjects of Slavery, Agents of Change: Women and Power in Gothic Novels and Slave Narratives, 1790–1865.* Athens: University of Georgia Press, 1992.

Young, Izola. "The Development of the Narrator as Cultural Hero in the Anti-Slavery Writings of Frederick Douglass." Dissertation, Howard University, 1987.

Books and Articles That Include Substantial Discussion of Ante-bellum Slave Narratives

Andrews, William L. *African American Autobiography: A Collection of Critical Essays.* Englewood Cliffs, New Jersey: Prentice-Hall, 1993.

————. "The Novelization of Voice in Early African American Narrative: *PMLA* 105 (1990): 23–34.

————. *To Tell a Free Story: The First Century of Afro-American Biography, 1760–1865.* Urbana: University of Illinois Press, 1986.

———. "Reunion in the Postbellum Slave Narrative: Frederick Douglass and Elizabeth Keckley." *Black American Literature Forum* 23 (1989): 5–16.

Awkward, Michael. "Negotiations of Power: White Critics, Black Texts, and the Self-Referential Impulse." *American Literary History* 2 (1990): 581–606.

Baker, Houston A., Jr. *Journey Back: Issues in Black Literature and Criticism.* Chicago: University of Chicago Press, 1980.

———. *Blues, Ideology, and Afro-American Literature: A Vernacular Theory.* Chicago: University of Chicago Press, 1984.

Barksdale, Richard K. "Black Autobiography and the Comic Vision." *Black American Literature Forum* 15 (1981): 22–28.

Braxton, Joanne M. *Black Women Writing Autobiography: A Tradition Within a Tradition.* Philadelphia: Temple University Press, 1989.

Carby, Hazel. *Reconstructing Womanhood: The Emergence of the Afro-American Woman Novelist.* New York: Oxford University Press, 1987.

Chinosole. "Black Autobiographical Writing: A Comparative Approach." Dissertation, University of Oregon, 1987.

Constanzo, Angelo. "Methods, Elements, and Effects of Early Black Autobiography." *A/B: Auto/Biography Studies* 2 (1986): 5–20.

Davis, Charles T., and Henry Louis Gates, Jr., eds. *The Slave's Narrative.* New York: Oxford University Press, 1985.

Dixon, Melvin. *Ride Out the Wilderness: Geography and Identity in Afro-American Literature.* Urbana: University of Illinois Press, 1987.

Gates, Henry Louis, Jr. *Figures in Black: Words, Signs and the "Racial" Self.* New York: Oxford University Press, 1987.

Fisher, Dexter, and Robert B. Stepto, eds. *Afro-American Literature: The Reconstruction of Instruction.* New York: Modern Language Association Press, 1979.

Foster, Frances Smith. *Written By Herself: Literary Production of African American Women, 1746–1892.* Bloomington: Indiana University Press, 1993.

Hajak, Friederike. "From Slave Narrative to Contemporary Afro-American Autobiography: Some Remarks on the Contribution of Black People to the Origins and Originality of American Culture." *The Origins and Originality of American Culture.* Edited by Tibor Frank. Budapest: Akademiai Kiado, 1984. 621–30.

Hedin, Raymond. "The Structuring of Emotion in Black American Fiction." *Novel* 16 (1982): 35–54.

Hull, Gloria, Patricia Bell Scott, and Barbara Smith, eds. *All the Women Are White, All the Blacks Are Men, But Some of Us Are Brave: Black Women's Studies.* Old Westbury, New York: Feminist Press, 1982.

Jackson, Blyden. *A History of Afro-American Literature: The Long Beginning, 1746–1895.* Baton Rouge: Louisiana State University Press, 1989.

Lee, A. Robert. "Black on White: The Emergence of an Afro-American Literary Voice." *Durham University Journal* 78 (1986): 335–44.

Martin, Reginald. " 'Total Life Is What We Want': The Progressive Stages of the Black Aesthetic in Literature." *South Atlantic Review* 51 (1986): 49–67.

Mason, Mary G. "Travel as Metaphor and Reality in Afro-American Women's Autobiography, 1850–1972." *Black American Literature Forum* 24 (1990): 337–56.

Olney, James, ed. *Studies in Autobiography.* New York: Oxford University Press, 1988.

Peterson, Carla L. "Capitalism, Black (Under)development, and the Production of the African-American Novel in the 1850s." *American Literary History* 4 (1992): 559–83.

Rampersad, Arnold. "Biography, Autobiography, and Afro-American Culture." *Yale Review* 65 (1976): 1–16.

Robinson, William H. "Earlier Black New England: The Literature of the Black I Am." *American Literature: The New England Heritage.* Edited by James Nagel and Richard Astro. New York: Garland, 1981. 81–99.

Sekora, John, and Houston A. Baker, Jr. "Written Off: Narratives, Master Texts, and Afro-American Writing from 1760–1945." *Studies in Black Literature* 1 (1984): 43–62.

Silverman, Jason H. " 'Truth is patient and time is just': Early Black Biography and Autobiography Reexamined." *Canadian Review of American Studies* 18 (1987): 255–63.

Smith, Valerie. *Self-Discovery and Authority in the Afro-American Narrative.* Cambridge: Harvard University Press, 1987.

Spillers, Hortense J. "Mama's Baby, Papa's Maybe: An American Grammar Book." *Diacritics* 17 (1987): 65–81.

Stepto, Robert B. *From Behind the Veil: A Study of Afro-American Narrative.* Urbana: University of Illinois Press, 1979.

Terry, Eugene. "Black Autobiography: Discernable Forms." *Okike: An African Journal of New Writing* 19 (1981): 6–10.

Tate, Claudia. "Allegories of Black Female Desire: or Rereading Nineteenth-Century Sentimental Narratives of Black Female Authority." *Changing Our Own Words: Essays on Criticism, Theory, and Writing by Black Women.* Edited by Cheryl A. Wall. New Brunswick: Rutgers University Press, 1989.

Washington, Mary Helen. *Invented Lives: Narratives of Black Women, 1860–1960.* New York: Anchor Press, 1987.

Individual Accounts

Henry Bibb
Stepto, Robert B. "Sharing the Thunder: The Literary Exchanges of Harriet Beecher Stowe, Henry Bibb, and Frederick Douglass." *New Essays on "Uncle Tom's Cabin."* Edited by Eric J. Sundquist. Cambridge: Cambridge University Press, 1986. 135-53.

Frederick Douglass
Andrews, William L., ed. *Critical Essays on Frederick Douglass.* Boston: G. K. Hall, 1991.

Bloom, Harold, ed. *Frederick Douglass's Narrative of the Life of Frederick Douglass.* New York: Chelsea, 1988.

Gibson, Donald. "Reconciling Public and Private in Frederick Douglass's *Narrative.*" *American Literature* 57 (1985): 549-69.

Goddu, Teresa A., and Craig V. Smith. "Scenes of Writing in Frederick Douglass's *Narrative:* Autobiography and the Creation of Self." *The Southern Review* 25 (1989): 822-40.

Jehlen, Myra. "Literature and Authority." *Conversations: Contemporary Critical Theory and the Teaching of Literature.* Edited by Charles Moran and Elizabeth F. Penfield. Urbana: National Council of Teachers of English, 1990. 7-18.

Leverenz, David. "Frederick Douglass's Self-Refashioning." *Criticism* 29 (1987): 341-70.

McDowell, Deborah E. "In the First Place: Making Frederick Douglass and the Afro-American Narrative Tradition." *African American Autobiography: A Collection of Critical Essays.* Edited by William L. Andrews. Englewood Cliffs: Prentice Hall, 1993. 36-58.

Martin, Waldo E., Jr. *The Mind of Frederick Douglass.* Chapel Hill: University of North Carolina Press, 1984.

Ripley, Peter. "The Autobiographical Writings of Frederick Douglass." *Southern Studies* 24 (1985): 5-29.

Sundquist, Eric, ed. *Frederick Douglass: New Literary and Historical Essays.* Cambridge: Harvard University Press, 1990.

Zeitz, Lisa Margaret. "Biblical Allusion and Imagery in Frederick Douglass's *Narrative.*" *College Language Association Journal* 25 (1981): 56-64.

Olaudah Equiano
Chinosole. "Tryin' To Get Over: Narrative Posture in Equiano's Autobiography." *The Art of the Slave Narrative.* Edited by John Sekora and Darwin T. Turner. Macomb: Western Illinois University, 1982. 45-54.

Costanzo, Angelo. *Surprizing Narrative: Olaudah Equiano and the Beginnings of Black Autobiography.* New York: Greenwood Press, 1987.

Koike, Sekio. "Olaudah Equiano: The Prototypal Christian Abolitionist Trans-figured from an African Heathen." *Kyusho American Literature* 20 (1979): 8–13.

Samuels, Wilfred D. "Disguised Voice in the *Interesting Narrative of Olaudah Equiano, or Gustavus Vassa, the African.*" *Black American Literature Forum* 19 (1985): 64–69.

James Gronniosaw

Gates, Henry Louis, Jr. "James Gronniosaw and the Trope of the Talking Book." *Southern Review* 22 (1986): 252–72.

Josiah Henson

Winks, Robin W. "The Making of a Fugitive Slave Narrative: Josiah Henson and Uncle Tom—A Case Study." *The Slave's Narrative.* Edited by Charles T. Davis and Henry Louis Gates, Jr. New York: Oxford University Press, 1985. 112–46.

Harriet Jacobs

Deck, Alice A. "Whose Book is This? Authorial Versus Editorial Control of Harriet Brent Jacobs' *Incidents in the Life of a Slave Girl: Written by Her-self.*" *Women's Studies International Forum* 10 (1987): 33–40.

Doherty, Thomas. "Harriet Jacobs' Narrative Strategies: *Incidents in the Life of a Slave Girl.*" *Southern Literary Journal* 19 (1986): 79–91.

Doriani, Beth Maclay. "Black Womanhood in Nineteenth-Century America: Subversion and Self-Construction in Two Women's Autobiographies." *American Quarterly* 43 (1991): 199–222.

Foreman, P. Gabrielle. "The Spoken and the Silenced in *Incidents in the Life of a Slave Girl* and *Our Nig.*" *Callaloo* 13 (1990): 313–24.

Foster, Frances Smith. "Harriet Jacobs's *Incidents* and the 'Careless Daughters' [and Sons] Who Read It." *The (Other) American Traditions: Nineteenth-Century American Women Writers.* Edited by Joyce Warren. New Brunswick, New Jersey: Rutgers University Press, 1993.

Garfield, Deborah, and Rafia Zafar. *Harriet Jacobs and Incidents in the Life of a Slave Girl: New Critical Essays.* Cambridge: Cambridge University Press, 1993.

Levy, Andrew. "Dialect and Convention: Harriet A. Jacobs's *Incidents in the Life of a Slave Girl.*" *Nineteenth-Century Literature* 45 (1990): 206–19.

McKay, Nellie Y. "The Girls Who Became the Women: Childhood Memories in the Autobiographies of Harriet Jacobs, Mary Church Terrell, and Anne Moody." *Tradition and the Talents of Women.* Edited by Florence Howe. Urbana: University of Illinois Press, 1991. 105–24.

Rosenberg, Warren. " 'Professor, Why Are You Wasting Our Time?': Teach-ing Jacobs's *Incidents in the Life of a Slave Girl.*" *Conversations: Contem-porary Critical Theory and the Teaching of Literature.* Edited by Charles

Moran and Elizabeth F. Penfield. Urbana: National Council of Teachers of English, 1990. 132–48.

Taves, Ann. "Spiritual Purity and Sexual Shame: Religious Themes in the Writings of Harriet Jacobs." *Church History* 56 (1987): 59–72.

Yellin, Jean Fagan. "Written By Herself: Harriet Jacobs' Slave Narrative." *American Literature* 53 (November 1981): 479–86.

Jermain Loguen

Hunter, Carol. *"The Rev. Jermain Loguen: As a Slave and as a Freeman:* A Narrative of Real Life." *Afro-Americans in New York Life and History* 13 (1989): 33–46.

James W. C. Pennington

Jugurtha, Lillie Butler. "Point of View in the Afro-American Slave Narratives: A Study of Narratives by Douglass and Pennington." *The Art of the Slave Narrative.* Edited by John Sekora and Darwin T. Turner. Macomb: Western Illinois University, 1982. 110–19.

Index

189

Wisconsin Studies in American Autobiography

William L. Andrews, General Editor

Robert F. Sayre
The Examined Self: Benjamin Franklin, Henry Adams, Henry James

Daniel B. Shea
Spiritual Autobiography in Early America

Lois Mark Stalvey
The Education of a WASP

Margaret Sams
Forbidden Family: A Wartime Memoir of the Philippines, 1941–1945
Edited, with an introduction, by Lynn Z. Bloom

Journeys in New Worlds: Early American Women's Narratives
Edited by William L. Andrews

Mark Twain
Mark Twain's Own Autobiography: The Chapters from the
North American Review
Edited, with an introduction, by Michael J. Kiskis

American Autobiography: Retrospect and Prospect
Edited by Paul John Eakin

Charlotte Perkins Gilman
The Living of Charlotte Perkins Gilman: An Autobiography
Introduction by Ann J. Lane

Caroline Seabury
The Diary of Caroline Seabury, 1854–1863
Edited, with an introduction, by Suzanne L. Bunkers

Cornelia Peake McDonald
*A Woman's Civil War: A Diary, with Reminiscences of the War,
from March 1862*
Edited, with an introduction, by Minrose C. Gwin

Marian Anderson
My Lord, What a Morning
Introduction by Nellie Y. McKay

American Women's Autobiography: Fea(s)ts of Memory
Edited, with an introduction, by Margo Culley

Frank Marshall Davis
Livin' the Blues: Memoirs of a Black Journalist and Poet
Edited, with an introduction, by John Edgar Tidwell

Joanne Jacobson
Authority and Alliance in the Letters of Henry Adams

Kamau Brathwaite
The Zea Mexican Diary
Foreword by Sandra Pochet Paquet

Genaro M. Padilla
*My History, Not Yours: The Formation of
Mexican American Autobiography*

Frances Smith Foster
*Witnessing Slavery: The Development of Ante-bellum
Slave Narratives*